MW01279934

View of fifth Floor of
Design Academy Eindhoven

HOUSE OF CONCEPTS

Design Academy Eindhoven

Edited by
Louise Schouwenberg
Gert Staal

Frame Publishers, Amsterdam 2008

PREFACE

'The secret is the individuality and autonomous structure of the academy and the resulting state of mind. With us there is little bureaucracy but much freedom of interpretation, and that energises everyone'. This is how Li Edelkoort, chairman of Design Academy Eindhoven's board of management since 1999, explained the success of her school. In a discussion with NRC Handelsblad she linked the intellectual freedom of the academy's education with the trend that she encountered at the time (mid-2006) in design in the Netherlands: 'We have become more imaginative and less moralistic. Holland may have its head in the clouds, but its feet are firmly on the ground – which is just as well when times are hard'.

So successful in two ways. Evidently recessions provide the most favourable conditions for the flowering of the design ability of the Low Countries. And in this environment a system of design training has taken root which passes on the key to the house of conceptualism to Dutch and non-Dutch alike. Barren concepts? Not if all is well. Although form and material usage often have a basis in scarcity, the best work done by students at Design Academy Eindhoven is characterised by a wealth of ideas. The value of the training finds expression in the least tangible aspects of the product: the associations that it evokes, the values that it communicates and the power of memory to which it appeals. The academy's best work sticks almost as well to the memory cells as to photographic paper.

It is interesting that just this conceptual quality has been able to blossom in a school which in the first instance was intended to supply industry in the Brabant region with usable product designs. It is true that the school based itself on design training models, particularly those developed in the United States, but it still retained an unmistakable provincial signature. For a long time – in fact well into the 1990s – AIVE students could not have imagined that they had studied at one of the world's most prized design training establishments. For that is how people see Design Academy Eindhoven today.

Naturally the presence of Philips meant that the then Academy for Industrial Design had Holland's greatest industrial complex as a neighbour. But apart from that, graduates in the years of post-war reconstruction could only offer their services to small companies, mainly active in the local market. Their products had no need to meet high cultural criteria. Functionality and affordability were much more important as characteristics of a well-designed industrial product.

And yet Eindhoven managed to turn itself around. In *House of Concepts* we attempt to learn from the current situation at Design Academy Eindhoven the characteristics which have given its training the special status that it now enjoys. A number of former students have done work which has won them a place in the vanguard of international design, and for this book we talked to them about the debt they owe to their training.

House of Concepts also documents the curriculum of the academy, and looks at the crucial role played by the designers who as sector heads have guided the school's different departments. By the time this book appears a number of prominent personalities will have left the teaching staff and been replaced by young designers. If it is true, as is often claimed, that the concept is burnt into the school's genes, this changing of the guard should take place without noticeable problems. For the moment it is too early to give an opinion. *House of Concepts* has no ambition to give a complete picture of the academy's recent development but rather to give a typical picture of its training and its 'products'. To that end we have chosen to provide representative snapshots rather than a complete stock list.

We describe the history of the school to show that the institution's present fame was built step by step and with great determination, not only by the present board of management but by its immediate predecessor, and most of all by Jan Lucassen and Jan van Duppen, who spent years polishing their ideal institution. It was they who took the first steps towards developing an international profile for the academy, implemented the reform of the curriculum, moved the school to its present location and succeeded in assembling an exceptional team of lecturers. From their ranks emerged Li Edelkoort, who subsequently succeeded in putting the school in the public eye and smartening it up to be the focus of Dutch Design. In recent years the two brands – Design Academy Eindhoven and Dutch Design – have become virtually synonymous. A world brand based not so much on the tangible qualities of products but on what they have to say. And what they have to say was designed in the Netherlands.

Louise Schouwenberg
Gert Staal

Susette Brabander
Man and Identity [2002]
—
Cross-over, 2002

XS, M, XL, 2002

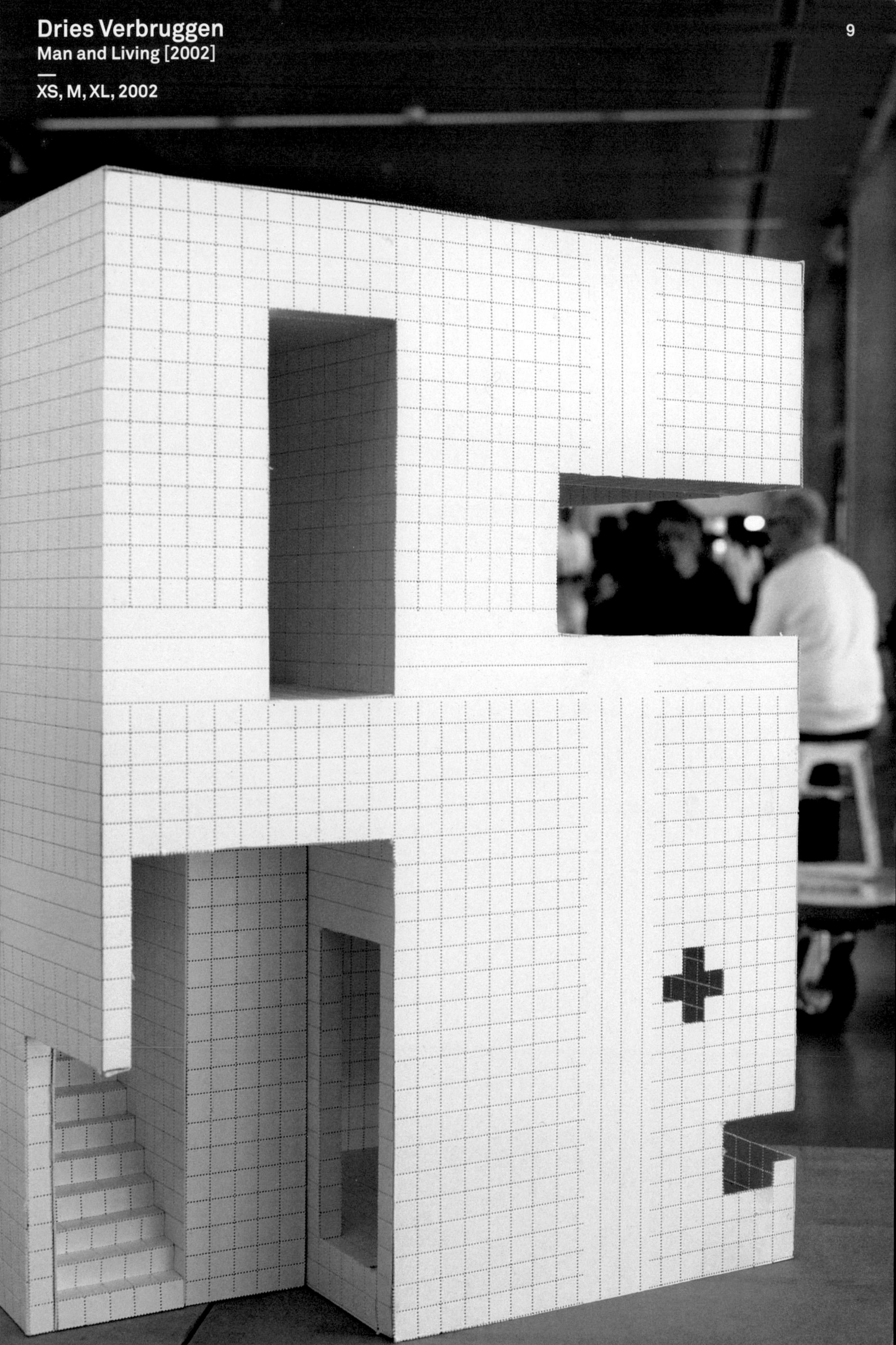

Lieke van Hooydonk
Man and Living [2002]

—

Counteract overpopulation by overbuilding, 2002

Caroline Gielen
Man and Living [2002]
—
Inbetween zones, 2002

Sannah Belzer
Man and Public Space [2002]
—
Wood curtain, 2002

Corridor of Design Academy Eindhoven during the Graduation Show 2002

Cathelijne Montens
Atelier [2002]
—
Tableware made of cast-iron, 2002

Wouter Scheublin
Atelier [2005]

Construction kit, 2005

Jeroen Verhoeven
Atelier [2005]
—
Cinderella, 2005

Eefje Ottenvanger
Man and Leisure [2002]
—
Cork bath, 2002

Early Ambitions, Academy for Industrial Design Eindhoven 1947–1998

Hedwig Saam

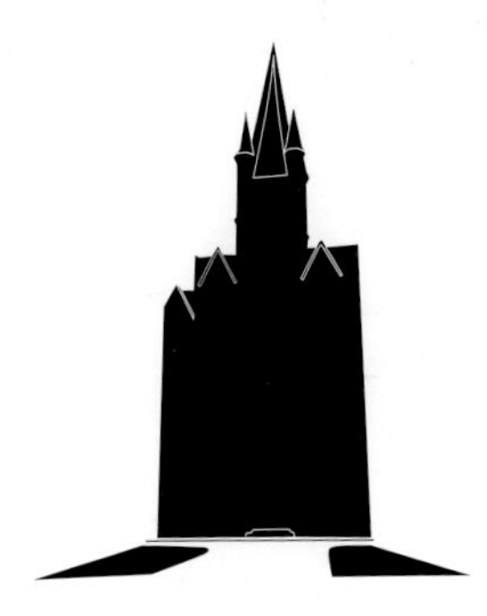

In September 1950 a unique school opens its doors (in Eindhoven's old city hall, Rechtestraat 24); the School of Industrial Arts in Eindhoven is the first school in the Netherlands to aim specifically at providing instruction in industrial design. Assuming the position of director is the relatively unknown René Smeets. During the 20 years of his directorship, Smeets is to play a crucial pioneering role in making the then unfamiliar discipline of industrial design part of the Dutch educational system and in garnering broad acceptance for this branch of education.

In post-war Eindhoven, ambitions held by the city council correspond with those of Philips Electronics. Despite a population of 125,000, the level of amenities in this place is decidedly not that of a big city. There is no shopping centre, no municipal theatre, only one hospital and a museum of no more than regional interest. Both Philips and the local government of Eindhoven are of the opinion that a city of this size needs an educational facility with an appeal that extends beyond the region. At Philips, this ambition is fed mainly by the company's need for a more highly educated workforce, as the firm's post-war operations in Eindhoven are to focus on administration and development. Up to this point, Philips has employed a two-pronged approach in an attempt to fill the required positions. The first step is to have better qualified people relocate to Eindhoven, after which they are to be further educated at a company school established by Philips before the onset of the war. Philips' ideal, however, is a municipal- and state-subsidized school of higher education, an ideal that coincides with the post-war aspirations of the municipality. Consequently, both parties actively lobby for the establishment of a technical university, as well as a polytechnic, in Eindhoven.

Immediately after the Second World War, the Dutch government – in particular those cabinets headed by Beel and Drees – sets as an objective the large-scale reorganization of the economic and social order. Social changes have nothing to do with converting to a state-controlled economy – for which both progressive political parties and various like-minded Dutch designers, such as Piet Zwart and Mart Stam, have been arguing during the war On the contrary, the reforms aim at achieving a more liberal economy, with a greater interest in private initiative and more power invested in the world of business, and especially industry. The minister of economic affairs, Jan van den Brink, only 33 years old in 1948, plays a starring role in the development of a multifarious industry meant to stimulate not only the manufacture of quality products for export, but also the fabrication of more traditional and artisanal products. Rather than the static Dutch economy of the 1930s, van den Brink envisions a much more dynamic society, while also warning of the alienating effects sure to accompany what he sees as unavoidable industrialization. In shaping his liberal industrialization policy, he undoubtedly recalls the difficulties faced by his father, who had been the director of a carpet factory during the Depression.

At the end of the Second World War, the Dutch government, with mental and financial support furnished by the American Marshall Plan, provides every opportunity for the development of large companies like Philips Electronics and Hoogovens Steel. In terms of size and recognition, Philips is perhaps the industrial flagship of the province of Noord-Brabant, but the smaller and medium-size manufacturers form an important, finely woven net made up of members that share not only the Roman Catholic faith but, even more, a community spirit and cultural principles. Long before the war begins, enlightened dignitaries, among whom cigar manufacturer Henri van Abbe, turn their attention to the cultural and social amenities of their town, not least as compensation for the negative effects of Eindhoven's emerging industrialization. (In 1936 Henri van Abbe donated a museum of modern art to the city which was named after him: Van Abbemuseum). After the Second World War, a number of manufacturers in textile, wooden articles and tobacco regroup in and around Eindhoven, including some in nearby Tilburg. In this relatively progressive climate, quickly the time is ripe for the establishment of new educational institutes aimed at serving both culture and the economy.

POLYTECHNIC SCHOOL OF INDUSTRIAL ARTS

In 1947, even before the mandatory Royal Decree has been issued, eager to set up the school the municipality of Eindhoven has the charter of foundation executed in the presence of a notary public, officially establishing the existence of the school. The anticipated Royal Decree, dated 23 May 1949, formally sanctions the opening of the Polytechnic School of Industrial Arts Foundation Eindhoven as a night school. On 19 December 1949, the school's board of governors selects Limburg glass artist René Smeets (1905–1976) as director. Initially, the board searches for suitable criteria on which to base its decision; there is, after all, no precedent that provides guidance. Ultimately, the board cites as definitive qualities Smeets's 'multifaceted and broad education; scholarly interest; merits in numerous areas of applied arts, of aesthetics and of the theory of form', calling him a 'competent educator with a good delivery, a pleasant and humane person who arduously practises smooth and facile manners'. Although the board is sorely tempted to appoint a celebrity from the art world, its choice of former serviceman Smeets is a deliberate one, no doubt underpinned by the expectation of a well-honed talent for organization, in light of his background. This relatively unknown figure is the first in the Netherlands to be given the responsibility of educating students in industrial arts and design, thus training them to take their places in Brabant's industrial operations.

Educated at Amsterdam's Art Academy, Smeets later devotes himself to stained glass and murals, often in collaboration with Mathieu Wigman and Charles Eyck. His interest in everything related to design is obvious early on. In 1941 he becomes the manager of ceramics workshop N.V. Russel Tiglia in Tegelen, where he trains his pupils to make decorative ceramic objects. He also serves as adviser to the Creative Handicraft Foundation in Delft. At the time of his appointment in December 1949, the board already has a list of activities waiting for him. Smeets is to begin making a list of initial necessities immediately, to have furniture produced, to draw up a prospectus, a curriculum and a timetable based on available data. Smeets has to determine the number of teachers required, interview possible candidates and select his staff. The same goes for the enrolment of pupils. Finally he is requested to plan and realize the interior organization and appearance of the school.

Having added the self-imposed task of creating good relations with the press, as soon as he's been appointed Smeets contacts the media. On 28 January 1950 he calls a press conference, the results of which are later described in the annual report as extremely satisfactory. Throughout his directorship, Smeets remains keenly aware of the importance of good relations with the press, quite regularly sending press releases and keeping a scrapbook of his press contacts. Local newspapers soon begin printing items that explain the objectives and the policy of the new school. In one of his very early contacts with the press, Smeets is quoted as saying the ultimate goal of the school is to 'help satisfy the need for effective, well-formed and inexpensive products for daily use, while also promoting export by making products that are easy to sell.'

Although not so clearly expressed in its officially stated objectives, Director Smeets obviously sees teaching pupils industrial design as the school's main task. In the publicity surrounding the opening of the school, Smeets emphasizes, time and again, the significance of the 'design' department: 'The most important department of this school is that of Industrial Design. Not that the three other departments are of marginal importance, but because a new subject is being taught here. The products that the Netherlands contributes to the world market have to meet extremely high demands. They must be practical, of good quality, agreeable and nicely shaped, and they should be easy to handle and pleasant to use. What is needed to achieve this are people with imagination, who can transform these demands into ideas and then translate ideas into an aesthetic form. Part of the goal of this school is to train such people and to educate them.'

In the school newspaper, Smeets goes on to say: 'It seems to me that one of the main tasks of an art school is to help train people with "style" ...people with a sense of culture and genuine refinement.' In the *Philipskoerier* Smeets compares the Dutch situation with that of other countries: 'In foreign countries – namely United States, England and Switzerland – the consumer places more value on the appearance of an industrial product than we do. And in light of the importance of a larger export of our products, it's necessary to pay even more attention to the design of serial- and mass-produced goods than is now the case.' Here, again, it is evident that Smeets considers his school's Industrial Design Department to be of great consequence.

What are the classes like that are meant to introduce pupils to this new course of study? Indeed, with no precedent to follow, it is exceptionally complicated to frame a good educational programme. The board makes orientation visits to polytechnic schools of industrial arts in Amsterdam, The Hague, Rotterdam, Arnhem and Maastricht. Under the leadership of L.C Kalff, C.E. – a member of the board and the general art director at Philips – a temporary curriculum is created as a guideline for the new director.

The five-year programme requires pupils to attend classes seven months a year, four evenings a week. The first two years provide a general foundation; at the end of the second year, the pupil selects one of the following departments:

A. Drawing and painting; graphic techniques
B. Modelling and sculpting
C. a. Industrial design
b. Textile design
D. Advertising design

In addition, the school offers courses in freehand drawing and painting and, on Saturday afternoons, a course leading to a primary-school teaching degree in drawing. In the press, Smeets airs his hopes for expansion, mentioning, among other things, stained glass (his discipline) and mosaics, fancywork for women, weaving and bookbinding.

Selecting teachers is not easy. The subject of industrial design is so new that experienced instructors do not exist. Nevertheless, the recruitment ad draws 92 applications, from which the director has to choose. The board expresses its preference for teachers previously employed by the local Sint Lucasgilde school of drawing. In very short order – the abridged course is set to begin in March 1950 – board members and director select Vermeeren, van Baar, v.d. Krogt and Louwers for the various drawing classes; Pot for advertising and publicity; van Rhijn for modelling and sculpting; Wiltschut for painting; and Jansen for mathematics, statics and dynamics. Smeets also teaches, of course.

Five pupils enrol in the abridged industrial design course. They do not find 'industrial design' listed as a course on their timetable, however. A great deal of attention is paid to drawing (decorative, letter, line, technical) and subjects like the theory of form and art history. On the one hand, this can be explained simply by noting the lack of teachers available for the subject of industrial design. Then, too, what Smeets has in mind is not a strictly functional approach to the subject. It's his opinion that human beings have an 'innate craving for decoration'. The industrial product, therefore, should also be decorated. In the autumn of 1950 – and in the years that follow, when the night school is operating at full swing – the timetable remains more or less unaltered. Industrial design classes with a distinctly aesthetic focus are taught by Smeets.

NEW INSIGHTS, TO BE FOUND IN THE UNITED STATES

In the years after 1950, Eindhoven's School of Industrial Arts continues its pursuit of a permanent structure. Not all courses are a success, and the same applies to the teachers. Director Smeets visits schools at home and abroad, in search of inspiration. With the ambition to open a day school in 1955, the need for a clear direction in the educational programme is becoming more and more apparent.

In 1953 Smeets is given the opportunity to visit the country that, according to him, has 'a 30-year head start' on the Netherlands: the United States. It is not Smeets who has initiated the trip. The Ministry of Economic Affairs (working under the auspices of the American Mutual Security Agency) has asked the Increase Productivity Contact Group to put together a committee for the purpose of visiting factories, schools and design agencies in the United States. One objective of this committee, led by Karel Sanders, is to discover why people in the United States seem to have more of a feel for industrial design and why manufacturers there are more inclined to produce functional items that are aesthetically sound as well.

The trip, which lasts five weeks, begins on 27 June, an unfavourable date. From the outset, visits scheduled for schools are plagued by the problem of summer holidays, which have already begun in the United States. Nonetheless, Smeets manages to have a number of highly satisfactory meetings with officials at the various schools on his list, and he finds the trip to be a very inspiring experience. Having returned home, Smeets writes an extensive report in which he includes his impressions and recommendations for education in the Netherlands.

In America, Smeets encounters a society that is completely convinced of the importance of industrial design. The motivation of the American manufacturer is driven completely by the thought that money spent on design means 'better business'. In the United States, he says, 'industrial design has become an indispensable instrument ... a tool of absolute essence to industry, especially in terms of sales. Designers have developed a pat method for getting their work sold; they calculate the cost price, do market and customer research – in short, they have developed a complete service intended to instil confidence in the manufacturer and to ensure their own success.' Smeets is forced to admit that this market-orientated approach does not always lead to aesthetically sound products, however. 'Even so, in the end the businessman uses industrial design only as a means to sell his product, and public taste is of overriding importance in the matter of sales.'

The American phenomenon is not that easy to fathom. The amount of kitsch that Smeets sees in the United States is startling, but he discerns the positive – and also weighty – influence of Bauhaus ideas as well. 'It is undeniable that these purifyingly clear, lucid concepts and methods are the reason that the level of American Design is so high.' And, he ascertains with delight, 'In a year's time, for example, more than 27 million classical-music gramophone records were sold in the United States; more and more Americans are attending university; the country has splendid museums; and so forth.' Many companies are investing their own money in expensive training programmes for designers, but Smeets still believes that such training belongs primarily in a nation's schools. Education in the United States is facing the same problems that are occurring in the Netherlands, though. Despite a broader acceptance of industrial design as an area of study, good teachers with experience are hard to find, and programmes offering a comprehensive, disciplined education – such as those for students of architecture and medicine – are nonexistent.

Nevertheless, Smeets is able to distil a collection of general conditions pertaining to the knowledge an American designer needs to function in practice. The educational programme should cultivate 'the fundamental ideas and basic elements of all visual works', offer an insight into 'tools, machines and methods for mass-production' and provide an understanding of 'problems related to sales, marketing and distribution of manufactured goods'. Smeets also points out the vital significance of versatility and 'a broad-based general education; stimulation to travel; an appreciation of music, theatre and all human achievements, of language and literature. In addition to contact with all sorts of people, a knowledge of great documents and books of world literature forms the foundation of a human character within which should dwell the artist, the engineer, the diplomat, the salesman, the philosopher and the psychologist.'

His recital is not complete, however, without a mention of the crucial importance of integration between education and industry. In the United States, Smeets sees how industry actively contributes to education, thus generating the necessary interaction between theory and practice. Students are given realistic assignments, and part of a school's teaching staff is made up of people from the world of industry. Only in this way, he says, can a student get the kind of education needed to become 'that special type of designer who will be 1/3 artist, 1/3 engineer and 1/3 salesman'.

To get a better insight into the practical experience of design, Smeets visits not only schools, but also a number of design agencies. What strikes him is the enormous expansiveness of the field that is covered by the American designer. His conclusion is that a designer's education should not be too specialized. His visits to design agencies also lead to other recommendations for education. Smeets is extremely impressed by the professional presentation methods and social skills of American designers. Particularly remarkable, he says, is the openness with which 'the labourer, the girl in the factory or the office meets and talks with bosses, managers and supervisors. Thus the educational programme should pay sharp attention to the way in which the future designer presents himself and his work, giving thought to correct appearance, polite behaviour, fluent and proper speech, also in public, suppleness and ease in his contacts with people'. Smeets also sees a major role reserved for photography, 'as a visual resource' that is of particular use during presentations.

Smeets ends his report on the United States by referring to the Educational Program for Industrial Design, a programme that corresponds precisely to his own conclusions and recommendations for educating students of design. Drawn up by Professor A.J. Kostellow, the programme comprises three basic elements.

1. **General Education**
2. **The Technique of Progress**
3. **Social and Economic Factors of Life**

In the first year, the student has the opportunity to develop his visual capabilities. Analogous to the Bauhaus method, this year is dominated by experimentation and analysis. The programme takes 'him closer to knowledge of the forces that influence the designs and the necessary inner discipline to work out the assigned problems'. In the second year, the experimental phase continues, but now the accent lies on recognizing the aesthetic potential of materials, forms and functions. In the third year, design assignments are of a more realistic nature. The student is ushered into a world of product research and reports. He spends the rest of the time painting and sculpting. In the fourth year, the student is confronted with actual problems, for which a more intensive form of collaboration with industry is essential. In addition, the programme places an emphasis on guiding design students in a general rather than in a specialized direction.

Filled with inspiration, Smeets returns from the United States, the land with which he is to remain in contact in his efforts to further develop the subject of industrial design. Smeets reports on his experiences in the local newspaper, conveying his unconcealed admiration for the American approach. In his mind, the visit has re-established the importance of industrial design to society, and Smeets is now hoping to persuade the Netherlands. He also has a keener eye for the type of education required. Smeets adds courses in photography, furniture design, typography, design and art history to the curriculum for the school year 54/55. Putting aside the desire to educate people with 'a sense of style', he now has a far more pragmatic view of industrial design as a discipline. But the real impact of the trip to the United States emerges only when Smeets opens the day school in September 1955.

DAY SCHOOL FOR INDUSTRIAL DESIGN

Ever since August 1953, Smeets has been keeping the Dutch press informed of the oncoming establishment of the first day school for industrial design. A few of his reports turn out to be false alarms, however. The actual event does not take place until September 1955. Smeets's carefully developed publicity campaign instantly goes into effect, and he bombards the regional and national press – as well as schools, businesses and trade unions – with information on the industrial designer, a modern, unknown profession poised to fill an oh-so-important role in society. Karel Sanders, director of the Institute of Industrial Design in Amsterdam, offers advice on implementing the publicity campaign, recruiting new teachers and planning the school timetable. Even before it opens its doors, media interest in the school is overwhelming, and Smeets has garnered the support of big businesses such as car manufacturer DAF, thus ensuring the necessary interaction between theory and practice.

The curriculum, which reads like a literal translation of Kostellow's Educational Program for Industrial Design, is divided into four parts.

1. General education. 'Series of courses meant to help the pupil acquaint himself with the past and present achievements of mankind in the areas of art, literature and science.'

2. Broad-based education in drawing, modelling and design. 'The future designer should learn to express himself in a fluent and competent manner using all materials and techniques.'

3. The technical and practical element of the programme. 'In this part of the curriculum, the pupil is to become familiar with the technological factors that facilitate mass-production; he is to learn to the best of his ability, both in theory and in practice, all there is to know about materials and techniques, insomuch as these are required by the commercial and industrial designer.' This phase of the programme also focuses on personal presentation, as well as on distribution and marketing methods.

4. Making the transition and adapting to actual practice. This phase includes vital interaction with the business world. In the final year of the programme, the pupil works as a trainee for various companies. 'During the period of study at school, the pursuit of a realistic insight into the problems of putting design into practice is fostered by making excursions to factories and businesses; working on realistic assignments, provided and explained by the companies; and attending lectures and classes given by people working in the profession.'

On the basis of these four cornerstones, upon which the educational programme rests, the day school has quite a multifaceted curriculum, unlike that of traditional schools of applied arts. Subjects such as economy, sociology and psychology are new and clearly based on the American model. Departments in the new day school are as follows:

A. General industrial design: training for designers and draughtsmen of the industrial serial- and mass-produced product
B. Commercial design: training for
  a: designers and draughtsmen in the areas of advertising, publicity, packaging and publishing (books)
  b: specialists in the areas of window-dressing, productpresentation, stand and exhibition construction
C. Textile design: training for designers in the textile industry and industries producing decorative, textile-related products.
  Sub-department a: weaving, knotting and braiding techniques.
  Sub-department b: printing techniques

Department A entails a five-year programme of study, including the fifth year as a trainee. The other two departments have four-year programmes 'in close contact with practical experience'. The first two years of the programme are devoted to general education, and a great deal of time is spent on experimentation. It is evident that along with American influences the *Vorkurs* of the Bauhaus have also been an inspiration. Smeets does adapt Bauhaus ideas to the Dutch situation, however. He is not willing to abandon decorative, nature-inspired patterns, for instance, a mortal sin in the eyes of the Bauhaus. Itten's renowned colour theory has been revised as well;

Smeets simply replaces it with his own version, in which nature serves as a model and the emphasis lies firmly on a harmonious and frugal application of colour.

SMEETS'S VIEWS ON WORK EXPERIENCE AND OTHER INDUSTRIAL DESIGN (ID) SCHOOLS

One of the fundamentals of the school is contact with the business world. Following his trip to the United States in 1953 and upon opening the day school, Director Smeets introduces a compulsory year of traineeship for students in the Industrial Design Department. After all, it's only through work experience that students can get a realistic look at their future profession. But there are other reasons for maintaining contacts between the school and the business community. The programme in industrial design needs intensive promotion, for in many instances companies are unfamiliar with the subject and understand even less how good design can be used to their benefit. Then, too, the school is hoping that businesses will provide students with realistic projects that they can tackle in the classroom.

Obviously, contacts are good with Philips Electronics, a firm represented in the school's first board of governors by L.C. Kalff, C.E. In a letter written in 1960, Smeets goes so far as to ask the head of Ir. Veersema Design Agency for financial help: 'When we have too little money in our budget to spend on a handsome prospectus or other publication, I should like to appeal to you for some additional resources.' From the outset, Smeets also keeps in touch with other businesses in Brabant. He's interested in DAF, for example, a company that operates in much the same way as American businesses do. In fact, Smeets is constantly on the move in his attempt to convince the business community of the importance of good design in general and, more specifically, to get companies involved in the school by, for example, 'press-ganging' their employees into joining his teaching staff. It's his way of laying a foundation on which future directors can continue building the school.

Smeets maintains close contacts with the business community and other organizations that can contribute to his promotion of industrial design. Karel Sanders, a personal friend and the director of the Institute of Industrial Design in Amsterdam, is a member of the advisory committee for the Eindhoven school. Sanders advises Smeets on matters ranging from the layout of an application form to possible visits to companies of interest to the school. Smeets is primarily concerned with the degree to which the Amsterdam institute can lend structure to the school and is eager to have publications issued by his friend's institute include the name of the Eindhoven school. For Smeets, having the Institute of Industrial Design involved in his school is a sign of recognition and a confirmation of his efforts to promote industrial design as a field of study.

In the early 1960s, there is talk of industrial design courses to be introduced at the Institute of Technology in Delft. A report issued in 1961, framed by the Education Committee on Industrial Design – a body that includes both L.C. Kalff and R. Smeets – further

Design Academy Eindhoven
Locations

Top left: Rechtestraat, 1961

Top right: Hemelrijken

Bottom left: Hermelijnstraat, 1974

Bottom right: Kanaalstraat, 1974

Opposite top: Elzentlaan, 1979

Opposite bottom: deWitteDame

explores the subject of educating 'the Industrial Designer in the Netherlands'. The committee not only wants to widen the view of industrial design as seen by those responsible for the country's industrial policies, but also argues for an educational programme at a university level, in addition to what is on offer at the academies in Eindhoven and The Hague. As a result, even future top-ranking executives will have a chance to 'get intimately acquainted with the notion and the significance of industrial design in all its facets'.

Despite Smeets's participation in framing the report, the following year he takes a 'more careful position' with respect to establishing an ID Department in Delft, 'because it makes no sense for other schools to enter into this when we're educating more than enough people'. The reason for this turnabout is not completely clear, but it may be prompted by the diminished economic perspectives of that moment. 'To date, graduates are still finding (not without much difficulty, for that matter) positions in industry, partly because we ourselves act as intermediary and "employment agency" to a considerable degree.'

Smeets reacts testily to other initiatives as well, such as an announcement made by the Institute for Applied Arts Education (IKNO) in Amsterdam, which suddenly claims to have an ID Department. Relations with the business community may be warm, but contacts with other schools of the opinion that the modern subject of 'design' belongs in their curricula are cool. Smeets finds an ally in the inspector of domestic science and technical education, A.G. van den Hoek, C.E. In a letter written in 1962, the latter states: 'I also feel that one school of industrial design in our country is enough.' In the same letter, he reassures Smeets with regard to the alleged competition. 'The IKNO has no department of industrial design, despite the use of such high-sounding language. There is no Royal Decree sanctioning the establishment and maintenance of such a department in association with the IKNO.'

In 1966 the scientific programme of industrial design at the Institute of Technology in Delft is finally a fact, albeit much later than expected. Remarkably enough, Smeets does not react to the establishment of the Academy of Art and Industry (AKI) in Twente in 1950, in the same year, *nota bene*, in which 'his' school begins operating. At the opening of the academy in Twente, the chairman of the East Netherlands Foundation of Applied Arts points out that the goal of this school is 'not to educate half artists' but to train people who can 'be of service to industry'. The Eindhoven archives produce no further reference to other contacts with the school in Twente, perhaps owing to the fact that the AKI never manages to distinguish itself in any significant way from conventional art academies and is not seen, therefore, as competition.

From the very beginning, Smeets maintains contacts with similar schools abroad, partly as a source of personal inspiration but more often because his foreign colleagues have an interest in the Netherlands' first school of industrial design. He regularly sends prospectuses to schools in Braunschweig and Düsseldorf, for example. Later, under the directorship of Houtman and Gilles, contacts with foreign schools assume a more structured form as the result of a student-exchange programme involving Eindhoven and schools abroad.

In 1961 the Ministry of Education, Cultural Affairs and Science (ECS) issues a report on education in the field of industrial design in the Netherlands. The report, framed by the Education Committee on Industrial Design, which includes Smeets, also addresses the prospect of work for designers: 'Unfortunately, exact figures on the need for industrial designers are not available.' As previously stated, the term 'industrial design' is still unfamiliar to many in the Dutch business community. Hence the survey contemplated by the Institute of Industrial Design would have had little effect at this time, as it would have failed to provide accurate information.

Despite its uncertainty as to the required number of designers, the report also expresses optimism: 'We should keep in mind, however, that were ID to be introduced on a larger scale the demand for well-trained designers should be able to be met. ... The needs of industry will also exhibit a certain differentiation. Some manufacturers will – and some already have – augmented their staffs with in-house industrial designers. Others will make use of freelance designers. There will be manufacturers with a need in this area for managerial figures in their technical offices and design departments. Finally, certain companies will have executive-level positions for people ... who will not only offer a sound evaluation of a firm's production policy but also be charged with determining principles and standards that apply to the form of the product in question. Altogether, this leads to differently orientated industrial designers. In general, all of them will have to possess, to some degree or another, qualities in areas that are technical, aesthetic, economic, social and cultural in nature.'

As made apparent by the cited passages of this report, the connection to practical experience is an important point of interest for the Education Committee on Industrial Design. The report delves into the quantitative, as well as the qualitative, need for designers. These issues also play a major role in the development of the Eindhoven school's educational programme. Responding to them, however, is extremely complicated. What exactly is 'practical experience'? Is it the product-development department of a large corporation? Is it a private studio from which one works for various clients? Or is it a situation in which products are both designed and manufactured by their creator? And how can one measure the need for industrial designers as they become increasingly more inventive in finding employment suited to their educational background? The scope of activity covered by industrial designers is immense and varies from aeroplanes to sunglasses.

THE 1960S
SOCIETY CHANGES, AND THE AIVE FOLLOWS SUIT

In the early 1960s, the day school for industrial design is still based on the same principles it adopted at the beginning, although the educational programme has gradually shifted to the programmatic and systematic side of design. Like their colleagues in the United

States and other European countries, Dutch students are also displaying a strong desire for schools and universities with a more democratic operating system.They demand a greater say in the ideology and the daily functioning of educational institutions. The established order, however, is unwilling to revise the existing system without a fight. This leads to a number of student sit-ins at universities. In 1968 – five years after the Secondary Education Act went into effect, entitling the Polytechnic School of Industrial Arts to call itself an academy – Academie Industriële Vormgeving Eindhoven (AIVE) is the first school in the Netherlands to experience a student sit-in.

On 28 May of that year, at 3 p.m., students begin their strike. They demand a say in school policy. Their demand is not completely unexpected, as school officials have previously attempted to open a dialogue with dissatisfied students by instituting a school council. Later, this council is divided into various committees, the most important of which – methodology and programming – are not open to student participation. In Smeets's absence, Deputy Director J. Vos is unwilling to make a decision concerning the admission of students to these two committees, and the situation explodes.

Nonetheless, neither the teaching staff nor the school management is wholly unhappy about this course of events. Deputy Director Vos gives the local press a positive statement. 'What do you want me to say? The strike clearly shows that they're deeply affected by the ups and downs of the school. What could be better than having so many people contemplating their profession? If they continue in this calm manner, the strike could lead to a new educational construct.' Smeets is less friendly: 'Anyone who's not satisfied can leave. The door is always open.' Later, he recalls the strike as being more interesting than unfortunate.

A new 'educational construct' is exactly what the striking students have in mind. Together, they discuss the calibre and content of the courses. A White Paper contains the results. On 10 June, the school management announces its intention to resume classes, and the students are in agreement. 'From this moment on, we [the students] want to wipe the slate clean and to work together building and developing our Academy, with no hard feelings.' It takes time, however, before all conflicts are resolved completely and a form of student participation is found that satisfies all parties involved. Smeets tries to appreciate the positive aspect of these developments, but in his heart he is deeply disappointed in the massive character of the rebellion and the support it received from the teaching staff. A director like Smeets, who stands at the top of the stairs each morning to greet his students and who unfailingly has his staff address him as 'director', no longer fits into what is then considered an anti-authoritarian juncture. The highly disciplined man – the founder and pioneer of education in industrial design who has been so far ahead of his time – suddenly degenerates into an anachronism. Unable to recover from the blow, he retires in 1970.

Smeets's departure marks the onset of a turbulent decade in the life of the academy. The élan of the early years fades, making place for consolidation and minor adjustments to the curriculum. Wim Gilles, Smeets's successor, is convinced of the need for a programme that is more university-like in nature. The educational changes he has in mind founder in the wake of opposition from the board of governors, and in1973 Gilles also leaves the academy. C.F.W. Houtman takes his place as director. Houtman's first big job is to draw up a new curriculum, which shows no inherent signs of modernization, however. In the late 1970s a wave of unrest moves through the student body. In 1978 several students write a letter to the board of governors criticizing the academy. They reproach the teaching staff, citing a lack of vision, competence and emotional involvement. The board does not reply to the letter.

Discontent continues to swell among the students. On 17 November 1981 they refuse to attend classes, demanding that 'a say and participation' be granted to 'students, teachers and personnel'. According to the students, the things they are being taught no longer correspond to practical experience. Courses in product design, in particular, have little to do with reality, and the Textile Department is considered too homely. The students demand a school council similar to the type now existing at Dutch universities. The board, however, argues that HBO schools (Dutch schools of higher vocational education) do not yet have such councils and says that anticipating the law is undesirable and would create 'a mess'.

But the board's blunt veto leads to a mess of its own making. On 4 December, students take over the school building, subsequently refusing entry to board members, school officials, teachers and remaining personnel. Demands have multiplied: board members are to hand in their resignations; the relevant ministry is to get involved in the school's affairs; the acting director, H.P.J. Verberkmoes, must be discharged; and the activists must be indemnified from any sanctions resulting from their occupation of the building. Classes resume on 12 January 1982. The representative advisory council is in place, and plagued by continuing criticism Verberkmoes is forced to step down as director. A triumvirate consisting of J. van Duppen, K. Ferwerda and W. Tak then fills the function of interim directorship. After one year, at the request of the board, former AIVE student Jan Lucassen is appointed the new director. He inherits the internal problems of his predecessors, while also having to cope with the changing role of industrial design and with government intervention, which is to have far-reaching consequences for art education. But in Lucassen, the academy once more has a director with a sense of vigour and a desire for innovation that hark back to his illustrious predecessor, René Smeets. During his years as director ('83–'99), he renews the curriculum entirely, draws international attention to the academy, and puts a definitive end to problems surrounding the location of the academy.

FROM AIVE TO DESIGN ACADEMY EINDHOVEN

Immediately after his appointment, Lucassen identifies the splits that threaten to cleave industrial design in two: he sees the industrial era, with its huge demand for products, while also recognizing the information-age-generated need for individual and more specific products that demand flexible manufacturing methods. According to Lucassen, the emergence of more and more types of products is constantly increasing the need for industrial designers. The new director forms an education committee whose membership includes Jan van Duppen (former interim director and later director of education) and Ulf Moritz (teacher of textile design). Within this group, it is mainly Moritz who stresses that the discipline of industrial design should revolve around human requirements. It's this view that forms the point of departure in the newly drawn up curriculum introduced by Lucassen. Courses in textile design and product presentation are replaced by eight departments that aim the spotlight at 'man': Man and Identity, Man and Living, Man and Food (changed later into Man and Well-Being, Man and Work (became Man and Activity), Man and Information (became Man and Communication), Man and Transport (became Man and Mobility), Man and Environment (became Man and Public Space) and Man and Leisure.

Lucassen now has a clean slate, and the historically evolved differences that separated the three old, independently operating departments – Product Development, Product Presentation and Textile Design – belong to the past. With his newly formed curriculum, he is the first and only person in art education to create a link between the user (the human being) and the user's field of interest, an approach unlike that of other academies, which set up their departments on the basis of differences among materials, techniques and skills. At the AIVE, emphasis is placed on the significance and the subjective perceptual aspects of products, as well as on their aesthetic qualities. Also receiving attention are ergonomics, technology and business administration. The new approach gives graduates the key to a much wider sphere of activity than had been available to students attending the academy before these changes were made.

In the '80s all students begin with two years of general studies, which provide an orientation to the subject matter, offer basic knowledge of materials, and serve to decondition the student. Beginning with the school year 92/93, the two years of general studies are reduced to one, after which students immediately select one of the eight departments in which design and subject modules are taught. At that point, new law dictates that the academy's programme of study is shortened from five to four years, the last of which features a compulsory traineeship and a graduation project.

To make it all happen, a great many new teachers are needed. Of the old guard, most of whom work full time, many are made redundant. They are replaced by well-known designers who teach at the academy only one or two days a week, in addition to running their own design practices. Their presence at the school automatically reinforces vital relations between business/work experience and education. At the same time, having designers of name associated with the school is of great importance to the quality and charisma of the AIVE. In the early 1980s, most of the academy's students originate in the region of Eindhoven, but when

1990 rolls around no other art academy in the Netherlands draws students from all corners of the country as well as the AIVE does. Courses are taught in modules, a method used by universities that makes it easier to attract visiting lecturers or, as a student, to transfer (permanently or temporarily) from one department to another. The ideal is for students to sharpen their skills in more than one department and thus acquire a broad-based education. Each of the design modules consists of three phases: an analytic phase in which students collect and analyse information; a creative phase in which hypotheses are made on the basis of the analysis, accompanied by flashes of intuition and unexpected points of view; and the implementation phase, with its focus on drawing and making models.

The academy's educational programme recognizes the importance of technology, but mainly as a resource that serves the designer. This is one of the primary differences between training to be an industrial designer at the AIVE or, for example, at the University of Technology Delft, which offers a programme heavy in technology and marketing. Jan van Duppen, AIVE's director of education, is especially aware of the growing importance for designers of conceptualization and artisanal work in the 1990s. Consequently, van Duppen attaches less importance to the making of scale models, despite their value as an instrument in the industrial and mass-produced manufacture of products. He is also vigilant about maintaining the open structure – no independent departments – that Lucassen introduced into the educational programme.

From the outset, the school has always had an art department (officially entitled Autonomous Design). In his contacts with the outside world, the first director, René Smeets, had been less than clear about this fact, and Jan Lucassen also characterizes the school to others as an institute of industrial design. Those within the academy, however, have long believed that art as a source of inspiration has a positive influence on the education of the industrial designer. In 1987, they still have high expectations for cross-pollination between the two disciplines. Ultimately, however, the presence of an art department actually threatens the school's independent identity. Time and again, Director Jan Lucassen points to the unique character of the school in his attempts to avoid amalgamation with other educational institutes for the arts. But the department in question is the very link that connects the AIVE with other academies and can be used, therefore, as a convincing argument in favour of amalgamation. To survive as an independent institute, it is better for the school to concentrate completely on industrial design. In 1990 the Autonomous Design Department is banished to Tilburg.

FIGHTING FOR IDENTITY

In the world of education, the late '80s are distinguished by schools amalgamating and becoming larger. In 1987 Minister Deetman issues the Division of Tasks and Concentration Report. He concludes that art education is characterized by a fragmentation of the supply, a low percentage of students who graduate, and too high costs.

Furthermore, too few graduates are able to find work. Deetman wants the educational institute itself to find a solution by means of voluntary amalgamations and agreements on division of tasks; he appoints the HBO Council as process coordinator. In its final report, the HBO Council does recognize the unique position of the AIVE, but nonetheless advises the school to find a partner for amalgamation. Lucassen lets the council know that he's not interested in amalgamating with another school. He believes the academy can function quite easily under its own steam. Keenly aware of the unique position that the AIVE holds within art education, he adamantly argues the point of incompatibility to avoid amalgamating with either the HBO Eindhoven or any of the other three academies in the province of Noord-Brabant.

Owing to Lucassen's standpoint, the academy loses its first opportunity, in 1988, to add postgraduate courses to its educational programme. At the beginning of the 1990s, however, it is not the Ministry of ECS that determines which schools may start postgraduate programmes. The Ministry of Welfare, Health and Culture assigns the task to the Council for Culture. To the disappointment of many involuntarily amalgamated schools, more than half the institutes authorized by the council to start postgraduate programmes are schools that have not been amalgamated. Among the fortunate is the AIVE, which can now offer postgraduate courses in industrial design and interior architecture.

On an ordinary day at the AIVE, Director of Education Jan van Duppen is the most visible of the school's officials. He is an excellent communicator, knows all his students by name and finds just the right tone in his contacts with individual members of the teaching staff. It is van Duppen and Ulf Moritz who are instrumental in recruiting the big names in design so crucial to the school's charisma. Having introduced the radical changes in curriculum at the AIVE, Jan Lucassen becomes the school's self-appointed ambassador. He lobbies at every conceivable level and consistently propagates the unique qualities of the school both at home and abroad. Lucassen successfully manages to prevent his academy from being swept away in the prevailing wave of amalgamation, but he fully realizes that his institute remains vulnerable. Ultimately he's able to combine, quite cleverly and creatively, his desire for an independent academy with the opportunities offered by the new Higher Vocational Education Act adopted in 1987. This act allows schools to develop so-called 'new undertakings', such as applied research, postgraduate studies, and a transfer of knowledge from school to business community and other target groups.

In 1988 Lucassen decides to set up an institute apart from the academy for these activities: the European Design Centre bv. Above all else, it is meant to be a centre of information and commerce for the application and exploitation of industrial design. An underlying but even more important objective is the 'third flow of funds': money made available to schools by business and industry. But the feasibility study, which is financed in part by a 400,000-guilder subsidy from the province of Noord-Brabant, shows that many initiatives of this kind already exist in the Netherlands. There is, however, quite a bit of interest in an information centre. In 1992 a revised version of the initially planned European Design Centre (EDC) opens its doors. The new institute consists of five departments.

- **Documentation/information centre**
- **Education centre for postgraduate and post-academic studies**
- **Research and development centre with a focus on new design methodologies and materials**
- **CAD centre for the study of computer use in 3D product design**
- **Transfer point that offers the academy's services to the business community, while also ensuring that the educational programme is geared as well as possible to the demands of business and industry**

Within the academy, Lucassen's brainchild is viewed with a certain amount of suspicion. Some people have the impression that the costs involved in establishing and maintaining the EDC might form a threat to the continuity of the school. But the EDC is based on precisely the opposite idea. In 1992 Dr B. de Nooijer, chairman of the board of the AIVE, puts it like this: 'If the academy wants to remain independent, and if we don't want to get caught in the wave of amalgamation that is inundating vocational education, we have to make the school a "centre of excellence".' Then, too, the EDC confirms and strengthens the international character of the school. A good example is the *EDC Newsletter*, a bilingual magazine, published by the institute, featuring international information on developments in the design world. Despite such positive side effects, the EDC is not the successful institute that Lucassen had hoped it would be. The EDC's focus on new technologies does not meet the interest of the students of that time and by the end of the '90s, the academy withdraws the postgraduate educational programme from the institute. Initially, the EDC manages to flourish thanks to generous subsidies from the European Community. Later, when the EC tightens the purse strings, the institute finds itself in trouble, and when, at the end of the '90s, the academy is no longer willing to cover the deficits, bankruptcy is declared. The EDC survives but the bond between EDC and the academy is entirely severed by then.

Still, the EDC experiment left its mark on the ambitions of the academy. Postgraduate education would help attract international students to Eindhoven and create the possibility to develop the school as a centre of excellence. On that basis the first modest attempts are made to set up a masters programme at the AIVE. Initially without much result, but, after the turn of the century, gradually becoming more and more successful.

EXHIBITIONS

Armed as ever with his singular vision and charismatic personality, Lucassen immediately places the academy in the international limelight, where it has always been for that matter, reaching out to students, media and the business community. As Smeets did before him, Lucassen employs all sorts of resources to grab the attention of media and subsidizers. One ploy is to issue publications featuring graduates' work and graduation exhibitions.

In the summer of 1955, Smeets already manages to organize the first exhibition of graduation projects – the work of night-school pupils at that time – and to mount the show in Eindhoven's Van Abbe Museum, *nota bene*. In his speech at the opening, Theo van Eupen, alderman for education, praises the freshness and originality of the designs. Among those participating are two of the school's first pupils, Frans van der Put and Jaap van Dam, who present a mock-up of a sports car of their design; it has a unique plastic body, and the young men see no reason why it shouldn't go into production the following year.

An even earlier exhibition of student work, also organized by Smeets, takes place in the school itself in 1952. In later years, graduation exhibitions are held at cultural centre De Krabbendans and at city hall. Director Smeets sees these shows as excellent PR vehicles that aid him in generating widespread interest in his school. At that time, the school is unique in the Netherlands, and in all of Europe only the Royal College of Art in London and the Hochschule in Ulm offer comparable programmes, as Smeets stresses in every article that features his exhibitions.

Following this promising start in the 1950s, the enthusiasm for graduation exhibitions as part of a public-relations plan diminishes, and such shows become chiefly internal events. Not surprisingly, Lucassen spots their potential once again in the late '80s. Eindhoven is no longer the industrial centre of the Netherlands, though. Lucassen fears that major companies, design agencies and the media will feel it's not worthwhile to travel from the Randstad (the umbrella term for the Netherlands' largest urban area) to provincial Eindhoven. He decides to take his academy's exhibitions to a place where they are guaranteed to get the attention they deserve. After a few years, they will have gained a sterling reputation and can return to Eindhoven. Among Lucassen's contacts at that time is the Kunsthal in Rotterdam, but his definitive choice is Amsterdam. In 1991 the first graduation show to be held at the Beurs van Berlage takes place.

ACCOMODATION FOR AN EDUCATIONAL ESTABLISHMENT

Like his predecessors, Lucassen places the academy's accommodation high on his list of priorities. The housing history of the academy is marked from day one by a shortage of space. When the school opens in 1950, it occupies Eindhoven's old city hall. In the constant scramble for space, certain activities take place in rooms unsuitable for them. At one point the print shop, a place filled with headache-causing fumes, is equipped with a large ventilator, but complaints of headaches continue to be heard. Years pass before it's discovered that all this time the ventilation duct has been emitting dirty fumes against a thick blind wall. At certain places in the building, extra ventilation is the last thing that anyone wants. The photography studio is located in the attic, where the roof leaks constantly and pigeons fly in and out. Those attending the school in the '50s will recall curtains with 2-metre-long 'hems' artistically clotted with smears of colour from hands and paintbrushes cleaned during class.

At regular intervals René Smeets directs the attention of the Eindhoven City Council to the poor state of maintenance at his school and to the increasingly pressing issue of too little space. New-build plans are postponed over and over again in favour of a series of moves to temporary locations, including an old kindergarten whose tiny toilets long remain in the memories of former pupils.

Although plans for a new building are shelved for the duration – as a result of all the moves and renovation projects – they are certainly not forgotten by Smeets. In 1966 the school's board of governors once more turns to the City Council. Stating its preference in a letter, the board makes clear that what it wants is a location in the vicinity of the 'Institute of Technology, on the one hand, and, on the other, the not-yet-built Institute of Higher Vocational Education' The main argument for an accommodation near the Institute of Technology is this school's close, longtime ties to the academy. Besides their close relationship, the institutes also share a need for facilities such as exhibition space, a large auditorium and collections of materials. Locating the two schools in close proximity to each other is a way to keep building costs within reason, while also realizing 'the fantasy cherished by the most progressive opinion leaders in the world, which is discussed at all the congresses and meetings'. 'It would be an act of great significance for the future,' write the authors of the letter, 'were the idea of a "Techneion", comprising both the higher technical and industrial design institutes, to be realized in Eindhoven.' Two years later (1968), the Ministry of Education and Science approves the purchase of a 7.5-hectare parcel of land not far from the Institute of Technology. But despite the detailed formulation of an 'educational programme of requirements for a new-build accommodation', complete with the request for a flexible layout, the plans are mothballed.

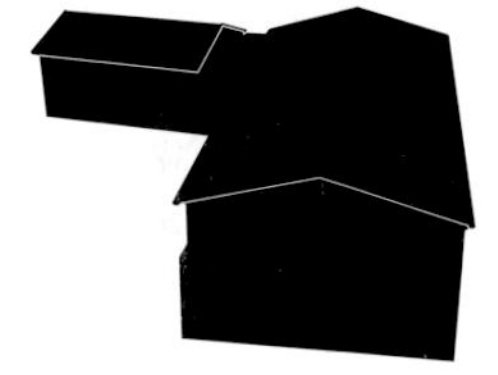

When Jan Lucassen takes his place as director, the school has been housed for about six years in the former Sint-Joris College and Sint-Catharina Lyceum, two schools under one roof, strictly separated, one for boys and one for girls. Not far from the Van Abbe Museum, the building, exemplary of the Amsterdam school of architecture and dating from 1924, has a perfectly symmetrical plan resulting from the rigorous division of the school into identical units for boys and girls. Even the playgrounds are separated from each other by a high wall. The richly detailed exterior is a perfect match for the new function the building receives in 1976.

In 1983 temporary buildings have long blocked the view of playgrounds outside the former school for boys and girls, and the academy is in dire need of more room. Being vacated by Philips at this time are a number of striking, Bauhaus-like buildings in the centre of Eindhoven. Initially, these remarkable buildings are threatened with demolition. But the removal of the light bulb factory on Emmasingel is soon spotted as a new opportunity for the academy. The Emmasingel Foundation is established, and its primary goal is to save the buildings. Another objective is to fill them with functions intended to integrate art and culture, information and technology, recreation and commerce. In 1993 the executive committee of the Emmasingel Foundation, assisted by an

advisory body that includes Lucassen, meets to discuss the future of the building complex. As a creative institute, the academy obviously is an ideal candidate for the colourful, multifunctional completion of the building, as envisioned by the foundation's executive committee. What's more, the academy sees an advisory role for itself with respect to the buildings' architecture and design. In 1998 the move takes place, and the academy underlines its international position by changing the name of the school to Design Academy Eindhoven.

SOURCES

BOOKS

Anon. Study of the Sint Lucasgilde in Eindhoven, 19th and early 20th centuries. Title and date unknown.

Eijck, T.M. *AIVE: The roaring eighties*. Utrecht, 1992.

Smits-Ort, J.M. *KIO 1952–1992: 40-jarige bestaansgeschiedenis Kring Industriele Ontwerpers*. Leiden, 1993.

van den Heuvel, J. *Voor de konsument of de industrie: Voorgeschiedenis en beginjaren van de AIVE 1945–1960*. Utrecht, 1986.

MAGAZINES

'De heer Smeets vertelt over: Industriële vormgeving in de Verenigde Staten. Vooral dienstig bij de sales promotion'. *Philipskoerier*, undated issue (probably 1953).

'Directeur Eindhovense Kunstnijverheidsschool terug uit Amerika: Industriële vormgeving is een economisch belang'. *Eindhovens Dagblad*, 29 August 1953.

'Een volkomen nieuw beroep: industriële ontwerper'. *Het rijk der vrouw*, 20 August 1959, p. 57.

'Het oog wil ook wat: Cursus industriële vormgeving eerste in Nederland. Kennismaking making met Rene Smeets directeur Kunstnijverheidsschool'. *Philipskoerier*, 11 February 1950.

'Industriële vormgeving gaat kijken in Amerika'. *Eindhovens Dagblad*, June 1953.

'Kunstnijverheidsschool vraagt de aandacht'. *Philipskoerier*, 19 July 1952.

Smeets, R. 'Ten geleide'. *Voorlopig contactorgaan van het leerlingencorps Middelbare Kunstnijverheidsschool*, Eindhoven, 1950.

ARCHIVE OF THE ACADEMY OF INDUSTRIAL DESIGN EINDHOVEN (AIVE)

Bijlage van de rekening en verantwoording over 1951. Avondschool voor Middelbaar Kunstnijverheidsonderwijs. Eindhoven, 1951.

Gegevens betreffende het cursusjaar 1963/64 van de dag- en avondschool. Eindhoven, 1964.

Gilles, W. *Brief aan de heren Elno, Houtman, Huygen,*

Truyen, Verberkmoes waarin Gilles oprichting van een bureau voor industriële vormgeving en productpresentatie van internationale allure bepleit. Ulft, 27 January 1960.
Gilles, W. *Prospectus AIVE*. Eindhoven, ca. 1970.
Gilles, W. *Toespraak bij de aanvaarding van het directoraat der Academie voor Industriële Vormgeving*. Eindhoven, 11 September 1970.
Goote M. *Brief aan de besturen van de rijksgesubsidieerde nijverheidsscholen*. 28 January 1952.
Houtman, C.F.W. (R. Burema and H. Eysink Smeets, eds.). 'Kunstenaars in het Stadhuis'. *Inforgaan*, Eindhoven, 1976.
Houtman, C.F.W. *Toespraak bij de aanvaarding van het directoraat der AIVE*. Eindhoven, 31 August 1973.
Intern onderzoek naar aantallen leerlingen per studierichting, sexe, vooropleiding, etc. aan de Academie voor Industriële Vormgeving Eindhoven. 1963.
Leerplan AIVE, 1972.
Leerplan AIVE, Dagonderwijs. Eindhoven, September 1973.
Leerplan School voor Industriële en Commerciële Vormgeving. (The word *Commerciële* has been crossed out and replaced by *Publiciteit, Etalage en Textiel*). 1 September 1954.
Lucassen, J. *Een visie op de AIVE*. Eindhoven, 17 February, 1984.
Meeter, A.P.D. *Brief aan het bestuur van MKS*. 24 July 1954.
Memorandum inzake consequenties invoering leerplan. Eindhoven, 5 June 1973.
Prospectus Academie voor Industriële Vormgeving Eindhoven. Eindhoven, 1970–73.
Prospectus AIVE. Eindhoven, 1980.
Smeets, R. *Brief aan Th. Van Eupen, wethouder Onderwijs en culturele zaken Eindhoven*. 7 October 1955.
Smeets, R. *Kleurstudie en kleurtoepassing: AIVE*. Date unknown.
Smeets, R. *Memorandum en toelichting agenda*. 27 September 1954.
Smeets, R. *Onderwijskundig programma en eisen aan nieuwbouw AIVE*. January 1968.
Smeets, R. *Plakboek publiciteit*. 1955.
Smeets, R. *Reglement van orde: AIVE*. Date unknown.
Smeets, R. *Stand plannen nieuwbouw*. 1954/55.
Smeets, R. *Verslag Amerikareis*. 1953.
Speech on the occasion of R. Smeets's retirement, possibly given by L.C. Kalff of the academy's board of governors. 1970.
Swinkels, G.H. *Brief aan College van B&W Eindhoven*. 1 June 1966.
Swinkels, G.H. *Brief aan Minister van Onderwijs, Kunsten en Wetenschappen*. 19 September 1951.
Swinkels, G.H. *Brief aan Minister van Onderwijs, Kunsten en Wetenschappen*. 14 March 1957.
van Poppel, A. *Brief van vader oud-student aan R. Smeets m.b.t gebrek aan waardering die Academie op dat moment in de praktijk geniet*. Helmond, 21 January 1960.
Verslag over het jaar 1950. Stichting Middelbare Kunstnijverheidsschool Eindhoven. Eindhoven, 1950.
Werkplan onderwijs AIVE. Eindhoven, 1973.

INTERVIEWS

Duppen, J. (1939). Former student, workshop assistant, teaching assistant, interim director, member of the board of governors of the Academy of Industrial Design Eindhoven (AIVE) and former director of education until his retirement in January 2001.
Kosman, Th. (1931). AIVE administrative director 1955–1991.
Lucassen, J. (1937). Former student 1956–1961, AIVE director 1984–1999.
Lucker, L. (1938). Former student 1956–1961, former head of the design department of OCE-Nederland bv.
Marinissen, A.H. (1933). Former student, former AIVE teacher, professor of industral design at the University of Technology Delft.
Peeters, P. AIVE Caretaker of the buildings 1953–1990.
van der Put, F. (1930), Former student 1950-1955, Founder/member of Philips Corporate Design Centre, 2nd in command 1960–90
van Haaren, H. (1930). Director of the Academy of Fine Arts Rotterdam 1982–1988, chairman of the board of governors of the Faculty of Arts and Architecture of Rotterdam University (known at the time as the College of Rotterdam and Environs) 1988–1993.

ACKNOWLEDGEMENTS

Many thanks to:
Prof. Dr T.M. Eliëns, head of collections Gemeente Museum Den Haag and Professor of the history of industrial design and crafts at the University of Leiden. Dr A. Martis, associate professor Faculty of Arts and Humanities/Arts, University Utrecht, for organizing a survey of graduates from the Academy of Industrial Design Eindhoven (1945–1980) and for carrying out this survey, with the help of their students, in 1992.
Dr T. de Rijk, Department of Industrial Design, University of Technology Delft, for his input and support.

Bas van Tol

C-Department [1985]

Top: Installation Buro Mod.Sec., 1987

Middle left: Performance at the opening of the Barcelona Pavilion as Ambassador of Modernism, 1986, in collaboration with Han Speckens

Middle right: City image of Amsterdam, 1991

Bottom: Interior ZBar, Design Academy Eindhoven, 1998

Top: Stand Danskina, Milan, 2003

Middle left: Club 11, Amsterdam, 2004

Middle right: Europa Bar, European Council, Brussel, 2004

Bottom: Restaurant As, Amsterdam, 2007

Christiane Müller

Man and Identity [1989]

Opposite top: Woolen hand tufted rug, Danskina, 1995

Opposite left bottom: Curtain fabric, Collezione Cesaro, 2001

Opposite right bottom: Colour Swatches

Right: Hand tufted woolen rug, in collaboration with Liset van der Scheer, Danskina, 1996

Bottom left: Presentation of rugs, Danskina, in collaboration with Bas van Tol, 2003

Bottom right: Embroidered woolen curtain, De Ploeg, 2006

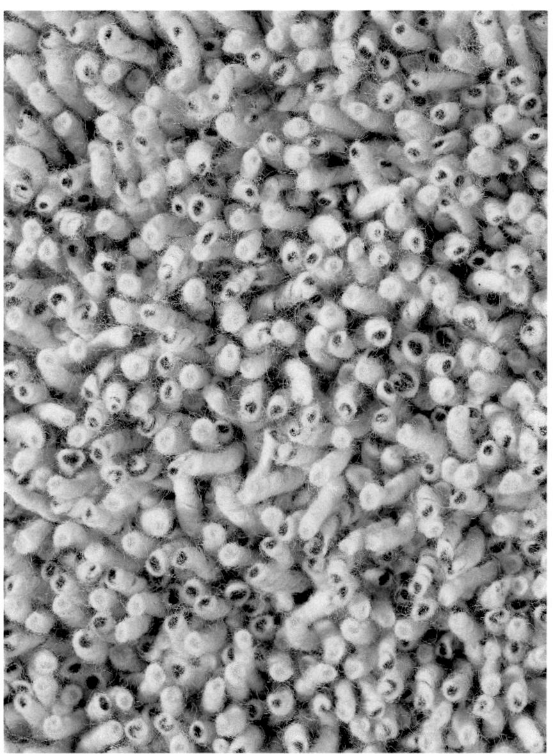

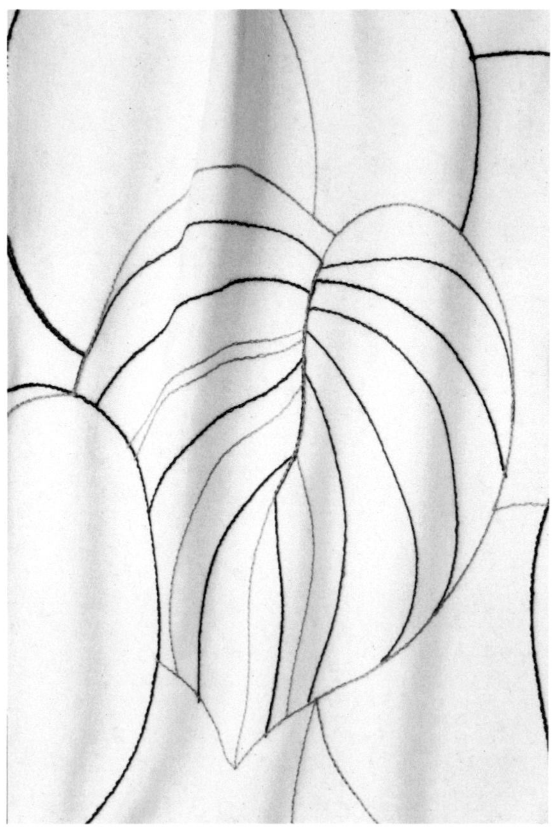

Bart Guldemond

A Department [1986]

Top left: Exhibition 'work of Joke van der Heyden and Bart Guldemond' in the house of Benno Premsela and Friso Broeksma, Amsterdam, 1992 (vases in collaboration with Vincent de Rijk)

Top right: Stand Metropolis M, KunstRai, Amsterdam, 1993

Left: Mis en scène fashion shows Orson & Bodil and 'SO by Alexander van Slobbe', in collaboration with Herman Verkerk, Paris, 1994–2001

Bottom: Exhibition design 'Mode, Vormgeving & Beeldende Kunst bijeen', in collaboration with Herman Verkerk, Centraal Museum Utrecht, 2000

Opposite top: Interior Vrij Glas Foundation, Zaandam, 2006

Opposite bottom: RSVP House, in collaboration with Joost Grootens, Almere, 2008

Top left: BV Bowl, ceramics and polyester, in collaboration with Bart Guldemond, 1988

Below: Ceramic series, 1994–2003

Bottom left and right: Prada Sponge, material research and prototypes for OMA, 2001

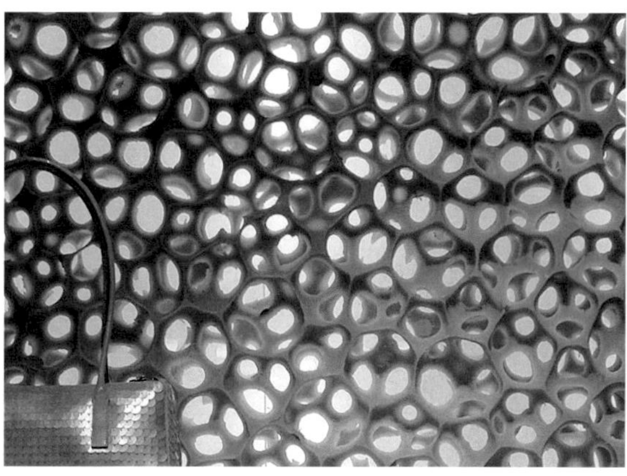

Left: Lighting object, polyester and aluminium, 2007 (commissioned by Kraayevanger Urbis Architecs)

Middle and bottom: OMA models; Très Grande Bibliotheque, 1989 (middle)
La Defence, 2006 (bottom)

‘The teaching staff still had modernist values at the back of their minds,’ says Jurgen Bey (1965), ‘simplicity, a minimum of twaddle and a keen attention to ideas.

In the late 1980s, Jurgen Bey (1965) graduated from the Academy of Industrial Design (AIVE), later to become the Design Academy Eindhoven, Man and Public Space department. Today Bey belongs to a group of Dutch designers who have gained international recognition. Various products from his oeuvre are considered design icons, and among his awards are the LAI (Lensvelt de Architect Interior Award) (2003), the Harrie Tillie Prize for design (2005) and the prestigious Prince Bernhard Culture Prize (2005). And yet Bey’s worldwide reputation is built not only on products but mainly on how he thinks and works. He’s an inspiration for the younger generation, and among his adherents are quite a few of his peers – even though it’s no secret that colleagues are normally critical of one another’s work.

Man and Public Space has always been a small department that has sent a relatively large group of good designers into the world. They’ve found work in all sorts of creative disciplines, designing products, exhibitions, sets and public spaces. A substantial group of graduates attended the Berlage Institute in Rotterdam, where they earned masters’ degrees in architecture and urban planning; still others climbed the administrative ladder in various organizations. Nearly all these ex-students are wildly enthusiastic about their education, and Bey is no exception. ‘The academy opened my eyes. It’s there that I learned to look at the world in a completely different way. The teaching staff included a nice mix of people: Marijke van de Wijst [then head of the department]; Hans van der Markt, whose theoretical input emerged with boundless energy and enthusiasm; and Désirée van Dijk, who injected spirituality into her classes and taught me to trust my intuition. They still had modernist values at the back of their minds: simplicity, a minimum of twaddle and a keen attention to ideas. In retrospect, I'm guessing that certain students didn't find it easy going. Those with a preference for decoration were in the wrong place, but I felt completely uplifted. When you went for something, there was nothing to stop you.' The department's modernist philosophy and a fascination for the narrative quality of objects came together in Bey's work: a strange symbiosis of poetry and functionality. Perhaps that's why he found his heroes – John Körmeling, Merijn Bolink, Job Koelewijn, Wim Delvoy – not in design circles but in the world of art.

Recognition for his work awaited Bey almost immediately after graduation in 1989. At that time, together with a handful of like-minded young designers, Bey became *the* face of Dutch conceptual design. Backed by a highly successful publicity campaign, the group was promoted internationally by the well-known platform Droog Design. Neither ease of use nor purely formal or aesthetic aspects determined the success of these designs. What counted most were the underlying ideas, sometimes presented in a humorous light and always as 'drily' and as lucidly as possible. From the outset, Bey differentiated himself from the others through his fascination for the wealth of references found in everyday objects. He rarely invented a new look for these basic products. Instead, he composed new stories and meanings by combining existing objects and forms, sometimes wrapped in a brand-new skin.

A small selection of Bey's designs starts with Kokon, a collection of old chairs and tables that reveal their origins beneath an elasticized synthetic skin; intimately united, they tell a tale that transcends their individual functions. The skin as an element that joins together various items also plays a role in Broken Family, which consists of the silver-plated pieces of different – and sometimes damaged – tea services; defects are irrelevant in this new family. No skin fuses the components of either Tree Trunk Bench or Light Shade, designs whose various parts are connected to one another in a more concrete way. The lamp, in particular, perfectly illustrates how Bey works: covering an old chandelier (or any other used lamp) is a contemporary plastic shade. When the lamp is switched on, the chandelier – the past – is visible; switch it off, and what you see is a reflective shade that mirrors its surroundings. Few products have been copied so often and so blatantly (and so badly), a fact that takes nothing away from the lamp's status as one of the bestselling products in Bey's oeuvre. Light Shade was followed by another successful design, the Oorstoel (Ear Chair), which Bey made in 2003 for Tilburg insurance company Interpolis (a subsidiary of Rabobank, originally established to lend financial support to farmers). As a reference to Rabobank's agrarian history, Bey gave the chair the form of a well-known armchair found in Dutch farmhouses. His interpretation, with its extended wings, allows for two or more chairs to be arranged to accommodate private conversations or meetings. Oorstoel satisfies the demands of today's flexible, variable office. It has claimed a place within the current supply of office furniture, and it is the

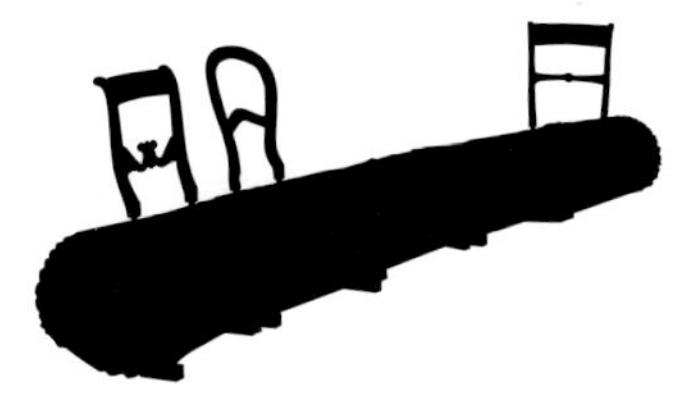

first product launched by furniture label Prooff, a collaborative effort between Bey's studio and SV Interieurgroep Rotterdam. Companies can commission Bey and his team to come up with specific solutions for specific situations: tailor-made work for an office world that Bey considers in need of creativity. Several ideas have already been developed in project presentations and drawings, such as plans that facilitate work in atypical locations like construction scaffolding, car parks and window-washers' platforms. Designs that prove to be more multipurpose than specific, like Oorstoel, will be included in the Prooff collection.

Where is Bey's career headed? Towards both education (London's Royal College of Art) and his studio (Studio Makkink&Bey). Early on, Bey realized quite a few projects for Droog Design, but that relationship has become far more sporadic. 'It's good to look at where you are on a regular basis and to see what's on the horizon. No doubt Droog fulfilled a terrific function for the world of design, but every now and again it's good to reconsider direction again. And the same applies to me.' His last project for Droog was the design of Simply Droog, a travelling exhibition that Bey completed in 2004 together with Ester van de Wiel and Sophie Krier. Nowadays, Bey and his team work for a diversity of clients, as well as on their own projects. Studio Makkink&Bey consists of Bey, partner/architect Rianne Makkink and a dozen or so young designers who either work full time for the studio or are involved in specific projects. Like Bey, most are former Design Academy Eindhoven students. Many did work placement at Makkink&Bey and were asked to join the firm after graduation.

One recent team project that corresponds well to Prooff's ambitions is Slow Car, a workstation on wheels. The auto was introduced in June 2007 at Art Basel as part of Swiss furniture manufacturer Vitra's Limited Series. Slow Car looks at work in a new light. The daily reality of kilometres-long traffic queues is going to get worse before it gets better, and the new method of working might also be suitable for campus-like zones. The little vision-conjuring car can be used as both a means of transport and a mobile workstation. 'I can picture, for instance, the car driving around Schiphol Airport from one place to another, with an occupant who doesn't have to stop working,' says Bey. Slow Car is based on the technology used to make vehicles for the disabled. 'There are so many ingenious solutions in that area. The cars are so manoeuvrable and have such a small turning circle, and the driver can raise and lower the car with a simple joystick. He can experience the trip as if it were a computer game. Isn't it a crying shame that most of these cars are so hideous? Designers are facing golden opportunities here. Visually, we've removed Slow Car from the category of vehicles for the disabled.'

Asked for his thoughts on the current Design Academy Eindhoven, Bey says that 'a school should be a place of concentration, an island that doesn't have to answer to reality just yet. You're removed from the real world for the time being, and that's good. You should be able to experiment at school and make a mess. That's what I miss at the academy today; it's too polished. Sometimes the school seems in danger of focusing too much on promotional activities, which can be detrimental to other necessary qualities. For instance, I think you shouldn't show students' work to the world so quickly. It's only new, and it's presented as though newness is a quality in itself.' For the past ten years, Bey himself has taught at Design Academy Eindhoven , in both the bachelors' and masters' programmes. He served one year as interim head of the Man and Living Department, and he gives workshops worldwide. Since 2006 he has worked as course director in the masters' programme of the Royal College of Art (RCA) in London, in the Design Products Department headed by Ron Arad. Bey spends two days a week at the school, where he contributes to the programme's direction and philosophy. 'People of many nationalities study in London. It's inspiring, and it hasn't led to a globalization of views on design. I don't believe in global design, but I do like a nice meeting of cultures. It adds that little something extra. Later, you all go your own way again. You're formed largely by your roots, so "locale" has a right to exist that should be cherished and not smoothed away. That terrible word "integration", for example, that pops up so often in politics – why does everything have to be unified, evened out? Diversity is wonderful. Unlike many other countries, England, and particularly London, allows various cultures to retain their differences. In that respect, it's a great place for me. We live in a round world. When I travel, I want to see something different, not just more of the same.'

Bey is careful in comparing Design Academy Eindhoven with the RCA. He can be vehement – a man of strong opinions – in speaking about education, but then he quickly weighs his words, saying it's never a question of either/or and always a matter of and/and. Bey prefers optimism to criticism, generosity to exclusion, and diversity to controversy, which may be unsatisfying to those who would like to hear explicit views from a designer who does indeed have such views. But the attitude suits a designer who would rather stir the imagination than persuade the mind to create negativity.

Louise Schouwenberg

Jurgen Bey

Man and Public Space [1989]

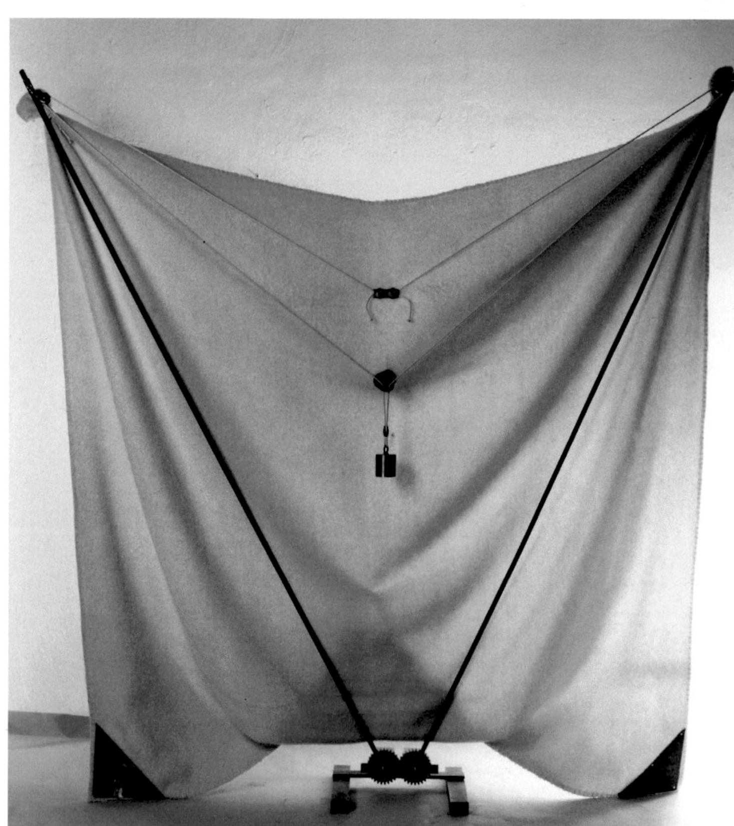

Above: Curtain, 1989

Left: Study Crate Cabinet, 2007
Wooden crate + old table and chair form an isolated space where ideas and thoughts are processed. Exhibition 'Designing Critical Design', Z33 Hasselt (B), 2007

Opposite top: Studio Makking & Bey, Rotterdam, 2007

Opposite bottom: Tea Bag Garden, 2007. Stacked bags of garden soil, cut open for plants. Exhibition 'Designing Critical Design', Z33 Hasselt (B), 2007

Opposite top: Catwalk and back wall for the Gaultier summer collection show 2004

Opposite bottom: Exhibition 'My Castle, My Home', Slot Zeist, 2001
Light Shade Shade, 1999
Kokon Furniture, 1999

Right: Stubborn Chair, 2007

Below: Minute-Crockery, 2003 (for Royal Tichelaar Makkum). The minutes of painting determine the ornaments and the price

Top: Tree Trunk Bench, 1999

Above: Study Crate Cabinet, 2007
Exhibition 'Designing Critical Design', Z33 Hasselt (B), 2007

Left: Ear-chair, 2002
(collection Prooff-SV)
Exhibition 'Designing Critical Design', Z33 Hasselt (B), 2007

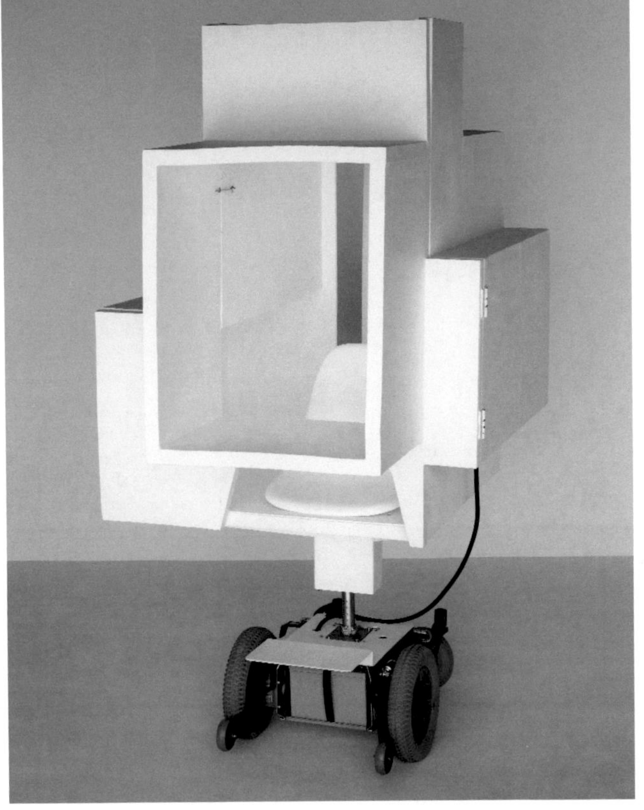

Top left: Linnen House, 2002

Above: Birdwatch Cabinet for a seven year old girl, 2007

Left: Slow Car, 2007 (Vitra Edition) Mobile working unit

Top left and right: Logo's stand Heimtex, 1992. In collaboration with Marijke Griffioen. Commissioned by Eveline Merkx

Left: Carpet in Concertgebouw Amsterdam, 2007
Commissioned by Merkx+Girod architects

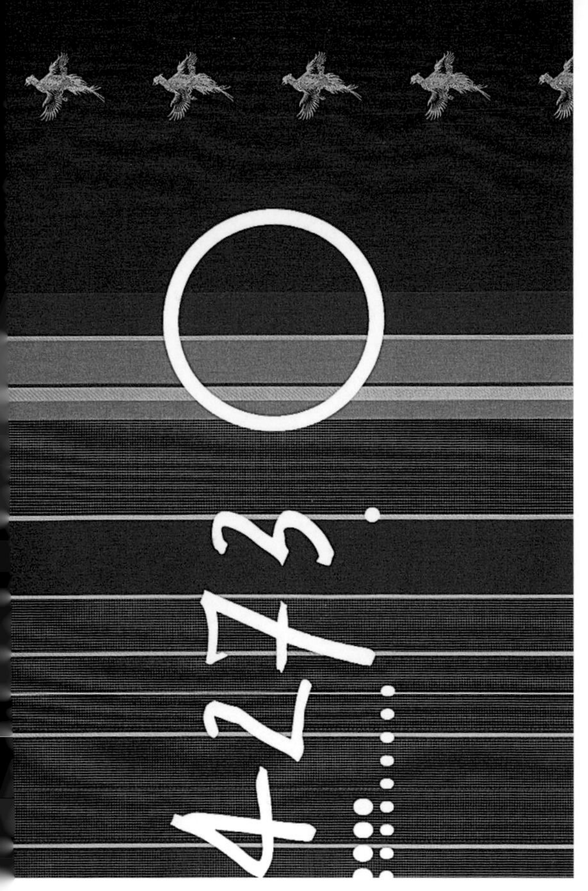

Above: Repeat, 2001
Fabrics for Maharam, New York
Design: JongeriusLab (Hella Jongerius, Edith van Berkel)

Top right: Works from permanent collection, 2005
Cooper-Hewitt, New York
Design: JongeriusLab (Hella Jongerius, Edith van Berkel)

Right: 'Nymphenburg Sketches', 2005. Nymphenburg Porzellan Manufaktur, Munich.
Design: JongeriusLab (Hella Jongerius, Edith van Berkel)

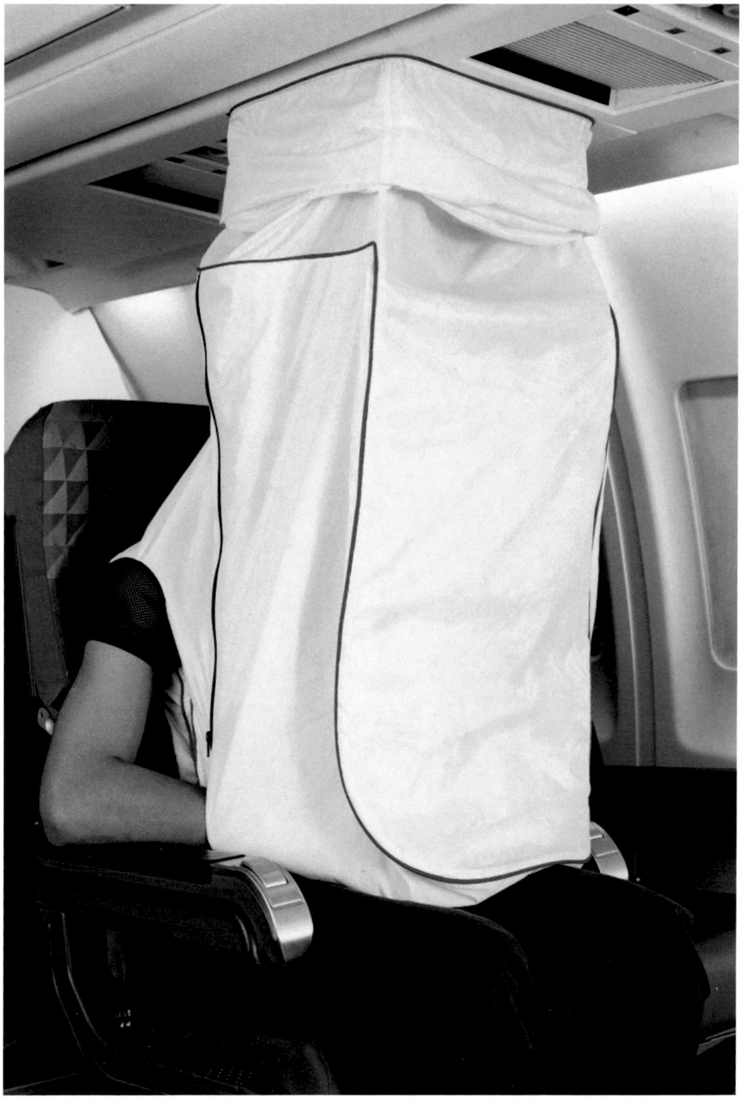

Above: Puzzle Pixel. The Romans in Budapest, 1997
Physical photomontage of European cities.

Left: NEST 747, 2001
In collaboration with Johan Prosje
Project 'Mobile Dreaming'
Organized by Auping Foundation

Top and left: Mobile Garden, Haarlem, 2002
In collaboration with Buro Mien Ruys (Marnix Tavenier)
Commissioned by Government Building Agency

Botom left and right: +Benches, 2005
Commissioned by CBK and the city of Rotterdam

Above: Rough-and-Ready, 1998

Left: TranSglass, 2007

Opposite left top:
Petit Jardin Armchair, 2007

Opposite right top:
Revolution Armchair, 2004

Opposite bottom:
Little Field of Flowers, 2006

Right: Blossom, 2003

Below: Happy Ever After, 2004

Bottom right: Witch, 2004

Opposite left top: Nectar, 2005

Opposite right top:
Garland Brass Black, 2002

Opposite left bottom:
Doll Chair McQueen, 2005

Opposite right bottom:
Nest, 2006

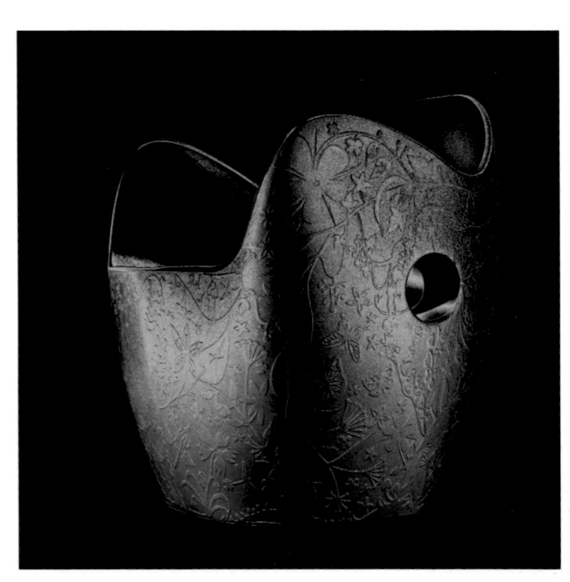

Piet Hein Eek (1967): . ‘We were trained to think free, keep all options open. The concept had to be good. You needed a solid concept to fall back on, no matter what’.

With 30 full-time employees and a good-sized furniture factory in Geldrop, Piet Hein Eek is no longer the freebooting designer of the early ’90s who seemed for a time to be the reincarnation of both Gerrit Rietveld and his assistant, Gerard van de Groenekan. In 1990, as a student at the Academy of Industrial Design Eindhoven (AIVE), Eek built a cabinet made of boards and slats found at scrapyards. A motley composition of colours and gradations of shabbiness. Eek not only recognized how attractive second-hand wood could be; he also looked for designs that would make reuse cost-effective. The project was not received by his instructors without the usual criticism, of course, but the obstinate student persevered – surely part of the reason that many view him as the academy’s number-one dissident. Eek’s projects were covered in the press, however, and little by little his designs began appearing in shops, galleries and living rooms.

‘That school’s always given me a bad feeling,’ he says, walking away to leave a note on a colleague’s desk. One more phone call, a quick scribble and Piet Hein Eek pauses to describe the school he entered in the mid-1980s. ‘In those days at the AIVE, you learned without really being taught. The first year and in particular the painting course, proved highly valuable to me. Through painting I learned to disregard the beauty of the detail as long as it didn’t comply with the overall quality of the work. We were trained to think free, keep all options open. The concept had to be good. You needed a solid concept to fall back on, no matter what.

‘At the time the academy and its teachers strongly advocated the importance of ideas as the only sound basis for design. Year after year the school produced new groups of designers who were forced into the same system of working and thinking. But you could argue about the quality of most of the ideas that have made Dutch design an internationally recognized brand. How sustainable did they prove to be for designers in the long run, and what did they add to the quality of their work? Looking back to that period, it is obvious that only the few front runners have survived, the trend has died away.

'The eighties and nineties were characterised by decadence and wealth. In contrast the simple ideas and concepts of many objects designed in the Netherlands felt like a breath of fresh air. And although their position has changed since the turmoil of 2001, they still seem to maintain a certain attraction.

'When I walk around the academy today, or lecture there, I inhale a sense of freedom and notice the students' strong personal motivation. The place has an academic atmosphere that was lacking when I was a student. It's become a spot where all sorts of stories can be told. You feel an individual energy, whereas two decades ago there was a collective energy at most, which led to a uniform sort of design and a bunch of nice-idea designers.'

His problem was a reluctance to conform. Consequently, he remembers life at school as a period of constant quarrelling. 'In retrospect the decision to use scrap wood for my final piece is perfectly understandable. I seem to spot the quality of materials and techniques that others take for granted or even ignore. To me, using scrap wood was anything but a nice idea. But unfortunately it was judged on that basis. I approached the project by accentuating the singularity of each board, although they were subject to the rules of the production process and the final product. The shape of cupboard is extremely simple. The pragmatics of my approach wasn't very well understood.'

Now, more than 15 years after that tumultuous debut, Piet Hein Eek claims an exceptional position among Dutch designers. Partly owing to his raw pragmatism and rejection of pretences, and partly to the clever way in which he's developed as both a designer *and* a manufacturer, all on his own initiative. Besides the people in his organization, Eek needs few others to make what he wants in the way that he wants it. Neither materials nor manufacturing methods restrict his operation, and he relies only on his own inventiveness to realize projects as diverse as a stage set, a school interior and a series of aluminium contract furniture. Eek makes scrap-wood sheds and small houses for the garden, as well as DIY furniture kits that are sold in department stores. He works with artists and architects and is involved in a number of ways with traditional workshops in developing countries.

Dutch design's 'no strings attached' era is over, declares the designer with satisfaction. Since the turn of the millennium, he notes another pressing matter that affects design. 'Up until 2001, you could say that design had been silent for a couple of decades,' he says. 'Social issues were completely ignored. Beginning in the '80s, people like Philippe Starck faced a virtually empty expressway. They had hardly any competition. By that time, consumers and subsidizers were prepared to embrace just about anything. As a designer, you got lost in either the decadence or the concept. Somebody suggested screwing a bare light bulb into the ceiling, and the world applauded. You had good gagsters, like Henk Stallinga, and a whole lot who weren't so funny. They were all unique, but I found most of their work utterly exhausting.'

Droog Design, he says, took full advantage of the moment. 'They filled an emotional void, as it were, by promoting extremely conceptual work. But it was 9/11 that really gave design a new focal point. When that happened, the light bulb in the ceiling was still good, but the need for simplification and for putting things into perspective became something entirely different. Something far more interesting. It's no longer a luxury to be restrained. Suddenly our work was playing a role in a fight against the consternation caused by an event that had caught society unawares.'

More and more often, Piet Hein Eek has the idea that his views on design and his approach to the work involved, which got him into trouble as a student, are now gaining recognition. It's something he first realized while working as a visiting lecturer at the academy several years ago. He tried to explain to his students the connection between designing and a far less familiar activity: making. 'How did that go? I had them do some real work. I asked them to give practical thinking a try – not only to come up with an idea for a product but also to do some concrete work on its realization. For most of them, this was something new. In two weeks' time we produced an enormous series of tables and chairs. At the end, the whole space was filled, probably as never before. Terrific! It was a great learning experience for me as well.'

Visitors to the factory in Geldrop walk into another jam-packed space. After being in business for some ten years, Eek & Ruijgrok is bursting at the seams. On the near horizon is the firm's relocation to a larger factory nearby, with more space for its many production lines. The move gives Eek an opportunity to take a close look at the structure of his organization. 'We started this operation in a state of total anarchy. Everybody did everything, and activities overlapped and crisscrossed where necessary. In those days, we were still convincing ourselves that each of us was equally responsibility for the business. We survived on the enthusiasm of our staff who did not cry out for organisational structures. For quite a while three-fourths of our production was custom-made items, but in the meantime we've had an increase in small-scale serial production, which requires a different type of organization. A fixed division of tasks. In my case, for instance, it means I'll never again be involved in the actual production process, but I am drawing more than ever.'

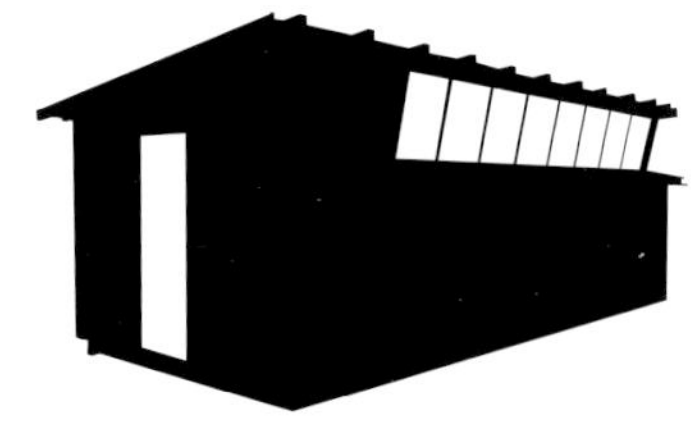

Reorganization or not, Eek & Ruijgrok's ability to produce custom-made products is a unique aspect of the enterprise. Eek assures us that in the area of prototypes, the company is virtually unrivalled. 'Materials, manufacturing methods and human skills are the basis of our designs. They satisfy the demand for custom-made solutions, but the thinking behind them is industrial, and the designs can be easily adapted to serial production. We do that better and cheaper than anyone else. In my opinion, that's exactly what a designer does. A current trend in the design world is to produce limited editions of a product at very high prices. More often than not this choice results from the recognition that the product would never sell in larger quantities at a normal price. I think a small batch should never be the answer to make a product feasible.'

In addition, Eek & Ruijgrok have succeeded in carving out a more and more recognizable niche in the market for Piet Hein Eek, the brand. A contented Eek confirms that practically all his designs bear the same three-word trademark. 'It's been that way since 1993. In the meantime, I think we must have between 20 and 30 Piet Hein Eek products with a life expectancy of at least another half century. They're going to outlive me.' Currently, his statement applies mainly to the Dutch market. About 80 per cent of what the company makes is sold in the Netherlands. But the international distribution network, carefully supervised by the headquarters in Geldrop, is growing. 'We require our international distributors to represent all our products,' says Eek. 'They can't choose, for example, between scrap-wood and aluminium furniture. I like to think of these joint efforts as friendships. They express the willingness of both sides to keep supporting the investment.'

'Designers,' says Eek, 'are usually slightly ahead of the times.' They sense what's lurking around the corner a fraction better or faster than the rest of us. Eek himself has more of an affinity with the artist, who wants to change the spirit of the times or to exert an influence on the 'everyday world'. Without a trace of irony, he says the designer is unimportant, with the possible exception of his ambition to touch people with his work. 'I try to send a signal about the way things are made and consumed. To do that, you have to be brave enough to oppose the spirit of the times.'

Eek sees the Design Academy Eindhoven's apparent move to become a brand as another indication of the spirit of the times. Evidently, there's an even keener understanding that the reputation of that brand reflects the quality and diversity of the individual students. 'The uniformity is ruptured. Compared with my own time at school, you see the enormous professionalization of today's academy, whose students learn to contemplate and to choose. Much attention is being paid to the craftsmanship: what's your subject, how are you going to make and present it? Even mediocre students perform and present at a high level, which is quite an achievement in comparison to the early nineties. What you contemplate, what you choose and how it's presented – all of that is still up to the individual student. The school provides the tools, but the student determines the character of the work.'

Gert Staal

—

Scrap wood cupboard, 1990

Top: Series of Door cupboards, 1992–1996

Above: Window cupboard, 1995

Right: Bathroom window cupboard

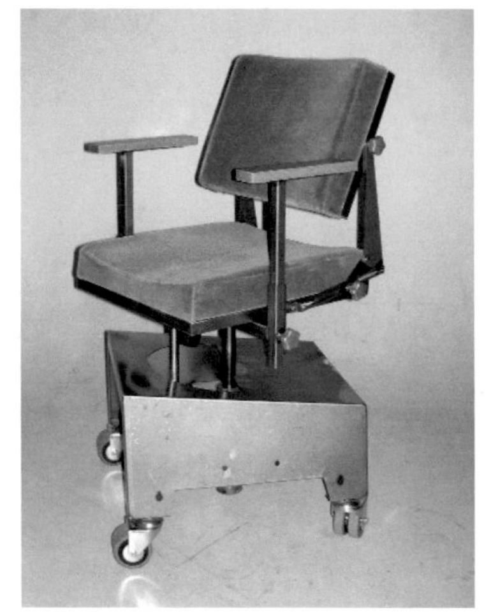

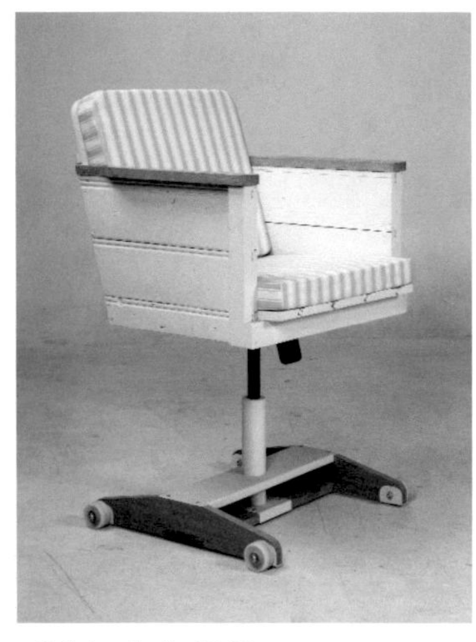

Crisis chair, 2003

Garden chair, 2002

Interpolis chair, 2002

Office chair Interpolis, 2002

Scrap wood canteen chair

Children's high chair, 1996

Aluminium chair, 1993

Children's rocking chair, 1996

Live and Play construction chair, 2001

Top: Garden house Zoetermeer, 1999

Aove: Ticket kiosk Kröller Müller Museum, 2002

Right: Garden house Floriade, 2002

Above and left:
Zambia project, 2005

Opposite left top:
Illustrator's office, 1998

Opposite right top:
Open-air theatre pavilion, 2005

Opposite left bottom:
Bakery shop, Amsterdam 1999

Opposite right bottom:
Bakery shop, Amsterdam 2001

U KUNT OOK
HIER BESTELLEN

KAHREL'S
THEE
GRONINGEN

Lucas Verweij

Man and Public Space [1992]

—

Right: Randstad Citymap, 1996. Map showing the Randstad, the urbanised area between Rotterdam, The Hague, Amsterdam and Utrecht, as a single city.

Below: Streetpieces for Almere, 2001. Proposal of Schie 2.0 (L. Verweij, J. Konings and T. Matton) to bring 'nature' back into a normal Dutch street, creating identity for the Vinex neighbourhood while abolishing private gardens.

Opposite top: Autarchic House, 1996–2001. Proposal of Schie 2.0 for a self sufficient house, which would facilitate a sustainable lifestyle as a natural habit.

Opposite bottom: Regelland, 1999. The project visualises the Netherlands as an overly well regulated country. Goal of this project by Schie 2.0 was to initiate discussion on sense and nonsense of the many rules and regulations versus the proper responsability of people. The project was shown at several locations, for instance in the ministery of Planning, The Hague, 2001.

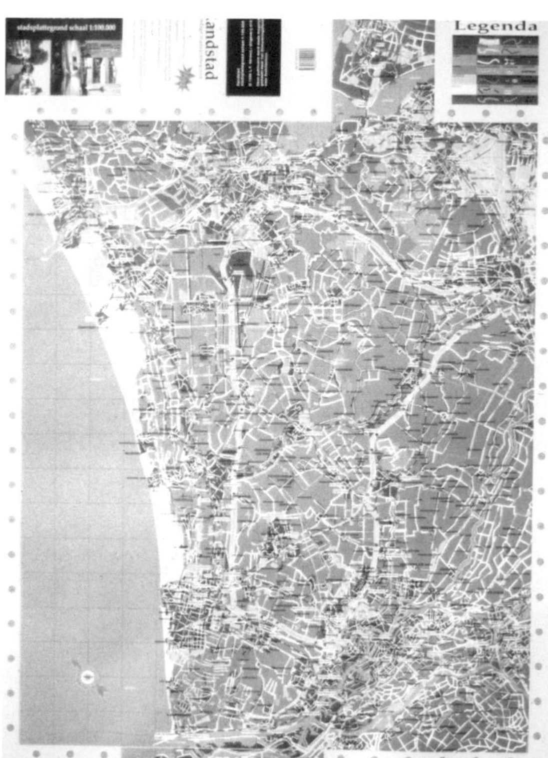

there is a restricted amount of
people who can enter holland
this way

Tradition was something to be ignored: 'We didn't give a shit about anything they told us,' says Richard Hutten (1967) 'But we were involved with design 24 hours a day.'

'I do what I am,' says Richard Hutten. Indeed, his work represents his personality, which is clear, playful and concise. A man of few words, Hutten never uses more means of expression than needed. Very much his own man, even as a student, he did not allow the Design Academy Eindhoven (then called AIVE) to change that fact. He belongs to a generation of designers that emerged in the early 1990s and, supported by Droog Design, redefined the profession. Within the context of design, he's achieved success and fame all over the world.

Hutten proudly and briefly mentions his description of what he does – 'no sign of design' – a motto pretty well known by this time. At the beginning of his career, this principle was easy to grasp. He derived everything he did from the archetypal table and turned its basic parts into various products. Observers couldn't see that a designer had been involved in making these objects. It didn't take long, however, before he started creating objects that *do* conform to the commonly accepted definition of 'design'. All the signs are there – surely justification for asking Hutten whether he can sustain his 'no sign' motto in the future.

Apparently he can, without effort. 'Look, this is what I do: I play with rules. I set them and see what happens in terms of both form and use. It's the reason why the exhibition about my work in Rotterdam's Kunsthal was entitled Homo Ludens, the playing man. My designs are very much like the goal in a soccer game, which is just a rectangle that you're supposed to put a ball through. All the complexities of the game evolve from that simple principle. If the goal had been designed with all kinds of exuberant frills, it would have added nothing to the game. So forget the frills. My designs are at the service of human behaviour. I don't solve problems; I create opportunities. It's rules

that count, and form helps me set them. I like to observe people interpreting them, and I just love it when they do something I hadn't foreseen. On the other hand, I have to admit that "no sign of design" does involve design, simply because everything that mankind has produced has been designed in one way or another, which means I have to take care to keep everything in balance. But form merely supports rules, as clearly as possible, and doesn't express some idea of beauty or style. What's more, I like the challenge of getting things done that have been called impossible.'

ELEPHANT

Quite good at keeping his designs in balance, Richard Hutten allows them to express precisely what they are. His designs are clear and sharply defined. Occasionally they seem to be in conflict with what the designer claims he's doing. Recently Hutten designed a shiny, bright-blue meeting table with very fat feet that consist of rounded shapes stacked one atop the other. In a rather radical way, the table seems to express the opposite of Hutten's previous explanation, but here again it's all about rules. 'This table is part of a meeting room I did for the Boijmans Van Beuningen Museum in Rotterdam,' he says. 'The idea was a space that would be over the top, just to make the people in it slightly uncomfortable. That way, meetings wouldn't last too long; ideally, the room would prompt people to get to the point quickly, to make a speedy exit and to be productive. The room was envisioned as a meeting machine, so to speak. Its principle is not unlike that of the interiors of McDonald's restaurants, where hamburger turnover is stimulated by an environment that's just pleasant enough for people to have an enjoyable but quick meal and to be on their way again, emptying a booth for the following customers. My overstated solution was a bright-red room furnished with a bright-blue table. The feet are actually enlarged machine parts, which express the "decision machine" concept.'

From a museum conference room to a white-plastic elephant is a giant leap, but here we are. Apart from the fact that it's a playful object, at first sight the elephant seems to be based on unfathomable rules. Although it sells very well, within the scope of Hutten's work this figuratively designed animal has to be the odd one out. Is it a coincidence that design pioneer Charles Eames also designed a small elephant, a children's seat made out of plywood? Eames had been exploring the properties of plywood in 1945, at the beginning of his career, two years after having designed his first product with it: a leg splint for wounded soldiers. Hutten had no previous knowledge of the esteemed designer's animals – it seems Eames didn't stop with elephants – he heard about them from a client.

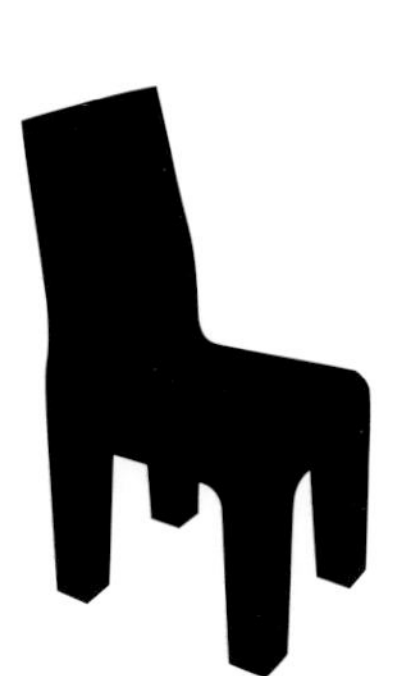

'Originally, it was part of a large building project I did in Amsterdam with MVRDV Architects,' says Hutten. 'The condominium has three large open atriums, eight storeys high, which provide an air of transparency. We thought of turning those vast spaces into parks that could be furnished as if they were oversized rooms. We put trees in large pots, for example, as blown-up plants, so to speak. The rooms are designed for sitting, eating and playing. While thinking about them, I happened to discover a toy elephant in my son's room, and it struck me as the perfect idea for a playroom object. A number of white elephants now function as lighting objects in the condominium, providing a cheerful atmosphere in the playing area, which occupants can look down on from their apartments. But there's a market for them as well.

At the furniture fair in Milan we put one on the street, chained to a post. Passers-by trying to steal it actually bent and damaged the post, but they didn't get the animal. Fascinating what this elephant evokes. As a matter of fact, just this morning I got a photograph from a man walking on the street carrying it over his shoulder, holding it by the trunk. I certainly hadn't realized you could carry it like that. And people tell me they love to sit on it, which again is not something I had in mind when I designed it. What's more, when my client told me Eames had done an elephant, it struck me that I'd inadvertently become part of the modernist tradition by designing an elephant.'

DESIGN SCHOOL IN KOREA
Tradition was not Hutten's main interest when he was studying to be a designer. To him and some of his fellow students – including Jurgen Bey, Jan Konings and Hella Jongerius – tradition was something to be ignored, at best. 'We motivated one another to experiment freely, and we didn't give a shit about anything they told us,' he says. 'But we were involved with design 24 hours a day. Our teachers found our attitude difficult to deal with. I remember designing a bedside table and discussing it in class. One of the teachers – it may have even been Gijs Bakker – asked: "Suppose you found this on the street, along with the rest of the rubbish; would you take it with you?" And I just stood there smiling. To me, the question was pointless.'

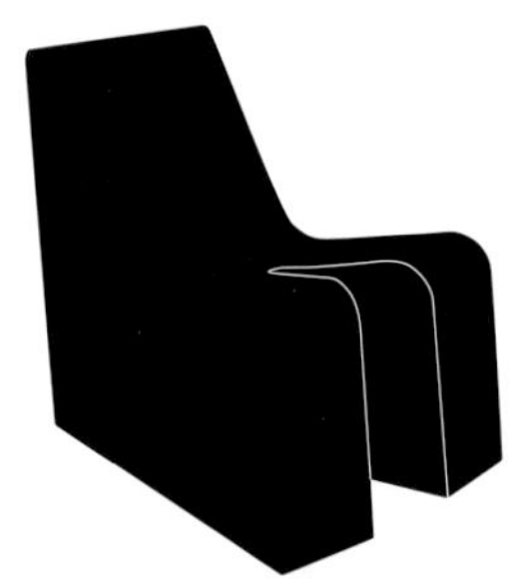

Currently, Richard Hutten is involved in establishing his own design academy in Korea. It's quite an ambitious project, which again involves the cooperation of MVRDV. 'It started with a conglomerate of companies, the Rhea Corporation, some five years ago,' says the founder of the new academy. 'It was going to be a design school plus shopping mall. We focused on a piece of land in Seoul. Unfortunately, city government officials wanted slush money, which they didn't get from us. In the end, the Rhea Corporation went bankrupt, and the mayor of the city even ended up in jail. We've recently picked up the plan again, and together with the Design Academy Eindhoven and the Academy of Arts and Design in Lausanne we're trying to get things moving. There's a new location in Busan, Korea's second largest city, which is right in the middle of the action. China and Japan are close by. We're still at the beginning. If it gets going, it will be a lifetime project.

'The main objective of the curriculum will be to stimulate creativity. Of course, you have to be creative in every profession and not everybody is equally talented. You can't make talent, but stimulation is viable. There are some cultural difficulties that have to be overcome. One is that Korean students are accustomed to teachers that tell them exactly what to do. At our academy, they'll have to learn to think for themselves. The other difficulty is akin to what Dutch soccer trainer Guus Hiddink had to deal with when he worked for the Korean national team. A player would pass the ball to the guy with the better reputation rather than to somebody with an opportunity to score. Reputation and status hamper creativity. I give my cell-phone number to everybody. That type of accessibility is a shock in itself. At the same time, I feel that I get more respect over there than I get here, being the person that I am, which is not the suit-and-tie type. If I wear a tie, nobody takes me seriously. As I said, I like to set the rules and afterwards I hope someone says to me: You played well.'

Ed van Hinte

Richard Hutten

Man and Living [1991]

—

Table concept

Top: Skyline Rotterdam, 1993

Bottom: The Cross, 1994

Top left: Table-chair, 1991

Top right: Sexy Relaxy, 2000

Above: Ding 22, 2000

Above: Zzzidt-object, 2000

Left: De Refter, Centraal Museum, Utrecht, 1999

Above: Parkrand housing block by MVRDV architects, 2007

Right: Parkrand outdoors design by Richard Hutten, 2007

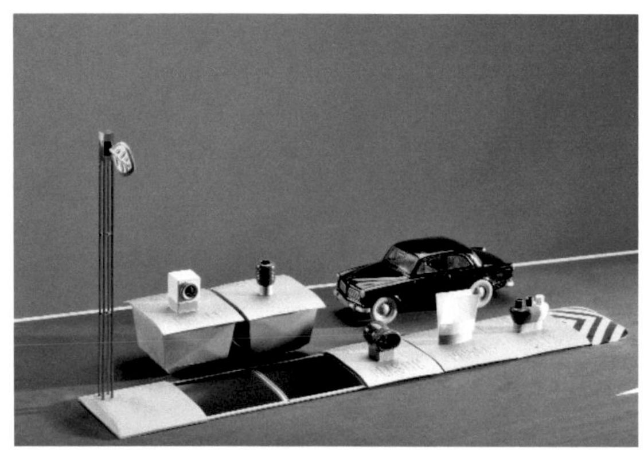

Left: Recycling as a branded experience, 1993. To be placed near supermarkets and along the cities edges

Middle: Gigasports, multi-brand sports superstore, Hong Kong, 2002–2004, 4 locations

Bottom: Yishion, storedesigns, Hong Kong, 2005, 3 locations

Top left: OmWorld, aromatherapy and homeware collection, Hong Kong, 2005

Top right: Crocs, footwear, Hong Kong, 2007, roll-out throughout Asia-Pacific 20+ locations

Above: Smartone-Vodafone, mobile communications service provider, Hong Kong, 2004–2007, 35 locations to date

Right: Carat, semi-precious stones jewellery presentation, Hong Kong, 2006, 3 locations

Hella Jongerius (1963) calls herself 'a mediocre student'. 'At the academy, I wasn't ambitious enough to really make things happen.'

'Lost and Found' was the title of a portrait of Hella Jongerius (1963) that appeared in *Frame* magazine in 2002. With nearly ten years of experience as a designer, Jongerius then stood at the threshold of an international career. Among the first contemporary designers to express interest in old production methods, she's reaping the benefits five year later, when such methods are generally accepted by many designers and predictions about her career have proved overly cautious. Whereas nearly all her earlier designs were private-initiative projects, major companies like Vitra, Maharam, Nymphenburg, Tichelaar, Ikea and Nike are now jostling to produce items with the Jongerius signature; she's won several awards (including the Kho Liang Ie Award 1997, the Rotterdam Design Prize 2003 and the French Prix du Créateur de l'année 2004); and her products feature in museum collections (including those of the Kruithuis in 's-Hertogenbosch and MoMA in New York) and are sold in the most prestigious galleries and shops. Without a doubt, Hella Jongerius has a top-ten position in the world of design.

Her career in a nutshell: a 1993 graduate of the Academy of Industrial Design Eindhoven (later named Design Academy Eindhoven), Man and Identity department (then under the leadership of Ulf Moritz), Jongerius calls herself 'a mediocre student'. 'Previously, I hadn't the slightest notion of what design was. It wouldn't be exaggerating to say that I was a cultural barbarian. At the academy, I wasn't ambitious enough to really make things happen. The decisive boost came from Lucas (fellow student Lucas Verweij, now married to Jongerius, then enrolled in the Man and Public Space department), who made me believe I had enough talent – I just needed the backbone to go with it.' It was soon evident that Jongerius had a good sense of the *Zeitgeist* – a spirit of the times that favoured her generation of Dutch designers. Although the international design world was profiting from the economic prosperity of the '90s and design was booming as never before, the Dutch were better able to legitimize the profession. Resisting the slick side of design, they emphasized the meanings and narratives beneath the skin of their creations. Among others who picked up on the phenomenon was Droog Design, an organization founded in the early '90s that provided a platform for and promoted the work of Jurgen Bey, Jan Konings, Marcel Wanders, Hella Jongerius and a handful of non-Dutch designers. And with success. Like other early Droog designers, Jongerius began with a familiar, archetypal language of form. But rather than concentrating primarily on ideas, she focused on materials and production methods, in the belief that the best ideas and stories demand intensive experimentation: the 'dirty hands' method. 'Material and intuition have always directed my work. As for the *way* I work, I sometimes seem to be more of an artist than a designer. I find the process as important as the final result. It's only when a material pushes the envelope and manages to break through that surprising possibilities and concepts surface. Working with a material in a certain way can not only produce an attractive design but also add a new dimension to the object. That's why I often work with decoration: the products' skin. Decoration isn't just about beauty – a common assumption – it can also generate meanings.' Exhaustive experimentation with materials – polyurethane, ceramics, glass, synthetic fibres, fabrics – led to a selection of products that included, design classics such as Hella's polyurethane bathmats, Soft Urn, Knitted Lamp, Embroidered Tablecloth and Polder Sofa.

A leitmotif in Jongerius's work is the search for a good balance between unadorned, mass-produced items and the handcrafted and often richly decorated one-off. Perhaps nothing has tested this ambition better than the four large vases she designed for Ikea. Unlike her experience with ceramic companies like Tichelaar, known for its quality products, the work for Ikea demanded a new approach to craftsmanship. Ikea's trademark – super-efficient packaging and low transport costs equal inexpensive products – does not apply to fragile vases in bulky packaging. Ikea was forced to reduce costs by having the vases made in Chinese factories. When initial samples failed to meet Jongerius's standards, the designer made several trips to China to supervise the operation on site. Although the resulting vases have been mass-produced on a large scale, they are still signature pieces by Hella Jongerius.

Economizing played a vital role in the Ikea project, but Jongerius has had to use her powers of persuasion when working with the more elite clients as well. Sometimes it's less about monitoring the quality of craftsmanship than about relinquishing it. One example is a 1998 project that began at the European Ceramic Work Centre in 's-Hertogenbosch. B-Service plays on the idea that old, partially damaged cups and saucers from Grandma's cupboard evoke more emotions than a perfect 12-piece tea service. Firing the pieces in an overly hot kiln produced a mismatched tea set: a family of one-offs. Jongerius then had to convince the ceramics industry (Tichelaar Makkum) that 'bad' kiln temperatures could produce 'good' objects. She also had to demonstrate the benefit of 'ineptitude' to craftspeople at Nymphenburg. After collecting patterns

and forms from the company archives, she asked the artisans to apply them in a fragmented way to new plates and bowls. ‘Mostly, I wanted to show the beauty of the company’s expertise and potential. But the people doing the work felt as though they were making unfinished pieces.’ Most of those who had to accept Jongerius’s ceramic designs were artisans. Her collaboration with American textile manufacturer Maharam meant locking horns with marketers. The first design was Repeat, a fabric with an extra large repeat interval that enables multiple pieces of furniture to be covered with the same fabric, yet no two are alike. ‘Repeat is a celebration of a product in all its richness,’ says Jongerius. ‘But more than just the concept or the treatment of a material, this is about an industrial process, about making something on a large scale and, not least, about gutsy marketing. Users are left with a lot of remnants, which could have made this fabric hard to sell.’

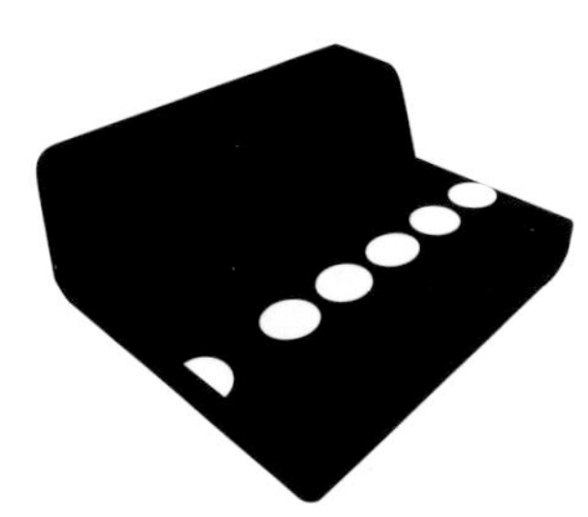

Although stories, meanings, material experiments and the balancing act between one-offs and mass-produced items still characterize the work of Jongerius, much has changed in the intervening years. In a recent project for Maharam, Layers, she came up with the decorative patterns herself rather than drawing on archival material or the iconography of her earlier products. An even more important change can be seen in the dimensions of her work. Joining her original, relatively small designs – crockery, vases, fabrics and the like – is a line of furniture and accessories for Vitra’s Home Collection, among which the well-publicized Polder Sofa. More recently, Jongerius designed a limited edition of strange objects with small details that refer to both functionality and the fantasy world. With products like these, Jongerius seems to be dragging a gradually evolving design phenomenon over its boundaries. In the past half century, the term ‘functionality’ has lost the ‘instrumental’ aspect of its original definition. Design is about image, about meanings that transcend purpose and utility, about context. This significance, this essential ability to cherish narrative objects – in a humdrum office garden, for example – is found in Jongerius’s Office Pets, which she insists are not art but functional objects. Even bolder is a related series of designs exhibited at the Kreo Gallery in Paris in the summer of 2007: wooden tables organically blended with abstract animal figures. Are they sculptural pieces with artistic pretensions or functional designs that add more to a room than a flat work surface?

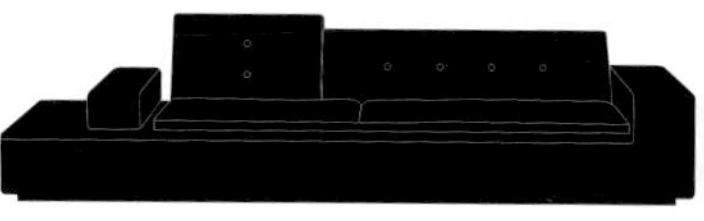

Vitra’s satisfaction with Jongerius is illustrated in her current position as the firm’s art director and material & colour consultant. Since 2006 she has been developing a palette for Vitra, selecting new fabrics and materials for old design classics (including the Eames Lounge Chair) and proposing new interpretations of pieces in the existing collection. She and others in her studio – Arian Brekveld, Edith van Berkel and Iris Toonen, all Design Academy Eindhoven (or AIVE) graduates – have worked on over 30 projects for Vitra, all of which are in production. ‘About half our time is spent working on such projects, and that might become even more. Vitra is a great company to work for. It’s fun to build the collection, especially because it means being involved in strategic corporate decision-making.’

No more than a mediocre student, Jongerius certainly didn't take long to prove she had all the qualities needed to make it big in the world of design. But what does she think of the youngest generation of academy graduates, some of whom feel the glare of the international limelight while still students and thus experience a completely different start to their careers? 'It wouldn't surprise me if it never got beyond those first products. Don't forget that that work was made in the rather safe environment of a school and under the very close supervision of instructors. Young designers like to disregard that fact, and they can be horribly arrogant at times. Things were not at all like that when Jurgen Bey, Piet Hein Eek and I got our degrees. We were far more modest, knowing that we'd have to prove ourselves in the real world.'

After she graduated, Jongerius taught for several years at the Design Academy Eindhoven, where she headed the Atelier department (currently part of the school's Compass division). At a time in which most of the academy's departments were still focusing more on shaping concepts than on realizing designs, Jongerius was concentrating hard on developing craftsmanship in her students. 'As a student, you must also learn to be of service and to master technical skills. I believe in a guild-like education in which students, supervised by experienced instructors, work on realistic projects rather than spending all their time on the conceptual aspects of an assignment. What they learn can be very useful – later, for example, when some of them specialize. I think the world will always need stars, but I also predict an increase in the demand for specialists, craftsmanship and team-workers. An educational programme has to anticipate that demand in its curricula, teaching methods and instructors.'

Louise Schouwenberg

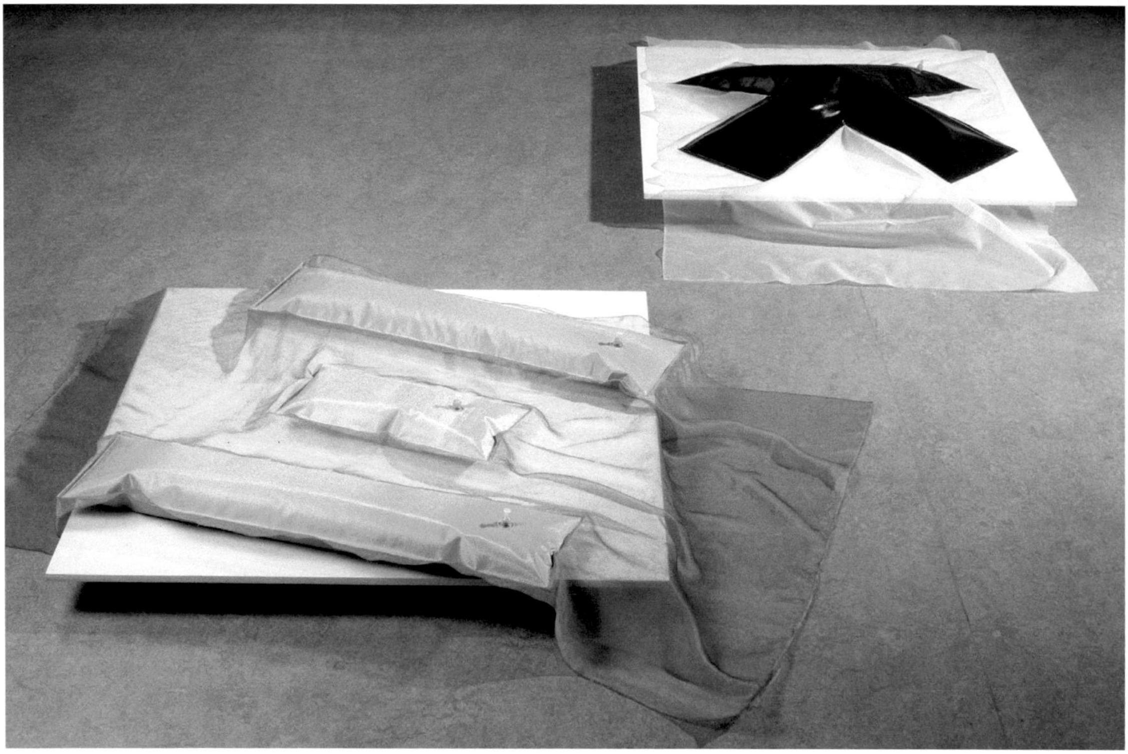

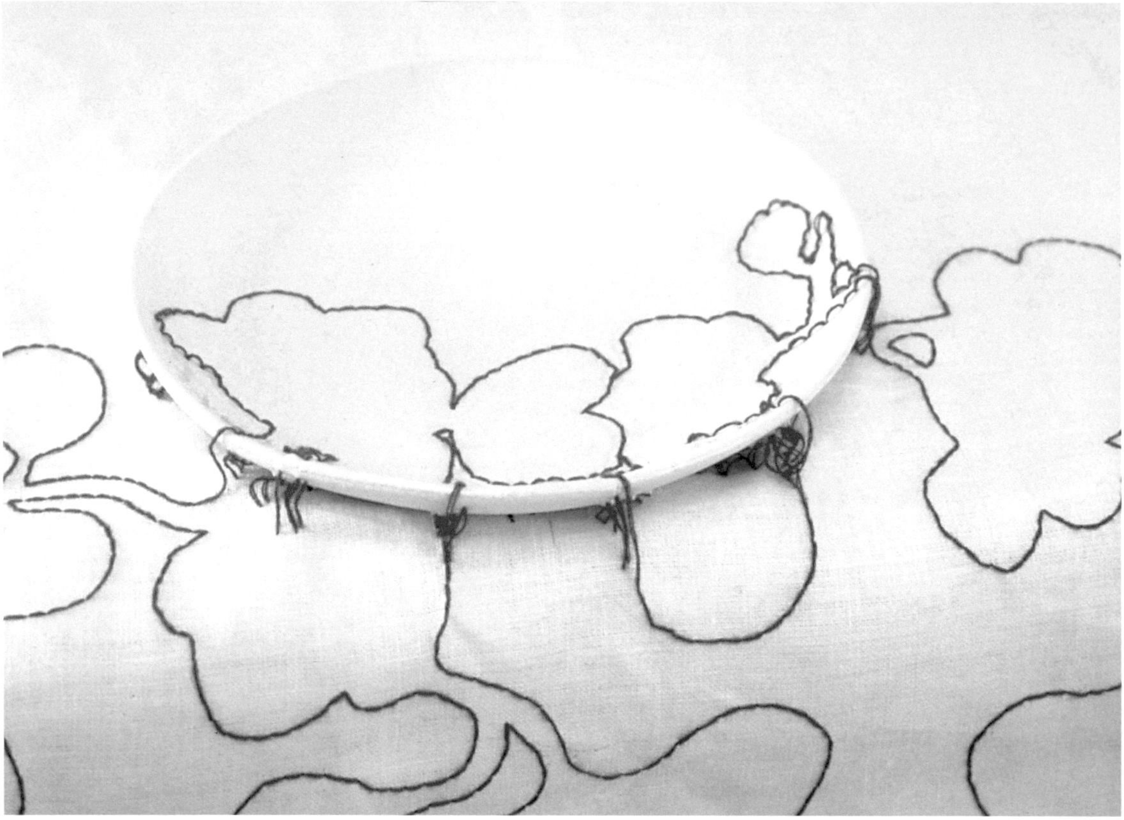

Opposite top:
Inflatable textile, 1993

Opposite bottom:
Embroidered Tablecloth, 2000

Above: Repeat (Maharam), 2001

Left: Works from permanent collection, 2005
Cooper–Hewitt, New York

Left: Delft Blue Jug, 2001

Below: Long Neck and Groove Bottle, 2000

Opposite top: Soft Urn, 1994

Opposite bottom: 'Jonsberg' Vases (Ikea), 2005

Opposite left top:
B-set dinner service, 1998

Opposite right top: Big White Pot and Red/White Vase

Opposite bottom: Majolica (Royal Tichelaar Makkum), 2005

Left:
Office Pets (Vitra Editions), 2007

Below: Polder Sofa (Vitra), 2005

Left: Park chair, 1994

Bottom: Big Talk, Amsterdam, 2006. The Bastion entrance of the Amstelpark is hidden behind a major highway, the A10. This 'non place' is made visible by the Neon letters. Commissioned by Amsterdams Fonds voor de Kunst and Stadsdeel ZuiderAmstel

Opposite page: Egmond aan Zee, 2001–2004. Design of stairs and pathways at the seashore, in cooperation with Veenenbos and Bosch landscape architects.

Baukje Trenning
Man and Identity [1994]

Opposite top: 1000 Dots and Smooth Waves, 1994. Concrete tiles, 2 × 2 m, Struyk Verwo Infra

Opposite bottom: Binary Fields (2002) and Floating Pebbles (1998). Concrete tiles, 60 × 60 cm, Zoontjens Beton

Top left: Tactiles, Pierce, 2001. Ceramic tiles, 15 × 15 cm, Royal Tichelaar Makkum

Top right: Art project for housing block by M3H Architects, concrete windowsills with imprint, Amsterdam, 2005

Left: Brick-for-a-brick, 2007. Bricks, Wienerberger/EKWC

Marcel Schmalgemeijer (1968): 'At the academy we learned that anything can be questioned. You design something, but you can immediately imagine it as something else.'

Marcel Schmalgemeijer (1968) graduated in 1993 from the Man and Public Space Department. His graduation projects were a series of remarkable open-space green areas and a travelling exhibition of 50 hats worn by Queen Beatrix, presented in a linear arrangement, much like a timeline, that indicated the date on which she had appeared in each hat. After leaving the academy, he took off in another direction: theatre design. 'I'd done a work placement with the Zuidelijk Toneel [a well-known Dutch theatre company], but initially my instructors didn't think that discipline fit into our department. To compensate, I trained at Neutelings & Roodbeen Architects and at industrial-design firm Kho Liang Ie. It wasn't until I presented my work-placement reports that the instructors saw theatre design as an interesting possibility.'

Looking back, Schmalgemeijer says he was an average student. 'I was still green and in awe of my teachers. I often had the feeling that I didn't get what was going on, and sometimes I struggled with the fast pace. I chose that department because I was interested in spaces and spatiality, an interest that deepened during my work for the Zuidelijk Toneel. In secondary school, I helped build stage sets for school performances. Ending up in the theatre seems only logical,' says Schmalgemeijer.

'What I like about scenography is that it allows you to think more abstractly. You build a temporary space with form, colour, material and light. Both performers and story can add meaning to that space. Then, too, you're not involved with all sorts of practical demands – like making a hooligan-proof or weather-resistant space. My designs are based on a script and/or on the

ideas of a director or choreographer. Conversely, my set design influences how the performers move – or *can* move – within that space. Some directors actually like having limitations imposed on them. It brings out their creativity. The actors in *Jan Rap en zijn Maat*, for example, rehearsed for two months on the completed set. The play takes place in a rehabilitation centre for disturbed adolescents. The set featured a large floor of upturned yellow crates, which was both awkward and somewhat dangerous. I envisioned the actors making all kinds of things with the crates and eventually wrecking it all. If I'd proposed that idea two weeks before the premiere, no one would have been able to work with it. The crates would have been superfluous. So the set had to be done early on to give them the opportunity to work with it.'

Recalling his start in the theatre, the designer says he was lucky to have worked with the best in the profession: Jan Versweyveld. 'He taught me how to build things, how thick a frame has to be if you want it to be stable. What materials to use. How lighting works. That a set for a travelling show has to fit into a trailer, that it must be simple enough to assemble in one day and to be dismantled even more quickly. I worked on ten or so productions with him and gained invaluable experience in the bargain. You could say that I learned the profession of scenography from him.' After four years with Versweyveld – two full time, two part time – Schmalgemeijer left to go his own way. 'When you work that long for someone, his way of thinking worms its way into your system. It took a deliberate effort to extract myself from that situation.'

The extraction process was a success. Schmalgemeijer has worked for well-known theatre companies like Toneelgroep Amsterdam; directors like Gerard Jan Rijnders, Pierre Audi, Olivier Provily and Peter de Baan; and choreographer Anouk van Dijk. In 2002 he won the Charlotte Köhler Award for theatre design, a prestigious incentive prize for young artists.

It's surprising, then, to hear him say that he has 'a kind of love-hate relationship with the theatre . . . a strange medium. You sit in an auditorium and look at a peepshow that's intended to evoke feelings of empathy. Somebody's up there acting sad or screaming loudly. The fact that it's all make believe does bother me sometimes. Seldom do I see a performance that touches or grabs me, even when the production is one I've worked on myself. It's often just a bit too clever. Or the story is boring. When a performance is good, though, it's the most powerful medium I know – and that's because it's live. It's happening right in front of you.'

Schmalgemeijer mentions Turks Fruit as one of his favourite shows, a musical for which he designed the sets. 'Compared with big musicals produced by Joop van den Ende, this was a relatively small-scale production. But made for a large audience. After working on a fair number of rather "artistic" projects, I wanted to make something for the general public. It was fun to come up with sets for them that were more abstract than what they were used to. *Turks Fruit* is about a passionate and powerful love between two people. At a certain point the relationship goes sour and one of the lovers dies of cancer. I suggested it be performed as though it were a rock concert. With a live band centre stage to beef up the sex factor. Before the intermission, I wanted the set to be one big love feast and afterwards a dismantled party room that paralleled the end of the relationship and death. Before the

intermission, several oversized objects appeared, gradually filling up the stage: a poppy, a festoon and a Chinese dragon. After that, things began disintegrating. The party was over, and props were ruined or had fallen down. Originally, the piece had been written as a film script, with many short scenes and various locations. Constantly changing sets can be distracting, though. I wanted to indicate location with as few means as possible. The basis of the set was a lot of black tables of different sizes. Depending on their positions, they served as cupboard, bed, easel or ordinary table – to signify a house, bedroom, studio or restaurant. The result was a rather abstract space that the viewer could complete mentally.'

In addition to theatre design, Schmalgemeijer makes art and designs events and exhibitions. Among his clients are the Centraal Museum Utrecht, SKOR (Foundation Art and Public Space), Montevideo, Het Princessehof Museum in Leeuwarden, and the Rijksmuseum in Amsterdam. 'Museums often want a combination of exhibition and theatre, so they look for someone who's familiar with creating spectacle and who can make a grand gesture.' One theme that required a theatrical solution was Deliciously Decadent, an exhibition that Schmalgemeijer designed in 2003 for Het Princessehof, the national ceramics museum. In three monumental halls, he crafted gigantic mountains of broken earthenware, glass and mirrors, respectively. Displayed among the shards were objects by artists and designers. Deliciously Decadent drew crowds of visitors, including many from the media, and a large part of its popularity can be attributed to Schmalgemeijer's remarkable interventions. In 2007 he designed Pretty Dutch, an ode to 18th-century Dutch porcelain for the same museum. This time Schmalgemeijer was asked to display a plethora of little cups, plates and vases in an attractive way. While researching the subject at the Gemeentemuseum in The Hague, he had to search for the Dutch porcelain exhibit. He was amazed that the items were so small that he'd missed them the first time around. Pressing his nose to the glass, he saw the quality of the little cups and their precisely painted decorations. For Pretty Dutch, Schmalgemeijer designed a large, flat, 'vertical' glass case in which the tiny objects were fastened to the backdrop like butterflies on display – an 'archive' of Dutch porcelain. On a wall across from the authentic objects, he projected a slide show in which a series of rotating porcelain pieces had been enlarged many times over. These images were meant to encourage visitors to study the items in the archive much more closely than they may have done otherwise. 'I wanted to help people look at the porcelain – to confront them immediately with the beauty of the details.' In a curious way, his installation reversed the conventions normally followed by a museum: here, the physical objects were illustrations of the projected images, as it were.

At the time of this interview, Schmalgemeijer is working on the design of HELD, an exhibition on Dutch heroes and hero worship. His client is the Rijksmuseum, and the location is the Nieuwe Kerk in Amsterdam. The exhibition compares showpieces from the collection of the Rijksmuseum, including a portrait of the famous 15th-century Dutch admiral, Michiel de Ruyter, with football matches starring popular hero Johan Cruijff and the book of condolences for controversial political hero Pim Fortuyn. 'The content is complex. The story that's being told is fragmented, and the subjects are quite diverse. It's my job to establish clear lines of thought and to accentuate certain matters. And to add the note of spectacle that's inherent to this theme, of course. Soon I'll be putting large panels into the church, which will lean against the columns at a slant, as if they've been propped there almost without thought. Each panel represents a monument of sorts, which conveys the story of a hero through paintings, writings and photographs. The binding element, positioned at the centre of the church, is a 40-metre-long orange grandstand featuring a door that leads to the exhibition. This is obviously a reference to the stadiums in which we honour today's heroes.'

Since leaving the academy in Eindhoven, Schmalgemeijer has built up a brilliant career that, as far as he's concerned, can continue to move in all directions: scenography for interesting theatrical productions, art for public spaces, graphic design, exhibitions and who knows what else? How has the academy contributed to his career? 'I learned an exploratory manner of design there, an attitude that's helped me a great deal. We learned that anything can be questioned. You design something, but you can immediately imagine it as something else. You can turn everything around in your head. I remember lining up a whole bunch of scale models for the design of a birdhouse. I didn't know which one to pick for further development. Hans van der Markt [instructor] said, "Why don't you use them all? Maybe they'd be really good as a series." I still work with scale models. It's the best way I know of to visualize a design. In our department at school, a lot of enthusiasm and industry went into making models. It was almost like a contest to see who could make the nicest one.'

Louise Schouwenberg

Above: Design for Open-space Green Areas, 1993

Right: Scenography of *Jan Rap en zijn Maat*, 2006

Opposite page: Scenography of *Turks Fruit* the musical, 2005

Opposite top: Façade of De Balie in Amsterdam where the 15th Cinekid filmfestival took place, 2001

Opposite bottom: Exhibition design 'HELD', De Nieuwe Kerk, Amsterdam, 2007

Top left and right: Exhibition design 'Deliciously Decadent', Museum Princessehof Leeuwarden, 2004. Shards of porcelain and glass were the carriers of contemporary artworks and designs

Left: Canadian Media Art Lounge/ Montevideo, Amsterdam, 2000

Below: Exhibition design 'Pretty Dutch', Museum Princessehof Leeuwarden, 2007

Arian Brekveld

Man and Living [1995]

Top: Tin vases, 1995

Middle: Poldersofa, 2005, Design: Jongeriuslab (Hella Jongerius, Arian Brekveld)

Left: Couch per metre, 2003

Above: Softlamp, 1996

Right: Wine cooler, 2000

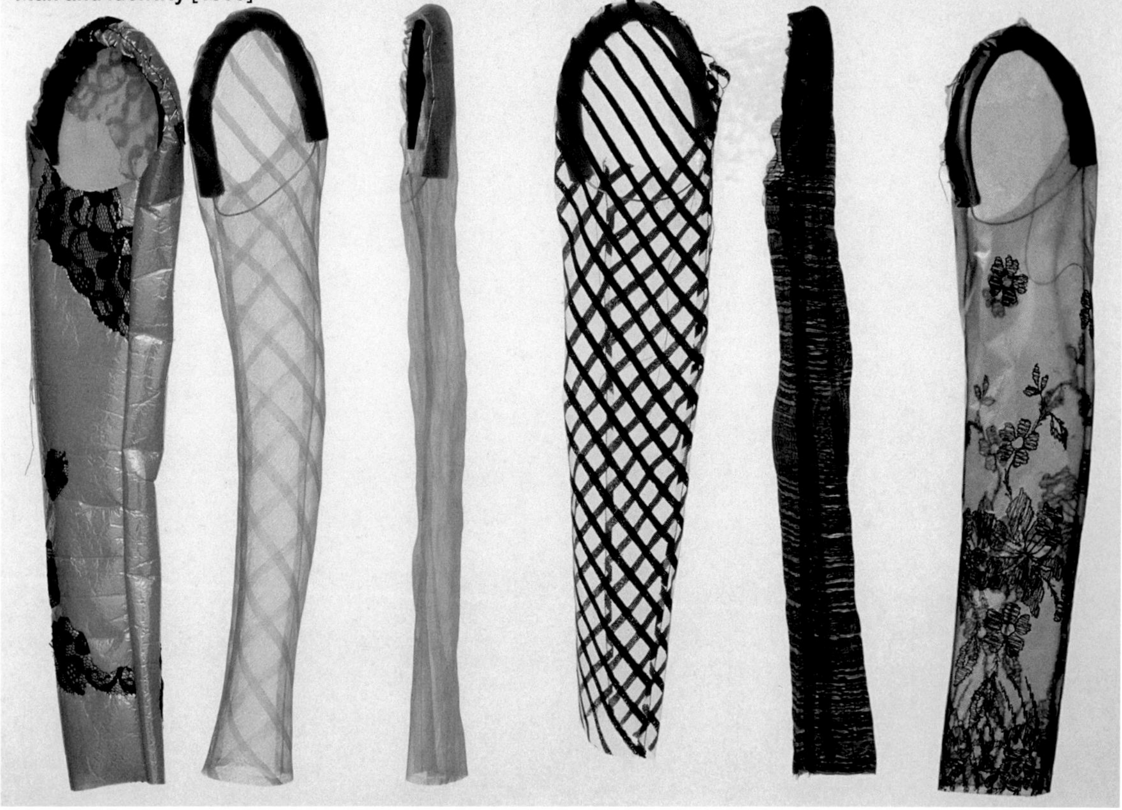

Marty Lamers
Man and Identity [1995]

Above: Collection of fabrics, 1995

Left: Handwoven fabrics for Expofil Fair, Paris, 1999. Presentation ‘Nouveaux Regards’

Top left: Sliver, 2002. Perspex curtain (design Marty Lamers/m3)

Top right: Angle, part of the collection Showroom Vol.2, 2007, JAB Anstoetz

Left: Edge, Rib, Acre, Grid, part of the collection Showroom Vol.1, 2007, JAB Anstoetz (Random light by Bertjan Pot)

Max Barenbrug (1965): ‘Mobility is a fundamental human right, and I wanted to find solutions for it. The departments of Leisure and Mobility touched on all aspects of design that I deal with today’

As the new millennium neared, he came, he saw and he conquered with a pushchair designed with fathers in mind. Today the Bugaboo is a commercial success in 42 countries, with the Netherlands, Great Britain, Italy, Spain and the United States leading the pack. The annual turnover continues to grow by leaps and bounds, reaching €55 million in 2006. The price of the pushchair, which starts at €629, is obviously not a drawback. What formula for success did Design Academy Eindhoven instructors whisper into Max Barenbrug's ear?

It's 1994. Max Barenbrug graduates from what is then still the Academy of Industrial Design (AIVE). He calls his final project the Multi Terrain Pushchair and is promptly named ‘best graduate of the year’. He's 29: old for a design student but young for an entrepreneur. His entrepreneurial character, however, was already evident when he entered the academy at the age of 24.

‘I'd been studying public administration,’ says Barenbrug, ‘but I got bogged down. I dropped out of that school as soon as I heard about the Academy of Industrial Design. Why public administration? Let's just call it a youthful blunder. I didn't know what I wanted, although I did have a passion for creative carpentry and construction. It just hadn't occurred to me that I could continue my education in that direction.’

Barenbrug threw himself into Mobility and Leisure, two relatively new fields of study. Taking place at that time was a gradual transformation of the

Academy of Industrial Design into the Design Academy Eindhoven, a school that, in brief, combined applied design and independent design. 'It wasn't automotive design that held my interest, but mobility,' says Barenbrug. 'Mobility is a fundamental human right, and I wanted to find solutions for it. Solutions in the form of products closely related to everyday life and daily use. In that respect, Mobility and Leisure were well-defined studies that touched on all the aspects of design that I deal with today: fashion, material, technology, brand perception – you name it.'

The deeper Barenbrug delved into the subject of mobility, the clearer it became to him that all demands made of bicycles, rollators, cars and the like were extremely subjective. 'Our instructors said to ignore the existing specifications of a certain product and to find new perceptual qualities to link to it. I have a vivid recollection of Har Scheffer, one of my favourite teachers, handing out A1-sized sheets of paper and asking us to put a dot on the paper in the right place. Doing it wrong meant the gallows. It was all about proportions, the golden section and so forth, and the fun was in discovering all those principles and calculations yourself. There lies the strength of this academy. The teachers give you the freedom to search while instilling in you a sense of composition, colour and material. Until at a certain moment you realize, on your own, that you're an independent designer. At that moment you're doing less searching than finding. Intuitively, you learn to find fresh solutions for problems both old and new.'

As a student, Barenbrug heard many of his classmates complain that what the teachers were pulling off wasn't pedagogically correct – making them work like mad with very little guidance. 'Some needed that extra boost, but they were at the wrong academy. As for me, I liked being pushed towards independence, and my classes were anything but impersonal. What distinguishes Design Academy Eindhoven instructors is an ability to reveal and convey passion, and to impart that feeling to students as well. And let's be honest, if you're not passionate about what you're studying, school is a punishment.'

Barenbrug saw many of his fellow students graduate and simply fall flat – 'talented and average alike'. To avoid the same trap, he set up a company. 'But I could do that more easily than the rest thanks to my graduation project, the Multi Terrain Pushchair, which I went on to develop, together with physician Eduard Zanen, into a sturdy baby buggy for fathers. I saw parents wrestling with unmanageable buggies – not functional, ugly. Made by manufacturers blind to the needs of parents. The prototype for the Bugaboo was a multifunctional chair, back carrier, car seat and buggy in one. And the bonus was a rugged appearance, which gave the user a different image.' The archetypal design made all the papers, but the buggy's manufacture proved to be commercially infeasible. Five years later the man was in business, under the motto 'it's dogged as does it'.

'From day one, my top business priority has been the creative process, followed by market research, marketing and engineering. This approach probably caused the long delay in our trek to success, but I have absolutely no regrets. It's this product that explains why we've been market leader in the high-end pushchair segment for eight years.'

Indeed, the Bugaboo has been the subject of very little advertising. After all, a good product sells itself. Following the introduction of the pushchair in the summer of 1999, European pavements, especially those in Amsterdam, were soon crawling with colourful buggies navigated by modern, self-assured parents, their babies riding high. When the pushchair appeared in the hit television series *Sex and the City*, the whole world sat up and took notice. The message was: hip parents buy Bugaboos. Among the hippest were Madonna, Brad Pitt, Zinédine Zidane, the Dutch princesses and popular Dutch singer Marco Borsato.

It's 2007. Barenbrug, at 42, is no longer plagued by growing pains. 'We have a hundred people working at our headquarters in Amsterdam, and another hundred at sales offices worldwide. The factory in Taiwan, where the buggies are assembled and shipped, has about two hundred more. Eduard and I have never set down a business plan – wouldn't know how. I just wanted to make my dream come true, and Eduard Zanen shared that ambition. How? By venturing into the unknown. Calvin and Hobbes (or in Dutch: Sjors and Sjimmie) in Taiwan – that's what it felt like when we arrived there in our pioneer days. Initially we outsourced the manufacturing, but it wasn't long before we saw the qualitative need for a factory of our own.'

His pioneer days are over. In recent years Bugaboo has become serious business. 'I'm no longer making 2D drawings on an Apple Performa 475 in Illustrator,' says Barenbrug. 'All the bright ideas that used to be mine alone are now the responsibility of a so-called "product management organization". And we're becoming more and more of an international player. We're setting up a factory in China at the moment. We want to insource as much as possible, which will give us optimal control over our corporate social responsibility.'

Barenbrug favours intuition over market research. 'I believe in creative input subsequently validated by research. I understand perfectly that when American dads want Bugaboo cupholders on their Bugaboo pushchairs, I shouldn't grouse about the disintegration of my transparent concept. In the early years, we did nothing about brand marketing, but in this and future phases it's got to be an integral part of the organization, of course.'

Speaking about the future: what are his plans? 'We'd love to expand the product line beyond baby transport. I'm interested in real industrial products for target groups. But it's going to take years. The more complex the process the better. Take note: design has to be an integral part of any business I'm in.'

Renson van Tilborg

Max Barenbrug
Man and Mobility [1994]

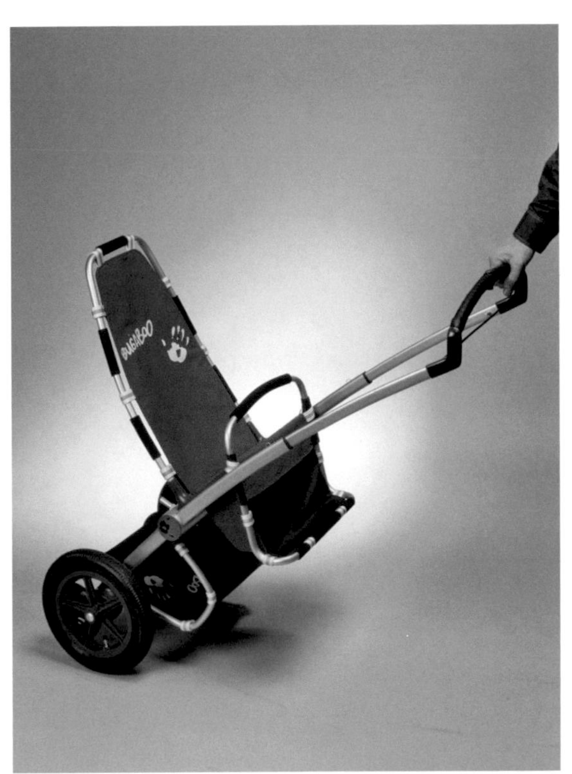

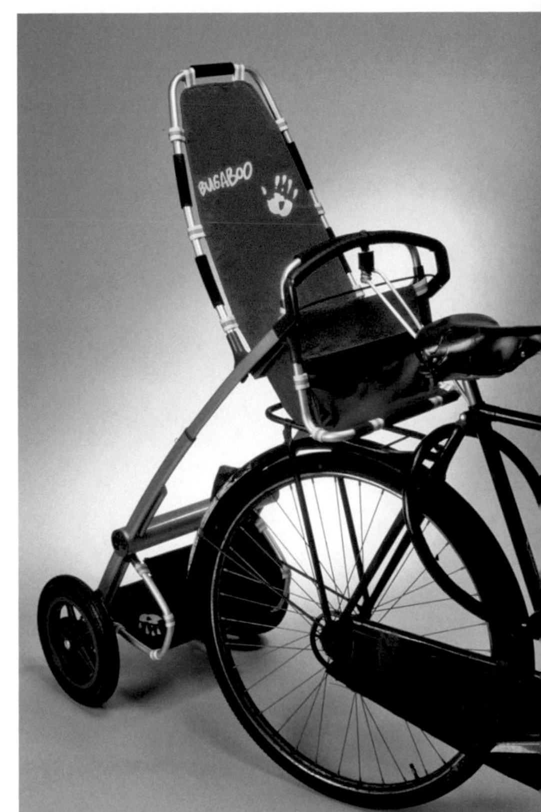

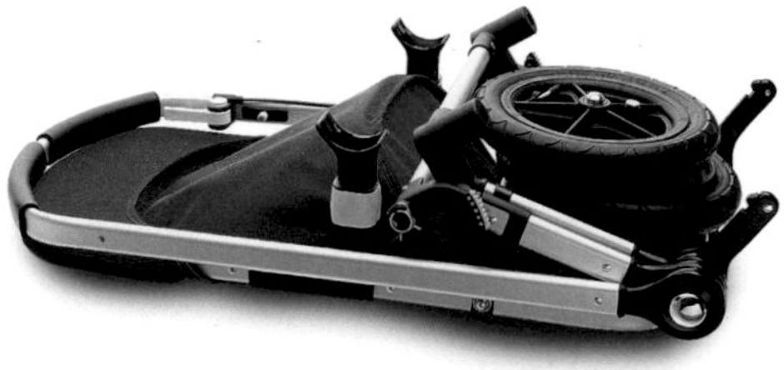

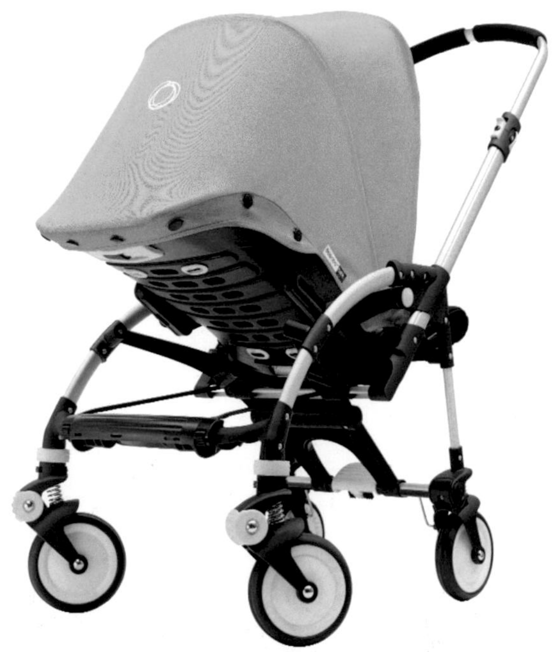

Opposite page: Bugaboo, 1997

Above: Bugaboo Cameleon

Right: Bugaboo Bee

Niels van Eijk
Man and Living [1997]

Miriam van der Lubbe
Man and Living [1995]

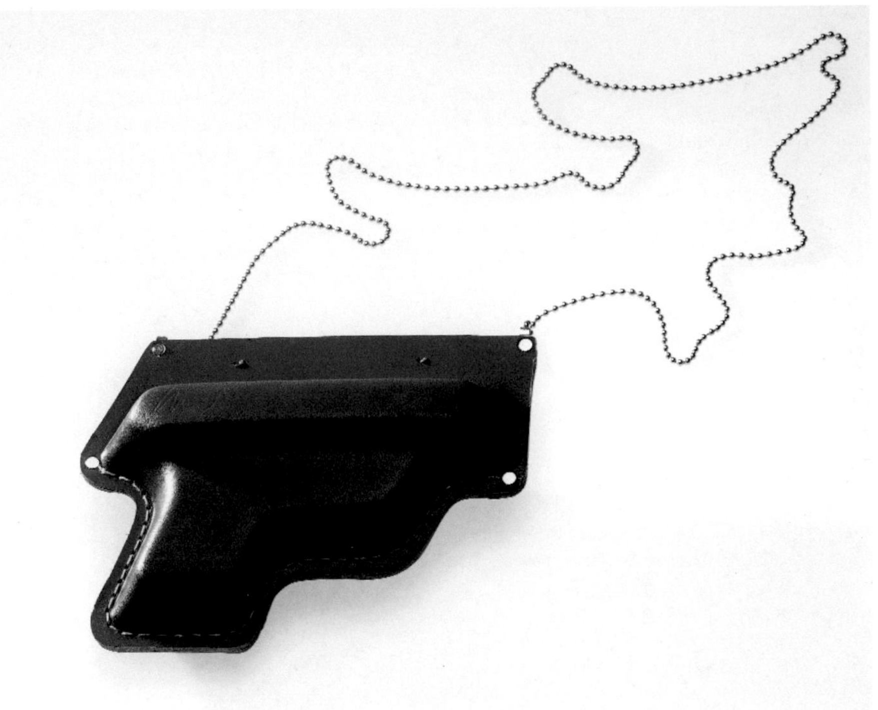

Opposite top: Cowchair, 1997

Opposite left bottom:
Stove designs, 1998–now

Opposite right bottom:
Bobbin Lace Lamp, 2002

Top: Lady's Bag Me and my Beretta, 1999

Left: Tea Set, 2000

Opposite page: Godogan, 2006

Above: With Love, 2006

Expansion and Exposure, Design Academy Eindhoven 1998–2007

Louise Schouwenberg

'Without question, currently the best design academy in the world', is what the New York Times said in 2003 about Design Academy Eindhoven. And in 2005 ICON, an English design and architecture magazine, placed Design Academy Eindhoven high on its list of the most influential organisations in the world of design. The jury members responsible praised the high quality of its graduates and lecturers. Design Academy Eindhoven, based in a small provincial city in the Netherlands, has built up an impressive reputation round the world. After all, this is the place whose students have included Tord Boontje, Hella Jongerius, Jurgen Bey, Piet Hein Eek, Richard Hutten, Job Smeets, Bertjan Pot, Wieki Somers, Maarten Baas, Joris Laarman, Demakersvan and many others. That is a relatively large group of well-known designers for such a small country. Is that an accident, or are the school's managers particularly good at promoting its students and ex-students and playing to the international media? The design world is used to showers of superlatives mainly intended for promotional purposes and not always able to claim any realistic investigation of the facts. One thing is certain: Design Academy Eindhoven, particularly in the last fifteen years, has become an indispensable feature of the international design world. For an explanation one could point to a happy combination of a number of developments, inside and outside the academy. Those directly involved, students and ex-students, department heads and lecturers, point primarily to the school's good organisation and special educational philosophy.

The school's charter was signed in 1947, its doors opened in 1950. From the time of his appointment at the end of 1949, Rene Smeets, the first director, strived to provide a high-quality course in industrial design. The promise would be fulfilled by him and his successors with ever increasing conviction. A strong position of the school in the international design world was ensured by the most recent directors, particularly the partnerships between Jan Lucassen & Jan van Duppen (1983–1999) and Lidewij Edelkoort (1999–) & Liesbeth in 't Hout (1999–2006); officially all four were directors. They were organised as a board of governors, chaired by Lucassen and now Edelkoort. High-quality courses in industrial design and a strong position in the international designworld was achieved by repeatedly guaranteeing the school's independence, by rigorously departing from the conventional approach taken by the discipline, by attracting the best people in the field as department heads and lecturers and by arranging international presentations which attracted much attention from the media. At the end of the 1990s these developments seemed to justify a new name and a new location: the Academy for Industrial Design (Academie voor Industriële Vormgeving – AIVE) became the Design Academy Eindhoven and in 1998 the school moved to its present location, the monumental property known as the White Lady (deWitteDame), a former Philips production site in the heart of Eindhoven. In 2006 Liesbeth in 't Hout left the academy to become director of the Amsterdam Fashion Institute (AMFI). Since then the management of Design Academy Eindhoven has consisted of general director, Lidewij Edelkoort, and director of education, Anne Mieke Eggenkamp.

Their view of education has remained broadly the same. Only time will tell whether the new organisation structure will lead to fundamental changes in future.[1]

SCHOOL, STAFF, PHILOSOPHY

school

The Netherlands offers a wide range of design courses, scattered over universities of technology, schools for higher vocational art education (HBOs), and vocational schools. Design Academy Eindhoven is classified as an HBO and in 2007 offers eight courses leading to a bachelor's degree (four year courses, but in reality many students take a longer period for their studies) and two courses leading to a master's degree. The level of the present bachelor's degree courses is however comparable in many respects with that of courses for a master's degree in other countries. Partly for this reason, but also because of the growth of the existing master's departments, the capacity of those departments is expected to increase substantially.

Design Academy Eindhoven differs from comparable Dutch education institutes with respect to the high level of independence which it managed to retain during a period in which most such schools were forced by the need to economise to become part of large comprehensive educational establishments. According to In 't Hout, this allowed Design Academy Eindhoven to keep out a good deal of bureaucracy. 'We had a lot of freedom. When Li (Lidewij Edelkoort) and I began, we wanted to keep everything as simple, transparent and clear as possible. This was one of the things that we could do because we were not part of a mega institution and so were not subject to all kinds of extra rules. We were flexible, could take decisions reasonably quickly and react to initiatives'. Another important difference from other institutions offering HBO-level design courses is that Design Academy Eindhoven is the only school devoted entirely to design. Comparable Dutch programmes in Arnhem, Breda, Rotterdam and Amsterdam are all provided by large art schools offering a wide range of creative courses. All of Design Academy Eindhoven's departments are design departments, which most likely explains the school's attractiveness for design students. Within the Netherlands Design Academy Eindhoven has for years possessed the largest student population (± 700 students) and can in several respects be said to occupy a leading position in design education in this country (and in the world, in terms of quality, if the New York Times is to be believed).

staff

According to everyone associated with Design Academy Eindhoven, one of the most important secrets of its success lies in the way its education is organised. After ten years' educational experience, the German textile designer Ulf Moritz (associated with the academy from 1970 to 2005) took the view that the school could only lose its provincial character if important people were attracted from the field. 'Gillissen, who was director at the time, brought me in as a lecturer for the textile department. Almost immediately he gave

[1] For more information about the school's history before 1998, see the chapter Early Ambitions

Jan van Duppen and me carte blanche to change the department so that it could provide a high-quality course in textiles. I was still young but had already acquired a respectable name as a designer. But we found ourselves surrounded mainly by lecturers who worked almost full-time, had been appointed for life and had absolutely no connection with the discipline any more. In 1983, when Jan Lucassen and Jan van Duppen took over the management of the school, we managed to do something about this. By then I was head of the textile department, but was asked by Lucassen and Van Duppen to join them in thinking about the school's policy. The academy needed people who really had no time for education because they were too busy with their own work and really didn't think much of the idea of working in Eindhoven. I still remember how in an Amsterdam café I talked Marijke van der Wijst, Frans de la Haye, Anthon Beeke and finally Lidewij Edelkoort into coming to work for AIVE. We had hardly anything to offer, the school still had neither name nor prestige. We therefore had to offer something different, in this case freedom and individual responsibility. And it worked. Suddenly we had a terrific set of professionals in Eindhoven to head up the departments'.

Interior designer Marijke van de Wijst: '*Marijke, you and I have no children, so we have time enough to teach* – these were the words with which Ulf finally persuaded me to come. At first I didn't want to. I had my own busy studio and Eindhoven did not attract me. But Ulf pointed out the opportunity that I would have to decide on the work done in the department Environment (later called the department Man and Public Space) to entirely suit my own views on the discipline. Until then the design of public space had consisted mainly of designing rubbish bins and traffic signs. Individual objects. I was given every opportunity to extend the scope of the profession. The point I kept on hammering away at with my students is that what matters is not products but context. And context demands a well-founded vision. As department head one must therefore be able to attract lecturers who can provide their own intelligent interpretation. I wanted to attract good theoreticians, architects and designers. I was given the freedom to do so, so I accepted the offer'.

Jewellery and product designer Gijs Bakker: 'Jan Lucassen pinched me from Delft University of Technology's industrial design department in 1987. Jan had big plans for the school which appealed to me, both for their content and the proposed organisation. Education In most parts of the world is awful, because it is provided by people who have been appointed for life. This is something you see in practically all American and English courses. Becoming head of a department almost always means saying goodbye to your professional practice because you are much too heavily loaded. Some schools require you to be involved in teaching three or even more days a week. So mainly mediocre people are interested. Lucassen realised quite early on that you would only draw in good people if you didn't load them too heavily'. In 't Hout: 'Likewise Lidewij and I felt that all one's energy should primarily be devoted to content, to the lectures. This means that department heads and lecturers should not have to be involved in bureaucratic rigmaroles.

So far even departmental coordinators have hardly been bothered by administrative issues. After all, we had a whole business organisation to take care of that sort of thing. In education you cannot offer people the kind of high salaries that can compete with what they could earn from their other work. Thus you have to make sure that running a department, teaching and the general environment are very attractive. Even the catering during the periodical evaluations of the student's works (taking place 3 to 6 times a year) must be fantastic. In due course the job must have prestige. Only then will you get in the top people from the design world'.

Since the 1980s the responsibility and freedom enjoyed by Design Academy Eindhoven department heads has extended primarily to the composition of the team of lecturers, the setting of the curriculum, the definition of the subjects on which lecturers and students are to work and presence at periodic appraisals. Outside these activities the heads are only sporadically to be found at the school. Moritz: 'That calls for mutual confidence. The lecturers did all the work, I was only the head. But I did put my stamp on the appraisals. Lecturers have a different, special relationship with students and so tend to judge them more positively. I came in as an outsider, stern-faced, and so was better able to assess their quality. I was the *primus inter pares*. From time to time other departments would have endless discussions because the head failed to take control or the lecturers were unwilling to accept control. Anyone who was not prepared to accept my authority was free to leave (as fate would have it Moritz left in 2006 after a furious argument with his team about whether to allow a student to pass. But with the date of his retirement already in sight – in the Netherlands lecturers on bachelor's degree courses are required to stand down in their 65th year – that argument made an appropriately violent end to a career in education that had always been intense)'.

Design Academy Eindhoven department heads generally do not lecture. Training is provided by a large group of designers, theoreticians and artists, each with a short-term contract to teach no more than one day a week (lectures are given by a total of more than a hundred people). Only a few have a permanent appointment. This approach encourages the necessary flow of people and guarantees intensive contact with the profession. Thus what applies to the department heads also applies to lecturers: they are chosen mainly for their professionalism and expertise but are, in Moritz's words, 'really not fated to be teachers'. In that respect Design Academy Eindhoven's educational team differs significantly from the equivalent teams at comparable educational establishments. Most courses in art and design in the Netherlands and elsewhere in the world have to deal with the phenomenon of *eternal* or *professional* lecturers, who slowly but surely find themselves occupied full-time in education. They train people for a profession in which they themselves no longer play an active role of any significance. That type of lecturer is hardly to be found at Design Academy Eindhoven. The results are obvious: both sceptics and devotees of the training are agreed that little ingrained routine is to

From left to right: Lonny van Rijswijck, Lotty Lindeman, Niels van Eijk, Piet Hein Eek, Miriam van der Lubbe, Nadine Sterk

be found in Design Academy Eindhoven, but rather great enthusiasm and pleasure and much willingness to embrace new initiatives. Edelkoort: 'You often hear lecturers say "I wish I could go back to school". It's always a very good sign if the staff is jealous of the training on offer!'

One exception is the training in the foundation course, for which a relatively large number of people are permanently employed. On the one hand this is a historically developed situation which the present management of the school, sometimes to its frustration, can do nothing about. Edelkoort: 'For this sort of training you need visionaries, people who have won their spurs in the field and are still active, but also people who can impart to students the basic aspects of the subject. Continuity has greater importance for the foundation course than for the design departments. But when people are about to be retired (because of age) I think that it would be a good thing to start to work with short-term contracts here as well. And I would prefer to replace departing designers by artists rather than more designers. In the early stages it is very important that people receive an artistic training in which they learn to think independently and to design freely. In their early years all of the people whom we now recognize as stars received intensive training from artists'.

The strategy of appointing (internationally) known designers as lecturers and department heads has turned out to be successful. Certainly the job of department head is currently seen as prestigious and the school has little trouble in attracting important names. And that has immediate consequences for the quality of the education. In 't Hout: 'There is a healthy kind of competition. Big names want to produce great designers. Because they were masters themselves they also want to train masters. Thus each department wants to be better than the rest, to be the department with the most attractive team of lecturers, the best projects and the most talented students. This encourages the departments to maintain a high standard. Gijs Bakker: 'I always found it important to propagate a distinct but undogmatic view of education. You must always set students a challenge, the bar can never be set high enough. But a vision must still allow space. You offer students a framework. Later they set their own frameworks. This applies not only to training but also to the profession. When a distinct line is set others can test and sharpen themselves against it. The worst thing is leniency. You must therefore select good teachers who are capable of taking on a fight. I still find one of the best proofs the case of Piet Hein Eek, one of my first students, who graduated in 1990. The two of us had a lot of difficulties with one another; he was completely unable to go along with my opinions on conceptual design. That gave rise to much discussion, but I am convinced that it was part of the reason that he became such a strong designer. He dug in his heels, and so was forced to develop a strong profile. When he sat his exams I received a threatening letter from him made up of letters that he had cut from newspapers. It read: 'Dear Gijs, if you don't like my bench, I set your house on fire!! Piet Hein Eek' (in Dutch: Beste Gijs, als je m'n bank niet mooi vindt, dan steek ik uw woning in de fik!!

Piet Hein Eek). That surely is a splendid proof that there was no rigid, homogenous thinking in our department!'

Whenever a Design Academy Eindhoven department gets a new head, it automatically means a change of attitude towards design and a change in the projects. In the Man and Well-Being department, the English designer, writer and trend-forecaster Ilse Crawford took over from the industrial designer Frans de la Haye in 1999. The Man and Leisure department, which had for years been headed by trend-forecaster Lidewij Edelkoort and coordinator Liesbeth in 't Hout (1992–1999), is led today by the artist Irene Droogleever Fortuyn. These changes of the guard have had unmistakable consequences for the educational flavour of the departments. The influence of department heads is perhaps easiest to see in the four departments whose heads have recently (2003–2006) left the academy, leaving a powerful legacy behind. Gijs Bakker spent years putting a conceptual stamp on the Man and Living department (Bakker headed this department until 2003. Since then he has led the master's degree department IM: Conceptual Design in Context. 'IM' refers to the 3 I's of design: Industrial, Interior and Identity design and to Master). Marijke van der Wijst helped the relatively small Man and Public Space department to achieve a significant position in the field of urban renewal. Under the leadership of textile designer Ulf Moritz, the Man and Identity department was a haven of beauty. And the charisma of graphic designer Anthon Beeke turned Man and Communication into a department where the term 'communication' was interpreted significantly more widely than the usual 'graphic design'. What their successors will bring to these departments cannot be forecast with any degree of confidence (recently interior designer Bas van Tol took over the Man and Living department, architect Liesbeth van der Pol took over the Man and Public Space department, textile designer Marty Lamers took over the Man and Identity department and graphic designer Annelys de Vet the Man and Communication department).[2]

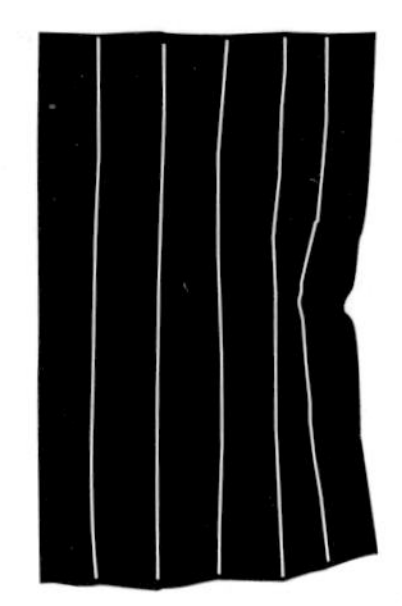

philosophy

In accordance with the prevailing views at the time, AIVE's courses were divided between the industrial, commercial (packaging, advertising etc.) and textile design departments. Both the names and the approach taken by the training reveal that the primary concern was with objects and production methods. All that changed in the 1980s when Lucassen was appointed director. He formed an education committee, whose membership included Jan van Duppen and Ulf Moritz, to work out a new philosophy. According to Moritz the most important recurring theme in the training should not be products and industrial production methods, but the people for whom the products were intended and the needs of the students. In 't Hout: 'Ulf was the founder of the academy's success. Every major change was actually set in motion by Ulf. And one of the great virtues of Jan Lucassen and Jan van Duppen was that they dared to follow his ideas'. During a meeting with management and department heads Moritz drew in the centre of a piece of paper a puny little human figure. In widening circles round it he drew the

[2] Further factual information about department heads and lecturers can be found in the chapter Curriculum.

domains and activities relating to a human being. First and foremost there would need to be a department in which people's identity, emotions and sensuality counted foremost. Next should come personal care, and shortly thereafter concern for the residential environment, leisure and communication. Finally, the outermost circles dealt with work, transport and public space. Initially most colleagues were sceptical about this approach but quite soon members of the profession, both inside and outside the Netherlands, became convinced of the radical changes that it would bring about.

The new vision was reflected first of all in the names of the bachelor's degree departments. After a few changes (for example Man and Essentials became Man and Well-Being, Man and Transport became Man and Mobility), by 2007 Design Academy Eindhoven has departments named Man and Identity, Man and Well-Being, Man and Living, Man and Leisure, Man and Communication, Man and Activity, Man and Mobility and Man and Public Space. (Since these names are long and all begin with the same two words, in practice they are often dropped. For the sake of simplicity this book will use the shorter form as well). The conventional design disciplines are still recognisable, so for example the greater part of graphic design comes under Communication, textiles come under Identity and product design is shared between a number of different departments. But the new department names leave room for more flexible ideas about their scope and even in due course for the emergence of new design disciplines. Moreover, while the department names may appear to precisely define the subjects they cover, in practice they overlap to some extent. Chairs, for example, are designed in both Man and Living and Man and Leisure, and car design is not exclusive to Man and Mobility. In some cases the name of the department is less relevant to its character and direction than the way in which the lecturers and the department head view design.

While the eight design departments provide training for various design disciplines, the students still take general subjects (including psychology, philosophy, economics, marketing, design history, drawing and sketching, CAD techniques, ceramics, textiles etc.) in what are known as the Kompas [Compass] departments, whose job is to provide direction and a foundation for the relevant design disciplines. Design Academy Eindhoven's master's degree courses have the same organisation as the bachelor's degree courses, though here the nomenclature is no longer strictly maintained. The master's degree programme has two departments, IM: Conceptual Design in Context (the larger department, with ± 55 students) and Man and Humanity (± 15 students). Here too most of the training takes place within the departments, while the general subjects and lectures take place in the equivalent of the Kompas departments, the so-called Source programme.[3]

Of course the new educational philosophy meant more than changing the names of the departments. It mainly affected the view on design, the type of designer that would be trained and the subjects on which people would work. Moreover it turned out to go well

[3] For more information see the chapter Curriculum.

with contemporary developments in the design world. Gijs Bakker: 'Until the beginning of the 1980s design was mostly problem solving (at most technical universities people still work in that way). Industry demands and designers answer by providing products which, as it were, follow logically from a set of preconditions. But even in the 1980s there was hardly any good industry in the Netherlands. This partly explains why in the design world a counter movement of designers was cautiously at work developing an independent professional practice, similar to that of artists. They started to produce products themselves and display them in exhibitions.

A directly related phenomenon was the growing tendency to develop products based on strong concepts. People were searching for ways to make design more relevant. Here the academy in Arnhem had played a pioneering role. Thus when we in Eindhoven began to concentrate on people instead of products, the idea went down well with the ambitions of self-producing conceptual designers. We would begin to train author-designers, whose designs would primarily be based on their own fascinations and ideas about what the world needs'.

External influences

At the end of the 1980s a small number of developments had an important effect on the design world and so on training for design. In the last decades of the 20th century the Western world experienced unparalleled economic growth; nobody at the time considered the possibility of any limit to that growth. The design world profited enormously from the increased prosperity and boundless optimism. Consumer society did designers no harm at all, as could be seen at every international design fair, where the general atmosphere was one of wealth and glamour. More and more all revolved around the surplus value of design and less around basic functionality, a surplus value which was mainly to be found in esthetics and cultural meanings. In the Netherlands the added value was to be found elsewhere. Young Dutch designers were unwilling to go on indiscriminately providing yet more products for the consumer market. Ideas became more important than functionality and comfort, and cultural value won out over economic gain. The new generation used unorthodox, autonomous products as an implicit commentary on the preconceptions of the design world and to comment on the problems in the world to which the elite were only too happy to shut their eyes. The West might well be prosperous, but in the rest of the world there was still much poverty. Moreover at the end of the 20th century it began to become apparent that unbridled consumption would eventually take its toll on the environment, with the result that the recycling of objects, shapes (archetypes) and materials became extremely popular amongst Dutch designers. Designs from this country had for years been known as sober and well justified (the modernistic slogan 'less is more' has always found a fertile breeding ground here), now different qualities were added, including critical commentary on developments in the world and the design profession. Within a short period of time design products would become autonomous creations, shown in media and within contexts that used to be confined to the arts.

In 1993 the new mentality amongst designers led to the foundation of Droog Design [Dry Design] by Renny Ramakers, a design theoretician, and Gijs Bakker, a jewellery and product designer. The platform for conceptual design would have much success in promoting Dutch design round the world and would begin to give it an image combining concepts, dry simplicity and a sense of humour. The influence exerted on education by the conceptualists was considerable. In the first place the new mentality naturally appealed to young people, and moreover many of the conceptualists began to lecture. At Design Academy Eindhoven Gijs Bakker was head of Living, one of the biggest departments, and many members of the first wave of conceptual designers, including Jurgen Bey, Jan Konings and Hella Jongerius, began to lecture quite soon after completing their own exams, so spreading a critical approach to the profession through almost all Design Academy Eindhoven departments.

For the departments' lecture programmes the influence of conceptual design and the Design Academy Eindhoven's changed views on education lead to an increased focus on the personal development of each individual student. But it also meant that the subjects became more ambitious and began to have ground in common with other disciplines (subjects varied from the responsibility of designers in relation to overproduction and ecology, overconsumption, craft versus industry, local versus global etc.).

To do justice to these demands, since the '90s training in the bachelor's degree departments is given mainly in the form of thematic assignments and weekly group discussions in which the developing ideas and proposals of individual students are discussed intensively. In the master's degree courses the subjects on which people work are generally more complex and therefore, apart from the focus on personal development of the students, the supervision and group discussions pay much attention to research and analysis.

While from the 1990s onwards conceptual design influenced most of the bachelor's degree departments, this was less true of the Activity and Mobility departments (led by industrial designers Óscar Peña and Axel van Enthoven, respectively), where the primary concern continued to be with technique. That might well explain why significantly less former students from these departments came into the limelight of international attention; this honour mainly fell to the lot of the conceptual, cultural designers. In 't Hout: 'For a conceptual approach from the profession you need the right people, and it must also suit the department. Van Enthoven for example is a fantastic designer, but his quality lies mainly in how he works with industry. We have given him every encouragement to exploit this connection with industry in his department, and that has resulted in the production of designers who have indeed been less visible but nonetheless do important work. People like Bakker, Van Der Wijst,

From left to right: Jurgen Bey, Ester van de Wiel, Sophie Krier, Bertjan Pot, Lucas Verweij, Chris Kabel, Hella Jongerius, Wieki Somers

Beeke and Moritz were clearly involved in much more than simply design. People of that kind are currently quite difficult to find. They were particularly well informed about what was going on in the visual arts where people are generally interested in ideas and not primarily in techniques or materials (though it should be noted that Moritz, more than the other three in his department, continued to hammer away at the importance of aesthetics and the proper treatment of materials). If a department like Living puts the emphasis on technique, there is always a risk of producing soulless products. But if you begin with people and dare to develop ideas about what occupies them, something new and surprising happens. The approach followed by the design profession in the 1990s had much in common with that followed by the visual arts. Yet it was still all about design, and that led to surprising changes in the design profession. Droog Design noticed particular developments in design and had much success with bringing them before the footlights. And the same thing was achieved by the academy's educational philosophy. Conceptual design and an educational approach directed at human beings are continuations of one another'.

DESIGN ACADEMY EINDHOVEN AND DEWITTEDAME

Since the 1990s the school has mainly directed its attention to the development of ideas, and this can be seen right up to the present day, both in the work of the students (see illustrations) and in the general atmosphere. Regardless of the time at which a visitor enters the monumental building named deWitteDame, he or she always notices that this is a place where people talk, talk and then talk some more. Small groups of students and lecturers, grouped around more or less empty tables in large open spaces, discuss ideas, research and graphic material that someone has brought along. Building and philosophy go well with one another. Even before moving to deWitteDame in 1998, untidiness was taboo at the academy. Thus people can still remember how the former location, built in the Amsterdam School style (St Joris college and St Catharina lyceum), had very well-ordered rooms, a kind of accountant's dream where there was even a designated area for subversive messages and posters. But while at that time the classrooms were still small and stuffy, deWitteDame was to provide significantly more opportunities for philosophy and practical concerns to be brought closer together.

DeWitteDame, a prestigious property, is located in the centre of Eindhoven. The architect, Dirk Rozenburg, was commissioned by Philips in 1928 to design the factory in the New Objectivity (*Neue Sachlichkeit*) style. The taut modernistic style of the building was to symbolise a new industrial élan in which the key concepts were efficiency and optimism. In 1953 the previously nameless building was painted white and shortly thereafter acquired its present name, deWitteDame. For tens of years Philips produced light bulbs there, but all that came to an end at the beginning of the 1980s, when the company moved its production facilities to other Philips locations, at home and abroad, and the building, like other former Philips buildings in Eindhoven, fell empty. A group of artists and art lovers took the initiative to look for an alternative use, which was eventually found with the arrival of Design Academy Eindhoven, Philips Corporate Design, Eindhoven Public Library and MU Art Foundation. The architect Bert Dirrix took responsibility for the rebuilding. He had the greater part of the building demolished, leaving only the concrete structure standing. The inside rooms he kept open and spacious, uninterrupted by walls, corridors and architectural partitions. The rooms provided a view through to everywhere, and columns, ventilation pipes and cables were deliberately left visible. This means that the building still has the feel of an industrial building which offers its current tenants many possibilities to arrange things to suit their own needs and ideas.

The transparency and spaciousness of deWitteDame turned out to go perfectly with new ideas about an open educational system that lays the emphasis not primarily on the literal manufacture of products but on ideas about people and their needs in a complex globalising world. That can for example be seen from the way the rooms are laid out. There are enclosed workshops here and there, scattered over the five floors, but classes mainly take place in large open rooms. The different departments have their own large tables inside flexibly defined floor areas, from which they have a good view of what is going on in other departments. Although there are no walls and hardly any enclosing partitions, it seems that the hundreds of students hardly disturb one another. The usual visual clutter and cacophony characteristic of courses in art and design round the world, are significantly less present here. In most cases cuttings, mock-ups and scale models only begin to turn up on the tables a few weeks before the term exams. And finally there are actual life-size everyday objects, some working, some not (in a conceptually oriented course it is always advisable to be careful about checking whether a chair can actually support a person's weight). For some years now there has been a cautious recurrence of the suggestion that more attention should be paid to experimentation with shapes and materials, and this has led to a slight change in the appearance of the classrooms. While some ten years ago they still looked suspiciously like efficient open-plan offices with a large number of computers and tables that were mainly empty, it is now increasingly striking that experiments with shapes and materials are still lying around even after closing time. The thought has finally got through to the House of Concepts that good ideas need to be properly packaged if they are to be convincing in the long-term.

DESIGN ACADEMY EINDHOVEN IN THE CITY

Educational establishments which are to some extent comparable with Design Academy Eindhoven as regards their aims and level of education include the Ecole cantonale d'art de Lausanne (ECAL), the Rhode Island School of Design (RISD) in Boston and Parsons in New York (which like Design Academy Eindhoven offer courses leading to bachelor's and master's degrees), the Royal College of

Art (RCA) in London and the Domus Academy in Milan (which only provide master's degree courses), all of which have their city as an extra attraction. Eindhoven, a rather dull provincial city in the middle of the Netherlands, is difficult to think of in such terms. It should however be noted that most students reluctantly describe it as a major advantage that Eindhoven offers little to distract them from their studies. While students do from time to time, and for the wrong reasons, choose more exciting towns like Amsterdam, London or Paris, people who come to Eindhoven are mostly strongly motivated. And once there they experience, as they put it themselves, that due to the lack of external stimuli the city encourages a high level of concentration on their studies and the student community functions like a close-knit family. After their studies however, most ex-students hurry back to the Randstad (referring to the group of larger cities in the Western part of the Netherlands, of which Rotterdam is particularly popular amongst designers) or go abroad.

To call a halt to the flight of designers, these days Eindhoven is trying to hold on to its creative potential, for example by converting the former Philips complex De Strijp into a trendy live-work district (Strijp S) with much attention to art and design (architects like Andrea Branzi, Alessandro Mendini and Peter Eisenman developed ideas for it). And then there is the former Physical Laboratory, now developing into a design and technology campus and providing workplaces for start-up design companies at low rents. Eindhoven makes efforts to profiling itself not only as a city of technology but also as the country's most important city of design. Although Philips, its most important trump, (responsible for turning the city into the proverbial 'city of light') has to a large extent already disappeared from the city, it still has other cards up its sleeve, such as two major training centres, Design Academy Eindhoven and Eindhoven University of Technology (Technische Universiteit Eindhoven – TU/e. The TU/e has only offered a course in industrial design since 2001. Design Academy Eindhoven was closely involved in establishing the distinctive features of that course, but now cooperation has ceased because of 'disappointing cross-fertilisation', in other words the management of Design Academy Eindhoven felt it was putting all its energy into the TU/e and getting little in return. Today cooperation only occurs incidentally). Then Eindhoven also has Philips' design department (Philips Design, based like Design Academy Eindhoven in deWitteDame), Designhouse (a cooperative effort between Design Academy Eindhoven and the Van Abbe museum), De Krabbedans art centre, the Yksi gallery, the restaurant De Witte Tafel (an experimental cooperation between Design Academy Eindhoven and a regional chefs' training school, for which Design Academy Eindhoven students take turns to arrange the layout). And a few years ago, on the initiative of Design Academy Eindhoven, the TUe and Philips Design, a materials library was set up which is intended in time to develop into a prestigious platform for designers, suppliers, educational and research institutes. There are also countless design organisations active in the city, including Design Platform Eindhoven which organises the

From left to right: Wim Poppinga, Baukje Trenning, Bas van Tol, Marije Vogelzang, Marty Lamers, Eibert Draisma, Frank Tjepkema, Edith van Berkel, Merlijn, Bas Warmoeskerken, Bart Guldemond, Marcel Schmalgemeijer, Janneke Hooymans

annual Design Week and other activities. The high points of the Design Week are the awarding of the Dutch design prizes and the most important public attraction, the Design Academy Eindhoven Graduation Show in deWitteDame building.

From 1991 tot 2001 the famous final exam exhibitions of the Design Academy Eindhoven were held in the Berlage Exchange building in Amsterdam, an expensive choice made because of the wish to attract more people to Eindhoven. In 't Hout: 'In 1991 it was an outstanding idea on the part of Jan Lucassen and Gijs Bakker to present the exam work in Amsterdam rather than Eindhoven. The public was just beginning to be aware of the academy and in Amsterdam many more people came to have a look. But from 1998 onwards we had our own splendid building, had already achieved a worldwide reputation and kept paying substantial sums of money for a presentation in Amsterdam. I was curious to see what the fame of the academy was worth, whether we were finally in a position to lure people all the way to Eindhoven. Moreover various organisations in Eindhoven would be happy to see us organise something in our own city. We asked the local authority to sponsor us, which they were very happy to do because they saw the need. At first it was really scary. I still remember how Li (Edelkoort) and I didn't dare go upstairs, because we were afraid that nobody would be there on the fifth floor where the Graduation Show was being held. But it was a great success right from the beginning'. In 2007 the Design Week attracted some 20.000 people to Eindhoven, and that was mainly attributable to Design Academy Eindhoven's Graduation Show.

DESIGN ACADEMY EINDHOVEN IN THE WORLD

At the time of his appointment in 1983, Jan Lucassen was instructed by the government to turn AIVE from a provincial school into a national design institution. When Lidewij Edelkoort was appointed in 1999, the task set by the academy's board was to establish the position of the school internationally. Moritz: 'The preparatory work had in fact been done by Lucassen and Van Duppen. Lucassen was charmingly macho, a real man, lively, a stayer who, like Li (Edelkoort), was afraid of nothing. He was for example responsible for the school's move to deWitteDame. He wanted to get somewhere, was unafraid, sold the old building and went off to a location which in terms of size was much more suitable, more practical and above all much more prestigious. And he already had revolutionary ideas about a master's degree course, which would be accomplished a few years after he left. He had vision, he was articulate. He travelled a good deal and established the school's first contacts outside the country, while Van Duppen ensured that everything was working well, that things were running smoothly'.

In 't Hout: 'We (Edelkoort and In 't Hout) were able to reap the benefits of things that Lucassen had set in motion. Li, like Lucassen, had vision and was prepared to take risks. I was always the more cautious one. In that respect I played the same sort of role as Jan van Duppen, who for a year still came regularly to the academy when Li and I had already been appointed as directors. He did a fantastic job of showing me the ropes. Van Duppen and I were the binding forces while Lucassen and Li represented vision and boldness'. Bakker too approved of the way that Edelkoort managed to widen Lucassen's approach, partly because she had at her disposal a large international network. 'She had first-class contacts with the international business world and brought the world of PR, styling and fashion to the school. That turned out to be exactly what was needed. Everything she took on she took on energetically. Since her arrival the work of the students is well photographed and documented in glamorous catalogues. And right from the start she made many presentations abroad and similarly began to turn up in all the best places. The first presentation of Design Academy Eindhoven in Milan for example took place in the via della Spiga, one of the city's most expensive streets. That had its effect. Work done at Design Academy Eindhoven is currently on show in exhibitions in places ranging from New York, Miami and Basel to Shanghai and Tokyo. And also each year in Milan, where the school produces thematic shows which attract much attention from the public and the press'. Since Edelkoort took charge of Design Academy Eindhoven not only have the students been successfully promoted round the world but also the school itself has set itself up internationally as representing a good brand. In 't Hout: 'There is nothing wrong with that. You still hear people who studied at AIVE saying that they graduated from Design Academy Eindhoven, because the name has come to have a good sound and former students are proud of it'.

For those who leave Design Academy Eindhoven Edelkoort sees many opportunities on offer. 'The profession is on the brink of a period of exponential growth. The boundaries are constantly being shifted. There is so much going on in the world at the moment and design has a major role to play. The profession is becoming more and more holistic, is finding its way into a variety of other professional fields and is becoming more important to strategic decision-making processes at all levels, in science, politics, economics and social processes. At the same time the profession has great opportunities on a smaller level as well. You see for example that industry is becoming increasingly sophisticated and globalisation is an unstoppable force, but at the same time local factors play an important role. The Dutch ceramics firm Tichelaar performs an exemplary function here. Old and new, expression, local colour; however global the world may become, the role of outsider remains very important. Tichelaar has made this role sophisticated by asking celebrities for special designs which can be used to demonstrate the firm's special character. The same kind of approach can also be adopted by other businesses. The Netherlands has to find a special way to distinguish itself and can do this as much by know-how as by creativity, which is where a special role is reserved for designers. Design entails more than physical products. In future designers will mainly be deployed as co-thinkers, working out conditions and making things possible. This is the kind of thing we want to prepare our students for. A school must provide it's students with the best tools for the future'.

While conceptual design is often criticised, particularly in the Netherlands, Edelkoort is convinced that a conceptual approach still creates the best conditions for a good future in design. 'A conceptual approach can even be used to radically improve industrial design. Apart from that field of expertise, former students can function in a variety of different roles because they are so well trained in conceptual thinking. They have learnt to base their thinking on content and autonomy. We still primarily treat the profession as an art, and that is what has brought design to its present high standard. I am convinced that the independent role of design can also be an economic factor. Design increasingly represents a different, symbolic value, and this is something that needs to be worked on. Within the academy the students are given a playground, i.e. freedom. As an academy you perfect as it were their personalities, the clay is still wet, something can still be done with it. Subsequently the imaginative finds it's way to other fields, not excluding industry, as can be seen for example from the success of Droog Design and the Moooi label'.

According to Edelkoort, an educational approach in which people are put first provides the best guarantee for a good relationship with social developments. A different way to achieve the same relationship is to work in cooperation with industry. What in the past took place only incidently has now, under Edelkoort, grown into a flourishing practice: the academy has a number of companies and organisations linked with it, which in return for a substantial sum of money have become Friends of the academy. (These companies include Renault, Swarofski, Nike, Forbo, Koninklijke Begeer and many others). 'In return students work on projects from which the company concerned can draw inspiration. The school keeps a watchful eye on the educational process and the conditions under which the cooperation takes place. Our relationship with industry is based on effort, not on results. We create a peep-show for industrialists; creative young people are challenged to think about industrial processes. But the educational element remains the most important thing. If a project leads to real commissions we get back round the table and ensure that the interests of the students are safeguarded. Thus these cooperative efforts do not mean squandering our efforts on industry. And it sometimes happens that afterwards former students find work with the same companies'.

As regards the future of Design Academy Eindhoven, trend forecaster Edelkoort sees it as bright: 'The standard of the students and applicants is improving. The profession is growing in terms of prestige and attractiveness, finally good money can be earned with it. For this reason we are getting in more and more higher educated students. The parameters for entering the profession have changed. The profession is about 100 years old, younger than photography for example, and is gradually becoming more adult. The importance of design can hardly be denied any more. And you can no longer do without Design Academy Eindhoven'. Gijs Bakker too thinks that the academy has acquired a value which has become indispensable to the profession. 'I think that in this respect the master's degree departments (which, after a few changes in the organisation, reached it's current form in 2003) will become more and more important. They can record the academy's body of ideas, including the knowledge acquired in the bachelor's degree departments, in a sort of databank, and spread it abroad. In the master's degree departments people are not just trained as author-designers but also develop strong investigative qualities. That means a widening of their horizons, but also an increase in the depth of whatever individual character the school has brought out. Practically all master students come here from abroad and want primarily to master Dutch Design (i.e. conceptual design). Subsequently they take all this knowledge and research back home with them, which will in due course have a visible effect on things that happen in those countries. I also think that the school provides a blueprint for what a good design course can achieve. We should really consider leasing the system to other academies'. Edelkoort: 'The pressure will certainly become greater, and we shall have to go on improving. We have the reputation of being the best school in the world. How do you keep such a reputation? How do you arm yourself against erosion? That will be a point of special interest for us in the near future'.

THE STUDENTS

Where do the Design Academy Eindhoven's better students end up? Over the years anyone who reads the inside pages regularly will have watched the progress of many former students. Who by now is unaware of Piet Hein Eek's cupboards, tables and chairs in recycled wood, Jurgen Bey's tree trunk cum bench and Kokon furniture, Hella Jongerius' vases and furniture, Tjep's Bling Bling, and the decorative lamps made of garlands of flowers by Tord Boontje, who studied in Eindhoven at the end of the 1980s and then left for London's Royal College of Art? Job Smeets' heavy bronze objects are world famous, as are the pieces of burnt furniture by Maarten Baas who committed a perfect act of patricide by setting fire to bits of design classics. Then there are Simon Heydens' moving wallpaper, Wieki Somers' poetic vases, Joris Laarman's decorative heating and the famous furniture by Demakersvan (Joep and Jeroen Verhoeven and Judith de Graauw).

A striking number of successful graduates studied in Living and Identity, two of the largest departments, in the somewhat smaller Leisure department or in Public Space, the school's smallest department, which paradoxically enough has for years enjoyed the best reputation. The expertise of the students does not as such bear witness to the specialties of the particular departments from which they graduated. For example, Katja Gruijters and Marije Vogelzang studied in the Leisure department, but since then they have both worked as food designers, a relatively new branch of design. Gruijters has worked for companies like Unilever, Heinz and Sara Lee DE. Vogelzang anticipated special things happening with food and opened her own restaurants with attached design studios in Rotterdam and Amsterdam. Designer Richard Hutten studied in the Living department, currently has a successful design firm and is busy setting up a design academy in Korea, in cooperation with the MRDV architects and Design Academy Eindhoven. Jurgen Bey, Marcel Schmalgemeijer and Lucas Verweij studied in Public Space, a department which has trained many designers who have mapped out their own very individual paths through the world. Bey's work touches on practically all design disciplines and is known as 'critical design'. Schmalgemeijer found work as a theatrical designer. And after his final exam Verweij worked for a short while in the twilight zone between art and design (the firm Schie 2.0, founded by Verweij, Ton Matton and Jan Konings, who studied in the Living department), then became a staff member at Premsela (the Dutch Platform for Design and Fashion) and is currently director of the Rotterdam Academy of Architecture, which offers a master's degree course in architecture.

Not all successful designers have achieved world fame themselves. For some of the academy's graduates it is mainly their designs that have become well known. For example Cindy van den Bremen's graduation project involved the design of trendy head coverings to allow young Muslim women to satisfy both their religious 'obligations' and their need to look fashionable. Basten Leijh's graduation project involved making a city bike, a project that was subsequently improved for bike manufacturer Giant. A prime example of a designer whose design became famous, rather than the designer himself, is Max Barenbrug, who designed the popular Bugaboo baby buggy, which even found its way into the Dutch royal family and the American sequal 'Sex and the City'. Tristan Frencken graduated from the Mobility department with a handy aid for wheelchair users, which featured in many magazines. More recent is the humanitarian project by Wouter Haarsma, who graduated from the master's degree course Man and Humanity. He developed an ingenious system in which coffee production, distribution and preparation are, as it were, telescoped into one another to generate more income for poor farmers.

Besides the well-known names and designs, since the completion of their studies many people have been working behind the scenes. For example, Monica Mulder has for years been working within the Ikea imperium as senior product and furniture designer. Arian Brekveld, Edith van Berkel and Iris Toonen, play an important role as designers behind the Jongeriuslab label. Willeke Jongejan works as a colour specialist for Sikkens and Flexa, Corrine van Gorsel as product designer for the German company Koziol. Corien Pompe is employed by Volvo and is one of the top designers responsible for strategic developments in the field of mobility. Baukje Trenning has for years been tempting the concrete industry into unorthodox applications of concrete in architecture and urban space and Christiane Müller acts as a consultant to large fabric manufacturers like Danskina and De Ploeg.

Apart from the names of people who studied here and products that were developed here there are countless projects, some of which were carried out in co-operation with companies or institutions, which can be described as important. For example, the master's degree department IM: Conceptual Design in Context, investigated

From left to right: Jeroen Verhoeven, Judith de Graauw, Joep Verhoeven, Richard Hutten, Joris Laarman, Vincent de Rijk, Christien Meindertsma, Arian Brekveld

thoroughly all of the design options for a new courthouse in Amsterdam, made proposals for temporary construction sites for the Dutch Railways and devised solutions for a problem district in Amsterdam (commissioned by the Ymere housing corporation).

PITFALLS AND SECRETS OF SUCCESS

Design Academy Eindhoven has its disadvantages. Not surprisingly, the disadvantages to some extent parallel the critical observations which can be made about the pitfalls of conceptual design. For example, an emphasis on the development of ideas only leads the best people to innovative visions and important designs. Amongst their weaker brethren the endless indulgence in navel-gazing often leads to all too rapid satisfaction with moralistic ideas, feeble jokes and a mass of gadgets, a phenomenon however that not only affects Design Academy Eindhoven, but can also be seen at other design education establishments around the world. As with art schools, only the best leave the academy with any chance of building up an independent professional practice capable of surviving in the long-term without government support. (In the Netherlands the most talented artists, designers and architects can receive substantial subsidies to help set up their studios or finance special projects. This arrangement regularly comes under fire, on the grounds that it would encourage complacency; supporters argue that without subsidies Dutch Design could not be so experimental. One thing is certain: practically no famous Dutch designer has managed to get through his or her early years without government support). Infected by the success of those who have graduated from the academy in earlier years, an independent professional practice is the dream of most designers leaving Design Academy Eindhoven. But this dream is regularly shattered because clients stay away and even the subsidy committees provide no money. Shorn of their illusions, many designers must go on to find employment elsewhere. And they are not all equally well trained for that. Because during their course the emphasis was mainly on personal development, students are generally able to put together first-class portfolios to present themselves in the best light, but sometimes lack a proper training in systematic methodology, strategy and technical know-how, qualities which the average student can benefit from after his or her study (the average student from a technical university generally has sufficient professional skills to find immediate employment in the field for which he or she has trained. Design Academy Eindhoven mainly provides a very good education for the better students). Also the great emphasis on the development of ideas that tempted many designers in the 1990s to work primarily with existing objects and archetypal forms had its price. It still seems difficult for students to take the Dutch word for design (*vormgeving* – giving shape) literally. Experimentation with sculptural shapes still relies heavily on the formal vocabulary of existing products. Yet with some caution it is possible to notice a change. Today, in 2007, everyone is at least aware that the physical creation process deserves attention. Another possible disadvantage is the lack of departments

for interior design, interaction design, graphic design (that comes under Communication, but is not treated as a separate design discipline) and autonomous art. As for the last, many designers flirt with the visual arts in their work but sometimes lack a proper assessment framework. Thus objects were displayed at the 2006 and 2007 Graduation Shows which according to the captions had the ambition to be both sculptures and everyday objects, while to the expert eye it was obvious that they could never survive in an artistic context. There are also a few things of arguable quality in the relatively young master's degree department Man and Humanity. This department attracts a relatively large number of well-intentioned do-gooders who do not always command the necessary level of design talent. Not surprisingly some ambitious projects for disadvantaged districts and poor countries have certainly not deserved to be described as either 'humanitarian' or as 'good design', in the full sense of the words. And finally the success achieved in recent years has sometimes given young graduates a premature arrogance which has not always been to the advantage of their powers of self-criticism.

But we began with the academy's quality and obvious success. So let us end there too. Apart from Marcel Wanders, Ineke Hans and Dick van Hoff, every internationally known Dutch designer – born after 1960 – studied in Eindhoven (Wanders spent six months studying at Design Academy Eindhoven but was sent away for suspected lack of talent, after which he continued his studies in Arnhem, where Hans and Van Hoff also studied). Design Academy Eindhoven's first internationally successful generation (which included Jurgen Bey, Piet Hein Eek, Richard Hutten, Hella Jongerius, and slightly later Job Smeets, Bertjan Pot, Frank Tjepkema and Wieki Somers) still took some time to achieve recognition. The products of the most recent generation (Maarten Baas, Kiki van Eijk, Joris Laarman, Demakersvan and others) were picked up by the media hardly before they had graduated. The academy's great popularity has meant that in recent years not one potential star designer has escaped the watchful eyes of the international media, the business world and the museums, which since the 1990s have had their eye on the cultural dimension of Dutch Design.

Most of those involved are agreed about the secret of the academy's success. The independence of its education guarantees a large measure of freedom and flexibility. By organising its education and atmosphere in the best possible way, the school has tempted important designers and artists to head its departments. The fact that lecturers lecture one day a week at most, guarantees that they remain firmly rooted in the profession and so provide a high quality education. And last, but certainly not least, an educational philosophy that puts people before products has become virtually synonymous with great attention to the development of ideas. All this has given rise to work and a mentality that have made an international impression. In the course of time this became sufficient to bring about a self-fulfilling prophecy: today the school's reputation tempts students and significant people in the profession to come from near and far to the provincial city of Eindhoven. The master's degree course is almost completely international, with barely 5% of the students coming from the Netherlands, which is something unique in the world. The popularity of the school has created the happy situation that it can choose from a large pool of potential lecturers and students (a luxury also enjoyed for example by the popular RCA in London). And that has given rise to a golden rule: any school that attracts the world's best designers-to-be is certain to produce the best designers.

SOURCES

BOOKS

Aaron Betsky and Adam Eeuwens, *False Flat. Why Dutch design is So Good.* Phaidon Press, London, 2004

J. van den Heuvel, *Voor de konsument of de industrie: Voorgeschiedenis en beginjaren van de AIVE 1945–1960*. Utrecht, 1986.

MAGAZINES

Alex Wiltshire, 'Design Academy Eindhoven'. *Icon*, january, 2006.

Cor Hospes, 'Redesigning Eindhoven'. *Bright Magazine,* 2005.

Nicky Bouwmeester, 'Eindhoven is focussing on Europe. Knowledge and Design'. *Smart Traveler*, 24 october 2005.

Peter de Graaf, 'Alle opvouwbare kandelaars verkocht (all foldable candles sold out)', Text focussing on the DAE and Eindhoven as the design capital of the Netherlands. *De Volkskrant*, 23 august 2005.

21 most influential, *Icon*, march 2005.

Alex Wiltshire, '3 days in the Netherlands', *Icon,* may 2004

Louise Schouwenberg, 'House of Concepts', *Frame Magazine*, 2003.

Stephen Treffingers, 'School For New Dutch Masters Turns Playful Into Paydirt', *New York Times*, 2 October 2003

ARCHIVE OF DESIGN ACADEMY EINDHOVEN – DAE

Brochures of the DAE 2000–2007

Graduation catalogues 1992–2007

INTERVIEWS / CONVERSATIONS

Lidewij Edelkoort (1950) former head of the Man and Leisure department 1992–1999, director DAE 1999–.

Liesbeth in 't Hout (1951) former coordinator of the Man and Leisure department 1992–1999, director of Education DAE 1999–2006.

Ulf Moritz (1939) former teacher and head of the Man and Identity department (was the Textile department of AIVE till 1983) 1970–2005.

Gijs Bakker (1942) former head of the Man and Living department 1987–2003, head of master department IM: Conceptual Design in Context 2003–.

Marijke van der Wijst (1940) former head of the Man and Public Space department 1987–2005.

Koos Flinterman (1950) former coordinator of the Man and Well-Being department 1995–2000, former coordinator of the Master department (Interior design, now part of the department IM: Conceptual Design in Context) 2000–2003, curator and organisor of many DAE projects, among which the school's annual presentations at the Salone del Mobile in Milan.

Hella Jongerius (1963) former student 1988–1993, teacher and head of the departments Atelier 2000–2003 and Man and Living 2003–2004.

Jurgen Bey (1965) former student 1984–1989, teacher of several bachelor departments 1998–2001 and master departments 2002–2005, interim head of the Man and Living department (in cooperation with Louise Schouwenberg) 2004–2005.

Lucas Verweij (1965) former student 1986–1991, former guest teacher of the Atelier department 2001.

Bart Guldemond (1962) former student 1980–1986, former teacher of the Man and Living department 1996–2006.

Marcel Schmalgemeijer (1968) former student 1987–1993.

Bertjan Pot (1975) former student 1992–1998.

Judith de Grauuw (1976) former student 1999–2005.

Jeroen Verhoeven (1976) former student 1998–2005.

Joep Verhoeven (1976) former student 1997–2005.

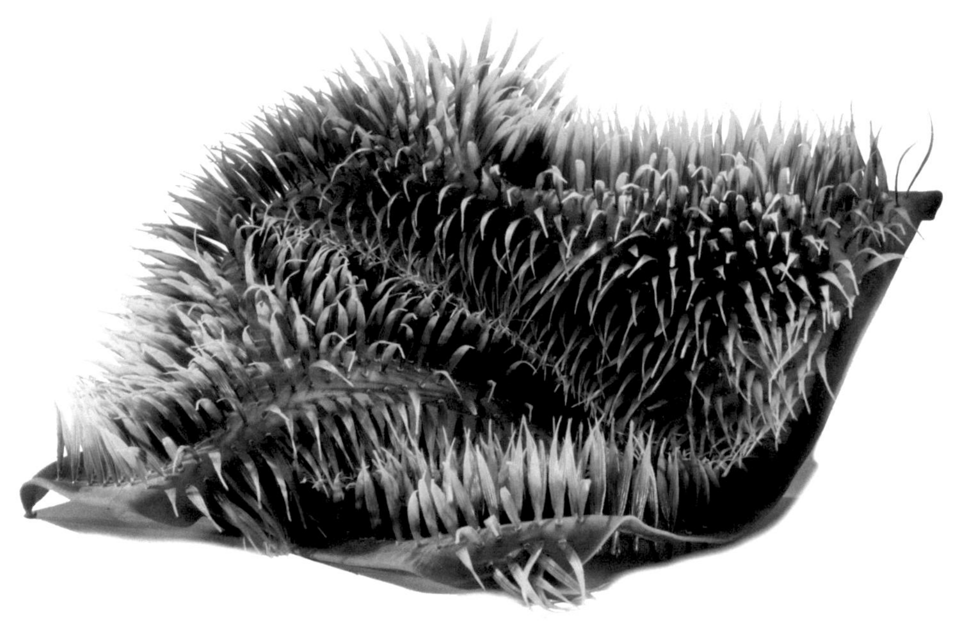

Above: Artificial plant, 1996

Left and below: Do Break, 2000
In collaboration with Peter van der Jagt

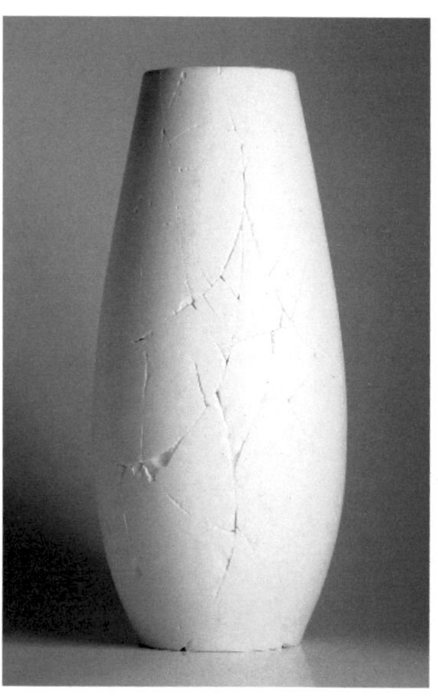

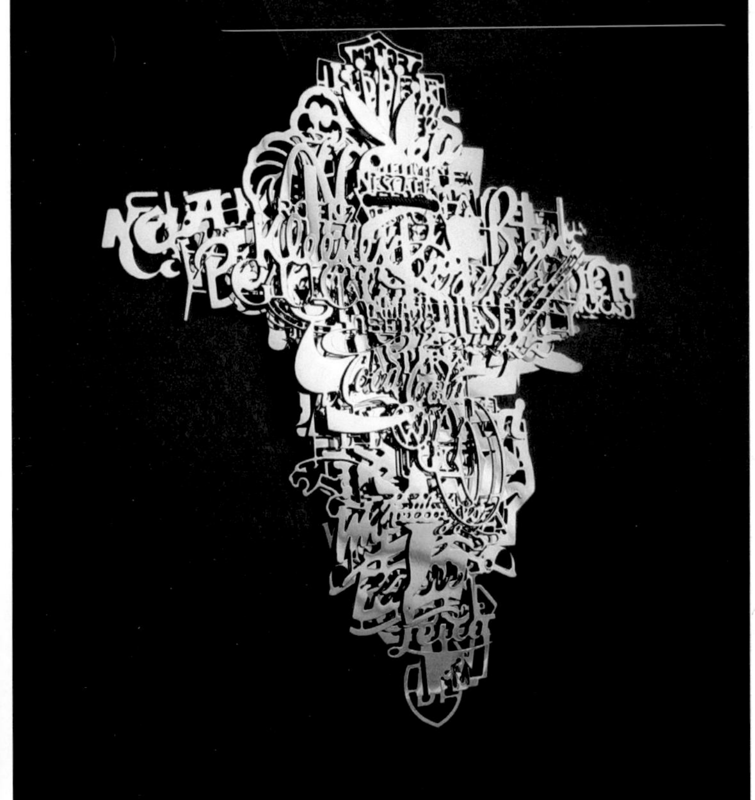

Above: Interior design restaurant Fabbrica, Rotterdam, 2006

Left: Bling Bling, 2003
Medallion for Chi Ha Paura

Airco Tree for the British Airways executive lounge, 2004
(Droog Design for British Airways)

ROC Economy, 2007
Design of the reception area of the economics department

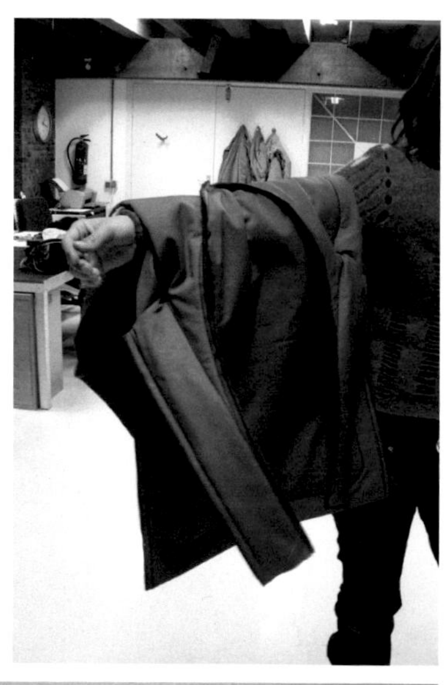

Top left: Bookcase, 1997

Top right: Costume Chair, 2005

Bottom left: French Carafe for Royal VKB, 2005

Bottom right: Suit Chair 1999

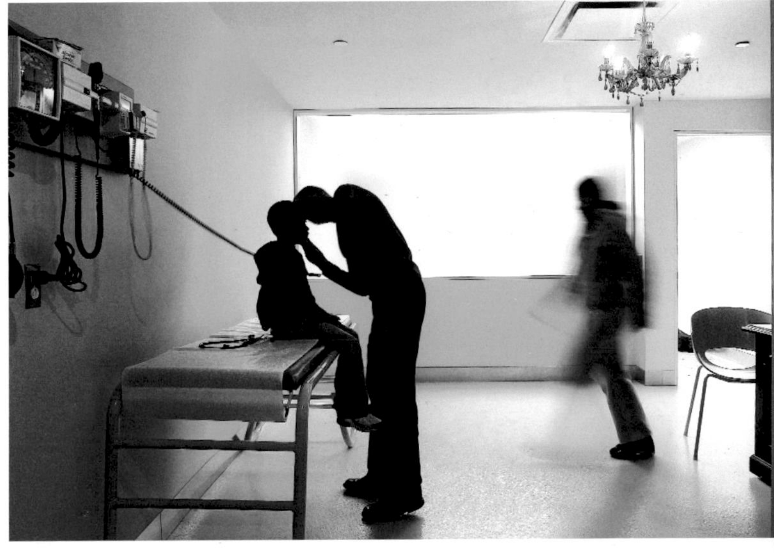

Paediatrics, Harlem New York, 2004

Top left: 'Play façade'

Top right: Waiting room and reception

Bottom left: Outside view of 'Play façade'

Bottom right: treatment room

Martinez gallery, Brooklyn New York, 2002

Top: Furniture wall

Middle left: Fireproof safety handrails

Middle right: Wrapped old staircase

Bottom: Exhibition design, City hall, The Hague, 2004

The 'Climclamberhangsitfoot-ballcurtaintheatretube'
Primary school De Paradijsvogel, Ypenburg Den Haag, 2006.
Hundred of meters of bright green tubes circle through the schoolyard and the assembly hall and can be used as benches, curtain rails, climbing frames and more.

Willeke Jongejan
Man and Living [1996]
—
Blinds, 1996

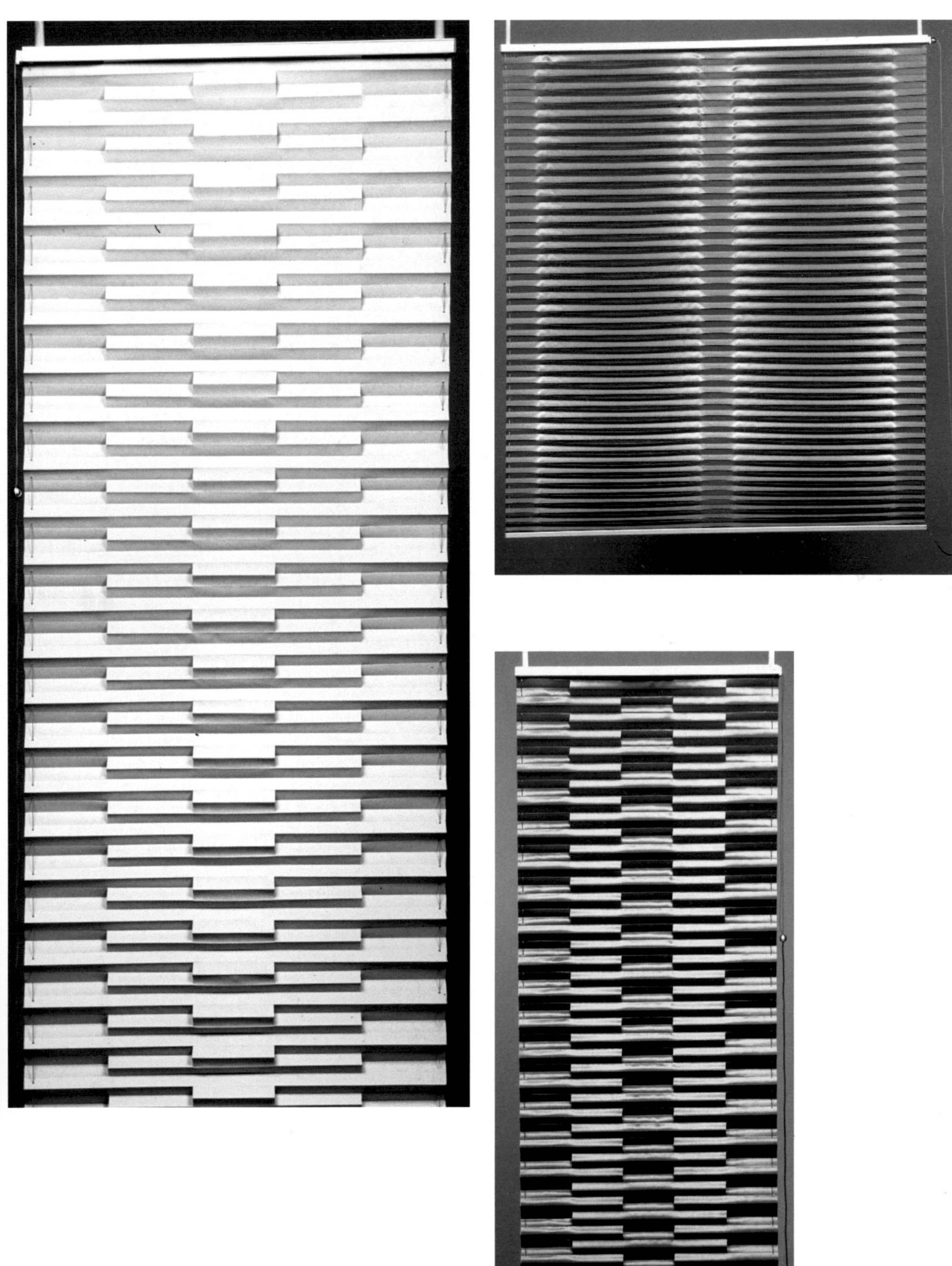

Nynke Tynagel (1977) and Job Smeets (1970): 'Li was the academy's first genuine cosmopolitan. Her views define the "designership" that we now aspire to: work driven by nothing other than a need to be unrestricted.'

Why his graduation project wasn't part of the 1996 exhibition that the academy had been holding annually in Amsterdam for years? A tormented grimace creases Job Smeets' face. Another one of those situations that forced him to swim against the tide.... 'That exhibition in the Beurs van Berlage was a tradition. But it meant nothing to me. My final project had appeared all over the place by then. I said I'd participate, but only if I could show a new piece of work. Those in charge at the time didn't like that idea. It had to be according to their rules. Fine, on one condition: since participation was evidently compulsory, I wanted 6,000 guilders to show my project. Never heard from them again.'

We'd just taken a short walk from Studio Job's atelier in the port area of Antwerp to a nearby restaurant. Both Smeets and his partner, Nynke Tynagel, are wearing snow-white trainers, fresh out of the box, as prescribed by the latest fashion code. Job's white T-shirt marks him as a 'Golden Boy'. The game of words and values is one they play with a passion at all times, in all places. It's part of Studio Job's oeuvre, part of the duo's decision to position themselves in the margin of the design world, and part of the constant shift between overstatement and understatement that characterizes both their designs and their conversation. 'Design is on no more than a modest – and not very high –

cultural echelon,' says Job. 'That may be the tragedy of the choice that Nynke and I made. The decision to become designers and then to battle relentlessly in an attempt to detach ourselves from everything associated with design: the material, the production process, the almighty manufacturer. At the end of the day, we're willing to rely on one authority only, and that's our own head. We want to be the curators of our own thoughts.'

At that moment, a couple of women at the studio are completing moulds for a series of concrete reliefs, an art commission for a building project in Amsterdam. A tiring task that requires precision, admits Job. And one typical of what goes on at the Antwerp atelier. 'We do girls' work here. The rough stuff is done by the guys at our workshop in Breda.'

For that matter, the studio in Antwerp is preparing for a forthcoming relocation to a 700-m² hall in another part of the city. The present space has become too small for Studio Job's ever-expanding operation. For the past few years, work by Tynagel and Smeets has drawn worldwide attention, which has had a decided influence on the scale of their activities. Recognition is growing for a perspective on design that was anything but widely accepted around the year 2000. 'I remember our solo presentation at the Milan furniture fair that year,' says Smeets. 'We put little red stickers on the designs we sold. In the context of a design fair, just doing that was pretty unusual. And even though not everybody understood the work itself, we felt we had to show our designs in Milan. I bought a suit especially for the occasion, the showroom was expensive and the production of our work had cost us a fortune. We barely had enough money to pitch our tiny tent at the Milan camp site.'

In 2000 Nynke Tynagel graduated from the Information department of the Design Academy Eindhoven, where she remembers learning a great deal from lecturer and graphic designer Anthon Beeke. Dominating her years at the Design Academy Eindhoven was the relocation of the school to deWitteDame, a building whose vast, open interiors were seen by officials at the academy as ideal spaces for a design school. 'Eliminating classrooms never had the effect that the director at that time, Jan Lucassen, envisioned,' recalls Tynagel. 'It simply didn't work. In my case, despite the chaos caused by the change of location, I got a good start at the academy. Soon after beginning my studies, however, I did start working for Studio Job, where I was given a lot of opportunities that undoubtedly enriched my education.'

Smeets believes it was then that the atmosphere at the school clearly began to change. 'When I arrived there, the place had absolutely no style. It was a straightforward, provincial school where not a soul had ever heard of public relations. If you wanted to ask one of the instructors a question, you had to make an appointment, so to speak. Departments like Living and Environment were run along strict lines. Living revolved around a "salon", where students worked according to a formula that everyone was expected to follow. Lidewij Edelkoort introduced a completely different regime in the new Man and Leisure department, from which I was in the first class to graduate in 1996. She offered us an empty playground and allowed us to find our own way. A few good teachers encouraged us to think freely and, in particular, to disregard the framework of existing design. That was one hundred per cent Li's vision, definitely not the school's. She was the academy's first genuine osmopolitan.

And she imparted that mentality to us. In retrospect, I realize that her views define the "designership" that we now aspire to: work driven by nothing other than a need to be unrestricted. Like Li, we've had to pay the price at times for that ambition. It's not a popular position to take, certainly not in the Netherlands.'

If former directors Lucassen and van Duppen deserve to be praised for anything, says Smeets, it's for the courage they showed in handing over the sceptre to Lidewij Edelkoort and Liesbeth in 't Hout. In doing so, they made the academy's 'international bent' a fact. 'In previous years, the academy had produced all the talent needed: people like Jurgen Bey, Piet Hein Eek and Hella Jongerius. In truth, the foundation for the success of Droog Design was laid in Eindhoven, and it's Droog who took the designers to Milan. Liesbeth and Lidewij were the ones who recognized the niche and who developed a very clever plan for the school, a plan that helped the academy attract funds and create exposure for the quality of its students. It was also good for the reputation of the academy itself.'

A brain-twister for Tynagel and Smeets is the secret of the Design Academy Eindhoven. 'I don't know,' says Job. 'Maybe the secret lies in its aura, which not only generates media attention but also seems to draw good teachers and students to the school. There's obviously a realization that you have to pull quality in before you can send it out again. And it's true: in that respect, the school has become exhibitionistic. Thanks in part to Droog and the academy, in terms of PR, Dutch design has reached great heights. In my mind the big question is whether we really have so much more quality to offer than designers elsewhere. We have more designers, but if there was a subsidy scheme supporting singers that matched the one that promotes designers, it's likely that the Netherlands would also have more singers.'

A remarkable side effect of the academy's position as an outstanding international institute is something that Nynke Tynagel sees in the trainees that work for them. 'Most trainees arrive with the idea that their time at Studio Job will be fun. It'll be a piece of cake – that's often their attitude. After working here for a month, they've usually put some of that pride in their pockets. More and more students from Eindhoven walk in with the idea that they're stars. A personal website, business cards, designs published in *Elle Wonen*. They've taken the glamour radiated by the school and made it all about themselves. But talent is the result of working endlessly on an idea, improving it, plugging away until you get the result you want. As a student, I didn't see that either, but it remains a part of our daily practice. Nose to the grindstone – and it may lead to nothing more than the top of the iceberg.'

Smeets believes that their work has helped to broaden the horizon of design to some extent. Their products, most of which can hardly be called functional, have opened the way to a new market of highly exclusive objects. He promises, though, that whatever the cost, Studio Job will avoid the perils of being typecast. 'Right now, when we've finally got the studio up and running, we have to guard against becoming a salon. We've got to be strong enough to ignore success and to take accountability for our actions. Are we still pursuing freedom? Managing to think outside the box in everything we do?'

Gert Staal

Job Smeets
Man and Leisure [1996]
—
Top: 'Easy Viewing', 1996

Nynke Tynagel
Man and Information [2000]
—
Below: Characters, 2000

Above: Elements collection, 1999

Presentation of furniture and objects at Galerie Binnen, Amsterdam, 2000

Left: Perished cabinet and screen, 2006

Below: Rock table, 2002

Opposite left top: Charm chain (with Viktor&Rolf), 2001

Opposite right top: Gold biscuit, cake of peace, 2006

Opposite bottom: Home work, domestic totems and tableaux, 2007

Left: Siver ware teapot (Bisazza collection) , 2007

Below: Paper furniture and chandelier (Moooi collection), 2006

Opposite left top: Charm chandelier (Swarovski collection), 2003

Opposite right top: Biscuit plates (Royal Tichelaar collection), 2006

Opposite bottom: Castle, 2003

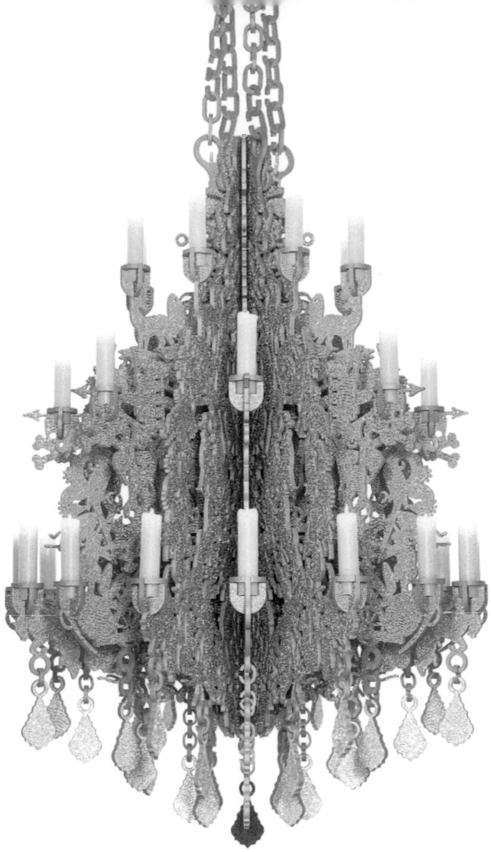

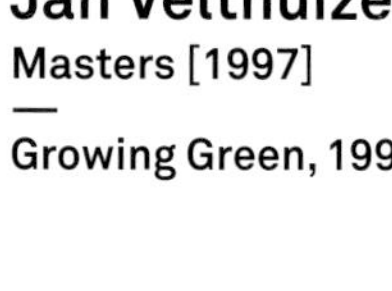

Jan Velthuizen
Masters [1997]
—
Growing Green, 1997

Marnix Oosterwelder

Man and Leisure [1997]

—

Dutch Funeral Culture, 1997

Monika Mulder

Man and Leisure [1997]

—

Gemini, 1997

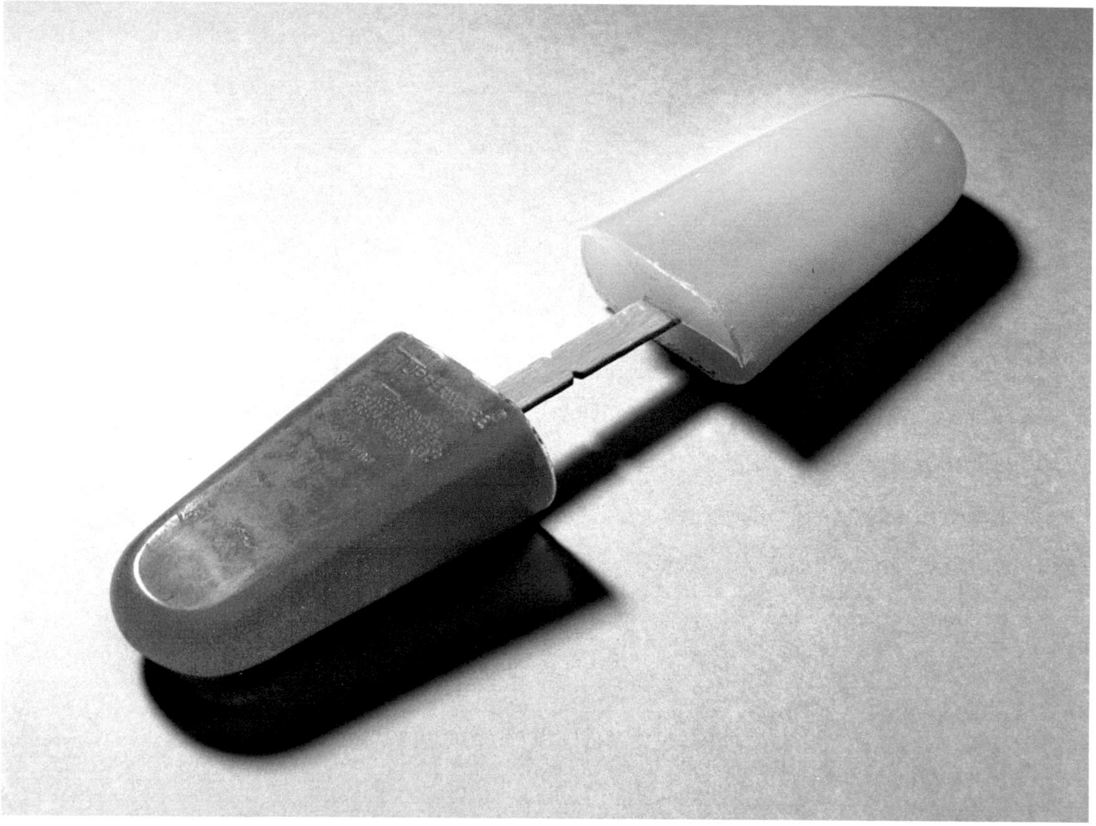

Danny Fang
Man and Leisure [1998]

—

Footwear from one shoelace, 1998

—

From old to new, 1998

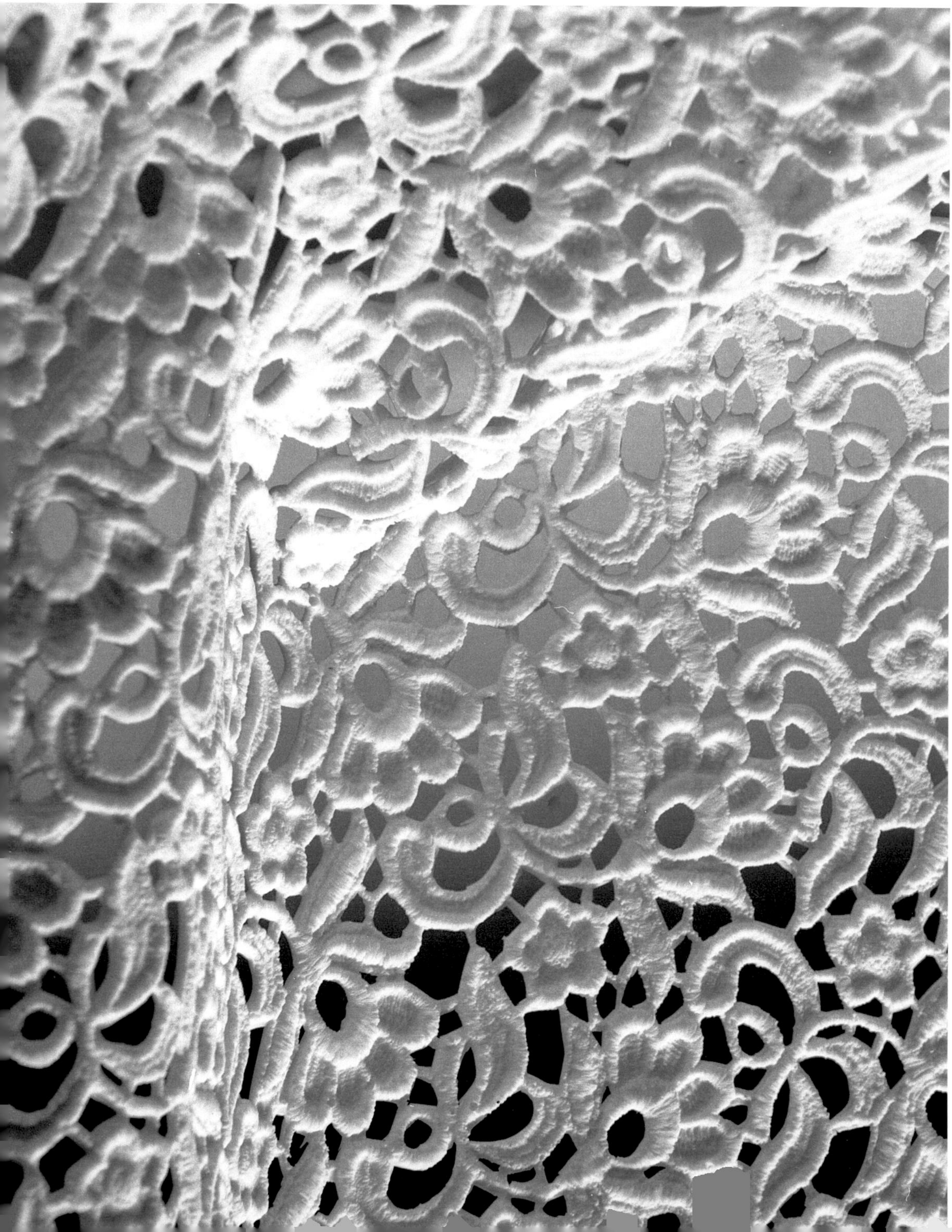

Cindy van den Bremen

Man and Well-Being [1999]

—

For safety reasons, Moslim girls are not allowed to wear head coverings in gym class. Van den Bremen designed Capsters, a line of sports head covers, which safely wrap around the head.

Marble Quarry 1998
Part of the series: Artificial Arcadia
(1998–2003)

Ringroad (Houston) 2005
Part of the series: Utopian Debris
(2002–2007)

Sebastiaan Straatsma

Man and Living [1999]

Right: Rubber no. 14, 1999

Below: Jelly Lamp, 2006
(In collaboration with Bertjan Pot)

Next page: Dustcollectors, 2007

'It was okay for things to look good. In retrospect, it's the reason why I opted for the Man and Identity department', says Bertjan Pot (1975)

'It was okay for things to look good. In retrospect, it's the reason why I opted for that department.' In the 1990s, when Bertjan Pot (1975) enrolled at the Design Academy Eindhoven (then called AIVE), he chose the Man and Identity department, one of the school's eight educational programmes. In those days, focusing attention on experimentation with materials and on the creation of beautiful objects was not an obvious priority in the school's other departments. So-called 'conceptual design' was not only wildly popular but also highly influential. Design had to be about something. Not only that, but there was a taboo on beauty for the sake of beauty and on too much thought given to the material qualities of a product. The atmosphere within the Man and Identity department was different. 'What I remember most is the liberating attention paid to beauty,' says Pot. 'There was no shame attached to making attractive designs.'

Asked for his opinion of the programme, Pot quickly slips into superlatives. 'My background had taught me absolutely nothing about design. The academy actually allowed me to develop as a person and not just as a designer. I learned a great deal from Ulf Moritz (then head of Man and Identity), my teachers and my fellow students. Most students in the department were girls, by the way. Obviously, textile design still doesn't appeal to guys.'

Pot and his peers, Wieki Somers among them, belong to a generation of Dutch designers that, unlike those that appeared before and after, began their careers on the sidelines, so to speak. The early '90s saw the international breakthrough of Marcel Wanders, Hella Jongerius, Jurgen Bey, Richard Hutten and, in their wake, Job Smeets. After a short period marked by little breaking news, at the dawn of the 21st century another handful of noteworthy Dutch designers (all educated in Eindhoven) emerged, among whom Maarten Baas, Joris Laarman and the Verhoeven brothers. The ink on their diplomas had barely dried before their products were making waves in international publications and at prestigious exhibitions. An exciting story, but one that has nothing to do with Bertjan Pot. 'I'm glad I wasn't immediately shoved into the limelight. A slower start allowed me to develop in a more relaxed manner, and I'm reaping the benefits now. I have self-confidence, know what my profession is all about, recognize my qualities. My products aren't nine-days wonders. The past two years have been really busy ones for me, but I've had no problem handling increased expectations. I sometimes wonder whether that would have been the case if I'd had instant success.' Strangely enough, he can't blame his early work for the initial lack of success. Pot's graduation project in 1998 was a series of balloon lamps that still fuel the imagination, nearly ten years later, and which feature all the characteristics of his later work.

His career in a nutshell. One year after graduating, Pot and fellow student Daniel White (who'd selected the Man and Activity department) set up design agency Monkey Boys. Encouraged by kudos from colleagues, the youngsters came up with products on their own initiative (including new models of the balloon lamps), which were shown at various design exhibitions. Clients weren't breaking down the doors to acquire their services, however; nor were the young creatives able to grab the attention of Droog Design (possibly one of the organization's historic errors), the hope of every young Dutch designer in the 1990s. And although nearly all recognized designers were well financed by the Dutch government in the early years of their careers, those in charge of subsidies were not particularly taken by the work of Monkey Boys. Three years into their partnership, White and Pot decided to go their separate ways. What had seemed so attractive at the outset – the breadth and diversity of their combined approaches – ultimately led to friction. Furthermore, their collaboration had produced few designs that united their talents within a single object. 'It was always obvious who had made what. Daniel was occupied mostly with sampling, whereas I was more into experimenting with materials. At a certain point, Daniel was fed up with being barely able to make ends meet, even though I was willing to keep trying.' With a trace of pride in his voice, Pot says he no longer needs subsidies; he's up to his neck in work – not only from museums and government agencies, but also from companies like Moooi, Cor Unum, Arco, Montis and Pallucco. The (inter)national media have discovered him (the 2007 spring issue of *The New York Times* featured an in-depth portrait of Pot), he's won two major Dutch awards (the Materiaalfondsprijs in 2003 and the Profielprijs in 2004), and several of his products have claimed a permanent place in the annals of design: Random Light, Carbon Chair and Slim Table. The same fate is surely in store for more recently completed designs, such as Non-Random Light and chairs dubbed Wieki, Slats and Skinny.

If you want to capture Bertjan Pot's work in a single word, a good choice would be 'skin'. Sometimes the skin functions as a structural component (Random Light and Carbon Chair for Moooi), occasionally it is no more than a tenuous film (Slim Table for Arco), and recently its primary purpose is to stir the imagination (Centerpieces for Cor Unum). The skin of certain products is such an intrinsic element that it melds with the construction to form an aspect of the design that demands countless preliminary studies. It all began with Pot's graduation project. For his balloon lamps, Pot soaked a circularly knitted net of glass fibre or another fabric in epoxy resin, filled it with inflated balloons, placed the whole thing in a plastic bag and vacuumed out

the air around the balloons, compressing them into a tight cluster. When the resin had hardened, he removed both plastic bag and balloons. The result was a rigid, seamless object with an opening for a light source. A similar marriage between skin and structure reappears in Pot's Random Light, which consists of a web of white strands, again soaked in epoxy resin, that encircle a hollow globe. Pot first manufactured Random Light himself, but when Moooi expressed interest in the design, manufacture was transferred to the Philippines, where low labour costs meant the lamps could be hand-wrapped. Low labour costs were accompanied by high transport costs, however. For a lamp that was being manufactured in increasingly larger batches, it paid to build an ingenious machine in the Netherlands that would do the random wrapping automatically, allowing the lamps to be made on Dutch soil once again. When Marcel Wanders asked whether Random Light could also be made in black, initial trials proved difficult enough to temporarily halt the project. (As of this writing, black is possible.) But Wanders' question did lead to important experiments with carbon fibre, a material so strong that Pot was able to make chairs out of it. The first of these, Random Chair, was soon followed by Carbon Copy, which replicates the Eames Plastic Chair. Here, too, the manufacturing process displays a nice mix of high-tech material and hands-on craftsmanship. Because of expected problems concerning copyrights, the chair hasn't gone into production, but it did pave the way for a highly successful design, Carbon Chair, which Pot developed in close collaboration with Marcel Wanders.

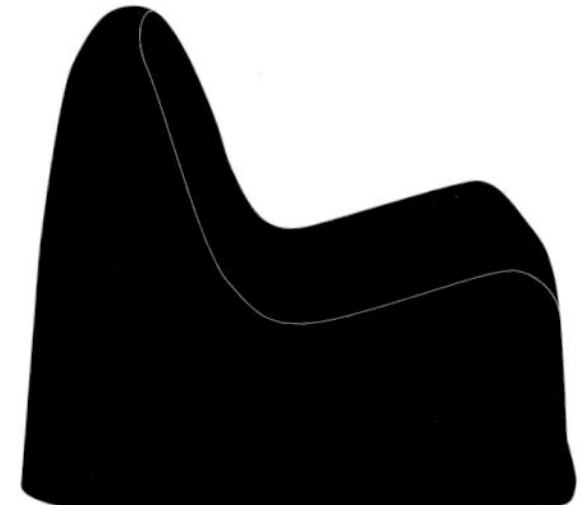

In the case of another successful product, the skin was added to the construction. In 2005 Pot was among a group of designers invited to create a centenary product for Arco, a manufacturer of high-quality wood furniture with a modernist look. 'During our tour of the factory, the director turned a chair around and showed us that the connecting piece between armrest and seat looks like wood but is, in fact, a steel strip covered in a wood veneer. In the eyes of this young designer, who had been taught to use materials in an "honest" way, it seemed at first like out-and-out deception. But I learned to work with it.' Slim Table has an elegant steel body clad completely in a paper-thin wood veneer that is essential to the character of the table.

The skin surrounding Pot's more recent products incites the fantasy rather than functioning as physical support or outer layer. According to Pot, products should tell an open-ended story that leaves us with something to ponder. His idea is visible in Centerpieces, objects designed for Dutch ceramics company Cor Unum. Pot made stacks of little plastic animals, dipped the lot into plaster of Paris several times, thus creating objects with a thickened skin. After digitally scanning the results, he enlarged the scanned images to make models for ceramic replicas. Because the contours of the plastic figures are blurred by the new skin, each Centerpiece has the look of an unfinished, attractive story. Or, as Pot puts it, 'of a beautiful fairy tale yet to be conceived'.

Louise Schouwenberg

—

Knitted Lamps, 1999

The Knitted Lamps, 1998

The Random Light, 1999

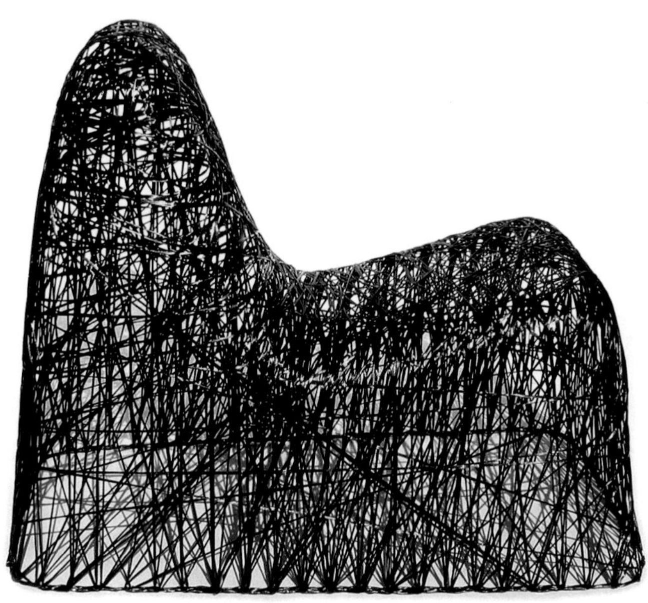

The Random Chair, 2003

The Carbon Cloud, 2005

From left to right:
The Carbon Bench, 2006

The Carbon Chair, 2004

Slim Table, 2005

Old Fruit Versatile, 2004

From left to right:
The Large-Foldup, 2002

The Seamless Chair, 2005

Konijnenlamp, 2006

Sticker sheets on glass: Graffiti for beginners, 2006

(table by Frank Bruggeman; vase by Sebastiaan Straatsma; chair by Chris Kabel)

Sophie Krier

Man and Identity [1999]

—

I take, I make, I fake, 1999

En Garde! A film, depicting Krier, a young woman, designer, engaged in a fight which by nature is paradoxical. The film was screened inside Fort Asperen during the exhibition Armour (2003). (Commissioner: Li Edelkoort; Camera, editing: Tim Klaasse;)

Nuits Blanches manifests itself as an on-site temporary dormitory (photograph taken during 100% Design, Van Nelle Ontwerpfabriek, 2004) which adopts empty spaces near fairs and festivals, as an ad hoc breeding ground for ideas and contacts. (Commissioner/Co-initiator: Sacha Winkel; collaborators: Novak Ontwerp, Vier, Onno Donkers, Proef and others)

Timo Breumelhof

Man and Leisure [2000]

—

Paraffin table, 2000

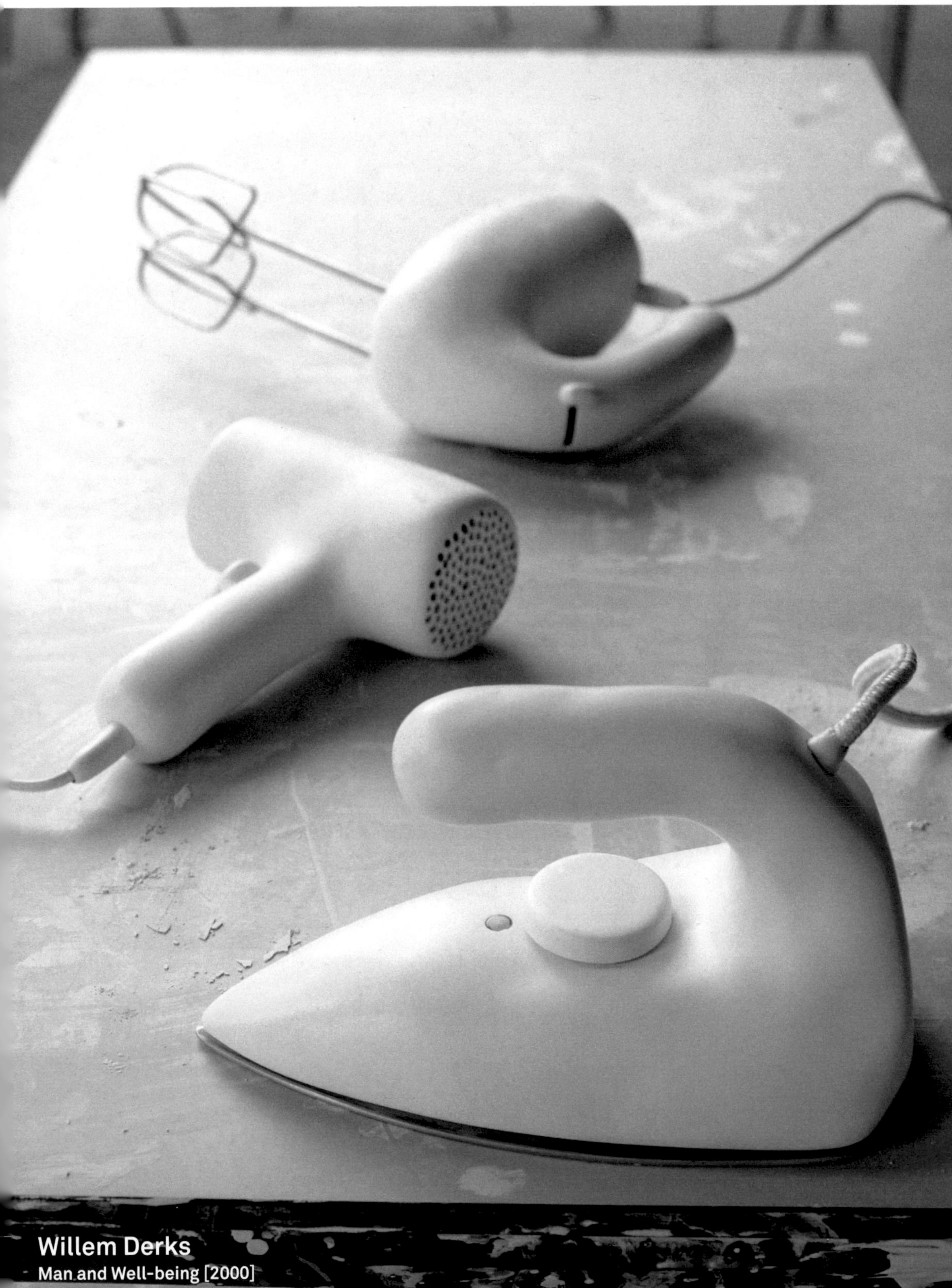

Willem Derks
Man and Well-being [2000]
—
My Archetypes, 2000

Ries Straver

Man and Communication [2000]

—

Extension, 2000

Desiree de Jong

Man and Identity [2000]

—

Second chance, 2000

Left: Muffins, 2000
When hard meets soft

Below: Bathboat, 2005

Opposite left top: Blossoms, 2004

Opposite right top: Mattress Stone Bottle, 2002

Opposite bottom: High Tea Pot, 2003

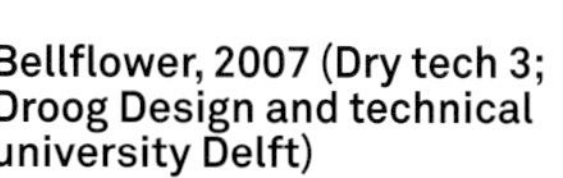

Bellflower, 2007 (Dry tech 3; Droog Design and technical university Delft)

Departed Glory, 2007

Kiki van Eijk
Man and Leisure [2000]
—
Living in a doll's house, 2000

Soft Cabinet, 2006

Soft Dressing Table, 2007

Nina Farkache

Man and Well-Being [2000]

—

Marble bench, 2000

Chantal van Heeswijk

Man and Living [2000]

—

Dyslexic furniture, 2000

Chris Kabel
Man and Living [2001]

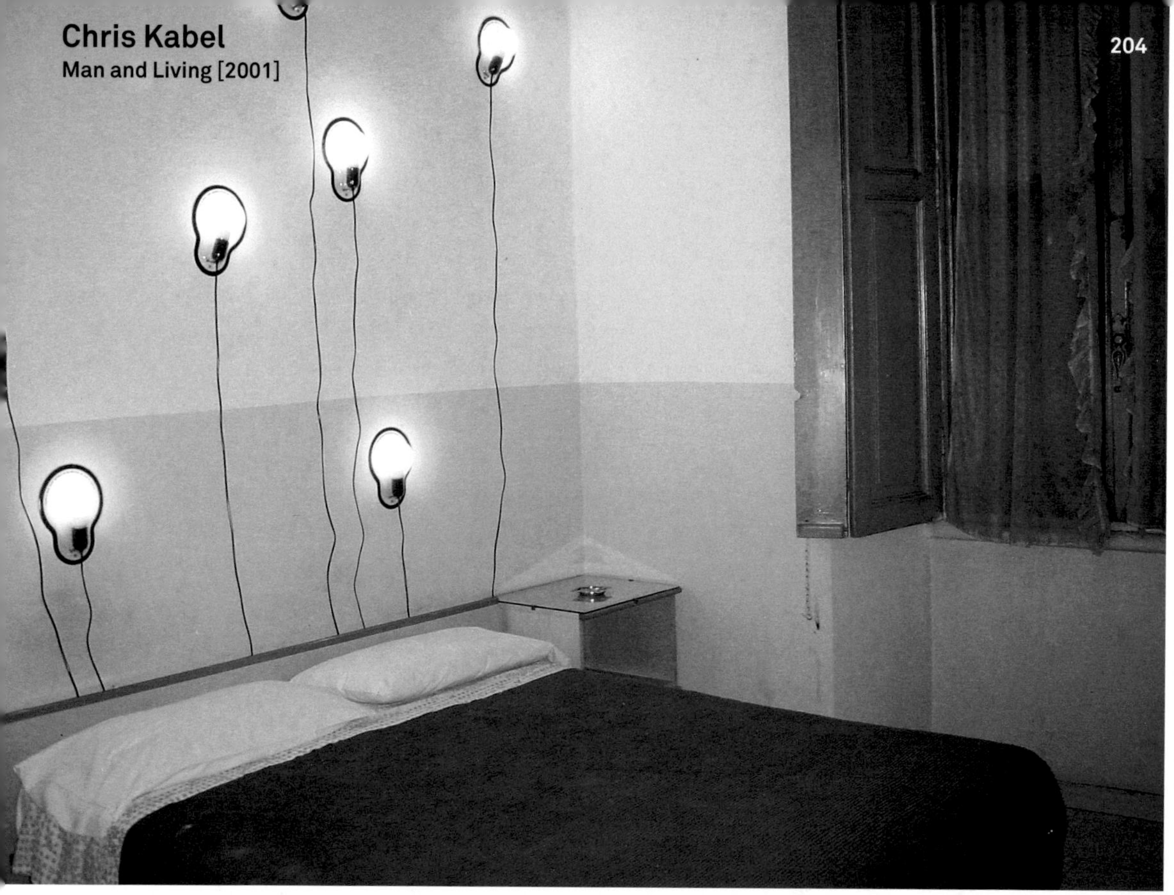

16

Opposite top: Sticky Lamp, 2001

Opposite bottom: Shady Lace, 2003

Left: Mesh Chair, 2005

Below: Flames, 2003

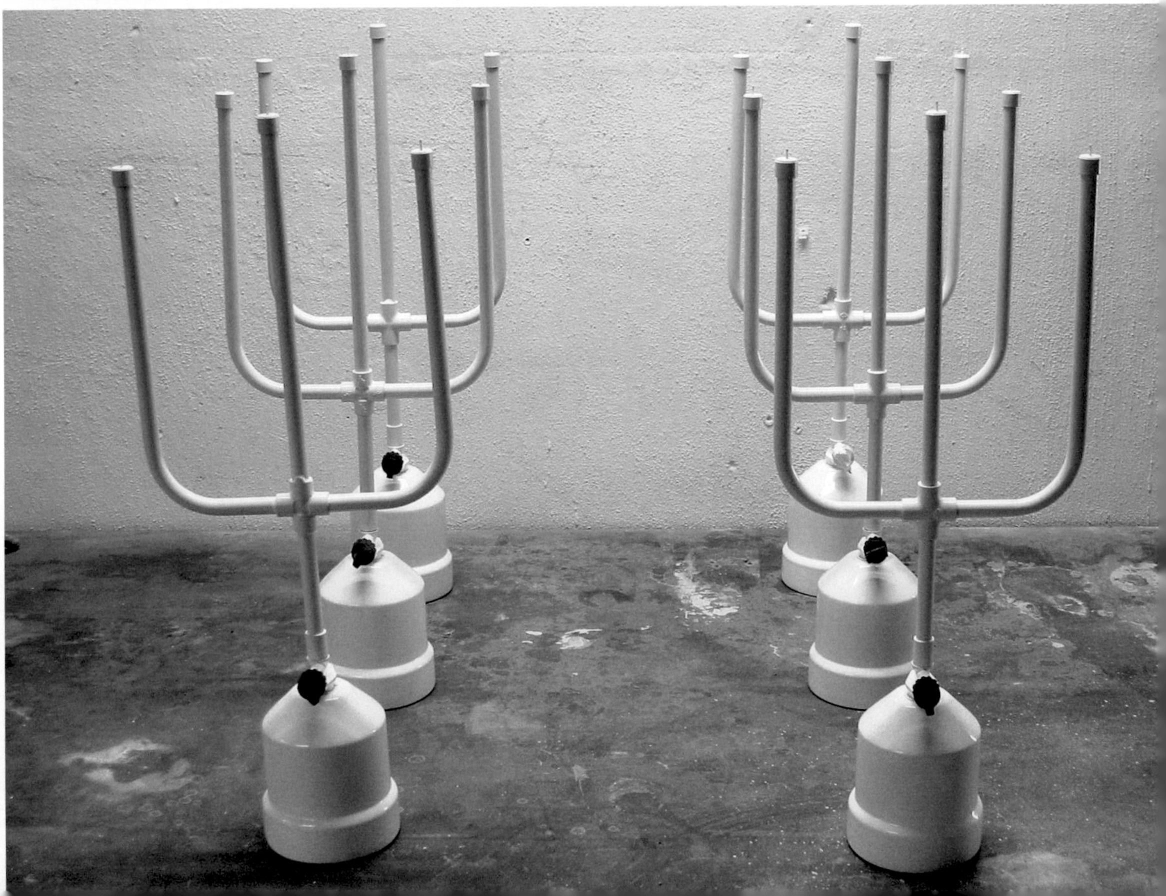

Laura Cramwinckel

Man and Public Space [2001]

—

Digital extrusion, 2001

Sannah Belzer

Man and Public Space [2002]

—

Wood curtain, 2002. The wooden curtain heralds the impending wrecking ball of the upcoming demolishing

Smoke, 2004
Burned pieces of furniture, preserved with clear epoxy.
Original design: Gerrit Rietveld's 1918 Red and Blue chair.

Clay Furniture, 2006

Sculpt, 2007

"Hey, chair, be a bookshelf!", 2005

‘Sometimes the Design Academy Eindhoven seems to be more of a brand than an educational institution,’ says Marije Vogelzang (1978). ‘On the other hand, I know from experience that it works.’

She prefers to call her designs ‘scenarios’. The work may be temporary and ephemeral, but at the moment it appears, it is no less carefully directed than a more permanent display. In recent years Marije Vogelzang and her company, Proef, have focused on ‘eating concepts’: her comprehensive productions include the preparation, presentation and enjoyment of food. Vogelzang prefers to design the whole chain of events, from the theme of the meal all the way through to the effects of her food on the diner’s metabolism.

‘To a certain degree, everything associated with a meal can be designed,’ says Vogelzang. ‘Is the weather nice? Is a person in love? Such things may be more difficult, but you *can* design the role of the main character in the event, the result of the food on his or her body, the sort of memories that can be evoked by specific dishes. I don’t like forcing people to do certain things or to act in a certain way during the meal, but I do try to entice them. By splitting up the classic combination of ham and melon and serving it on half plates, for example. If you want some of both, you have to share with another person. If you have only ham and you want only melon, you have to trade with someone. It’s in ways like this that I try designing environments and conditions that allow me to influence people psychologically.’

On hearing the term 'eating concepts', even a poorly informed outsider immediately suspects that the root of her efforts can be traced to the Design Academy Eindhoven. At no other school in the world is such a strong emphasis placed on 'the concept'. In recent decades, the academy's graduates have bombarded the world with sleeping concepts, parking concepts, wall and seating concepts, growth concepts and other conceptual images. Often their focus on conceptuality became the brunt of critical reflection. Accused of avoiding the requirements normally demanded of products, the work was labelled 'noncommittal': these were 'ideas', not 'products'.

In quite a few cases, it was precisely this conceptual attitude that allowed Design Academy Eindhoven students to respond to the existing package of products and services with a counteroffer that commanded attention and that helped expand the established criteria applied to design. Not based solely on the new terminology, but rather on the actual impact of the work. More than many an industrially sanctioned product, these were often designs that managed to worm their way into the viewer's memory; to prove, in an almost irrational way, their 'propriety' and 'timeliness'; and to be genuine media magnets. As a result of these various factors, the typically conceptual work that bolstered the Eindhoven academy's reputation assumed a clear presence in the minds of many design watchers. Although they seldom got their hands on the actual products or even saw them with their own eyes, they discussed the designs less and less in terms of their substantive nature. The presence of these designs in the media more than compensated for the relative absence of conceptual work in the tangible reality of shops and department stores.

Marije Vogelzang had little idea of what lay in store for her when in 1995, at the age of 17, she entered the academy. She was unaware of the school's reputation. A major reason for her choice, she admits, was the desire to leave her birthplace, Enschede. 'I certainly didn't select this academy deliberately. What attracted me was the expectation that here was a place I could indulge my childlike instinct to create. I wanted to spend time designing clothes, jewellery and the like. Besides that – it sounds ridiculous now, but it was real at the time – I thought it would be fun.' Twelve years later, she finds herself as the winner of the EDBR Prize, which is part of the Rotterdam Design Prize 2007, a rather prestigious award granted to designers who have carved out a prominent position for themselves with their oeuvres. For Marije Vogelzang, the prize means, among other things, that a coherent series of products takes its significance not only from the aesthetic quality of a single product but also, and above all, from the attitude that complements the work. Meanwhile, she's learned that even entrepreneurship contributes to that attitude. With increasing success, she runs her aptly named firm, Proef (Dutch for 'taste'), 'although I still don't know whether the knack of managing a company is something that has to be mastered or whether it's ultimately going to be an obstacle to my career as a designer'.

Fun? That is no longer the first word that comes to mind when she thinks of the academy. Everywhere she looked Vogelzang saw how fellow students, even in their first year at school, got carried away to the wildest extremes. 'You were encouraged in all sorts of ways to push the envelope. Also with respect to developing a competitive spirit. With some people it bordered on the obsessive; missing a single day at school sent them on a guilt trip.' She cherishes a special memory of first-year drawing classes, which she found a mystery at the time. Why was a future designer asked to pick up a pen and put dots on a sheet of paper, over and over again? Only later did she realize how important this apparently simply exercise, called 'visual grammar', had been in developing her sense of rhythm, spacing and balance.

Hard work went hand in hand with hard criticism. At the end of her first year in Eindhoven, Vogelzang was in trouble. She was on the verge of being asked to leave, and she now knows why. 'If only I'd worked more and boozed less. If only I'd showed up for class more often, like the others. In those days, I was mainly a knitting fanatic with a somewhat overactive social life.'

Nonetheless, she persevered, and the transition from her first year to her second, when she entered the Man and Leisure department, also marked an upgrade in her school results. From that moment on, she was where she belonged. 'It's there that I got the room to do only those things that I found exciting. The conceptual approach to work was stressed more and more, and the actual process of making things less and less. The same shift was reflected in a closing of the workshops. During that period I could design a religion, for example. It was fantastic to be able to contemplate something that abstract. Suddenly, my education was a perfect match for what I most liked to do. I'm not a builder, not a maker. I see myself as a scenarist, and maybe even that label is too limiting. In the future, perhaps I should cook a lot less and get more involved in philosophy.'

Looking back, she has no trouble describing the quality of her education. 'You learned – at least in the Leisure department – to experiment and mess about. Because there wasn't a lot of supervision, you might find yourself caught in a trap – of your own making, of course – and have to extricate yourself without help. It taught you to get orientated fast, also with respect to your fellow students. In a practical sense, they may have been a more important source of information than the instructors. You learned techniques, the tricks of the trade, from your peers. Lecturers mainly represented a certain perspective on design. Everyone played a role in everyone else's creative development. Ultimately, though, you and you alone were the determining factor.'

In 1999, a year before she graduated, Marije Vogelzang realized her first food design. The funeral dinner she created appeared at the furniture fair in Milan as part of the academy's presentation. 'At that time, food wasn't a self-evident subject for a designer. I had virtually no idea of the consequences of a choice I'd actually made quite intuitively. That must have played a part in my decision to make my graduation project about clothing and *not* about food.' Meanwhile, the work done by Proef demonstrates that her later decision to go with food has opened the

doors to an exceptionally rich profession. She becomes increasingly aware of the layers of meaning in food design with every passing day. 'Food is tied to everything: there's a link with politics, with ecology, with social relationships, with health, memory – you name it. The idea has developed slowly, and I really haven't been able to take stock of the full magnitude of what it might mean. I've only just begun.'

The greatest satisfaction, she says, is in seeing people put the food she designed and prepared into their mouths. 'That's the foundation of what I do.' A growing recognition for her work within the world of design is gradually becoming noticeable in her firm's commissions as well. Not only the quantity of projects keeps growing; the increase in quality is even greater. And a culinary world with a deeply conservative attitude has also shown its appreciation for Proef, which runs a highly successful luncheonette in Rotterdam. More important, however, are projects that exhilarate and surprise both participants and designer. An example is the buffet she prepared with recipes and ingredients used during the Second World War: her collection of titbits for people who experienced the war evoked a wide range of memories and, in so doing, created a truly extraordinary moment.

What are her thoughts on the Design Academy Eindhoven's influence on her personal development and on the way in which the school positions itself today, seven years after her graduation? 'When you look at the position currently assumed by the school, it's no wonder that some people have their doubts. Isn't it all a bit over the top? Sometimes the Design Academy Eindhoven seems to be more of a brand than an educational institution. On the other hand, I know from experience that it works. I have more credibility as a designer because of my background. In my opinion, the credit goes to Lidewij Edelkoort, who started as head of the Leisure department and later became the face of the whole academy. In any case, the school's growing visibility is obviously the reason why more and more people want to attend the academy, and an increase in popularity is allowing the school to implement a more selective admissions policy. Looking around me, I'm convinced that not everyone benefits from the Design Academy Eindhoven approach. But students who feel at home there can go far, with or without the help of individual teachers. After graduation, I worked for a while for Hella Jongerius, who likes to tell stories with her products, which is exactly what I want to do. I believe our need for narratives began at the academy. I still collaborate with Droog Design. They give me the opportunity to do my own thing. It may not amount to much, but it's good fun!'

The conversation with Marije Vogelzang comes to an abrupt end when a colleague points to the clock. In just a few minutes, the designer must leave to pick up her child at the crèche. Vogelzang takes this opportunity to make another pointed remark. 'Of all the people in my class at the Design Academy Eindhoven, I'm one of the very few with a child. Seems as though almost no one has had the courage. Apparently they're all afraid that kids will hinder their careers.'

Gert Staal

Marije Vogelzang

Man and Leisure [2000]

—

'Titshirt', 2000

Interior and exterior of Proef restaurants in Rotterdam and Amsterdam

Top: Food-concept 'Elements', 2003

Right: Food-concept 'War food', 2005

Middle: Food-concept for the Armour exhibition at Fort Asperen, 2003

Bottom: White funeral lunch at the Salone del Mobile, 1999

Top: Christmas dinner at Droog Design, 2005

Below: Christmas dinner at Droog Design, 2006

Susette Brabander
Man and Identity [2002]
—
Cross-over, 2002

Cathelijne Montens

Atelier [2002]

Soap buildings, 2002

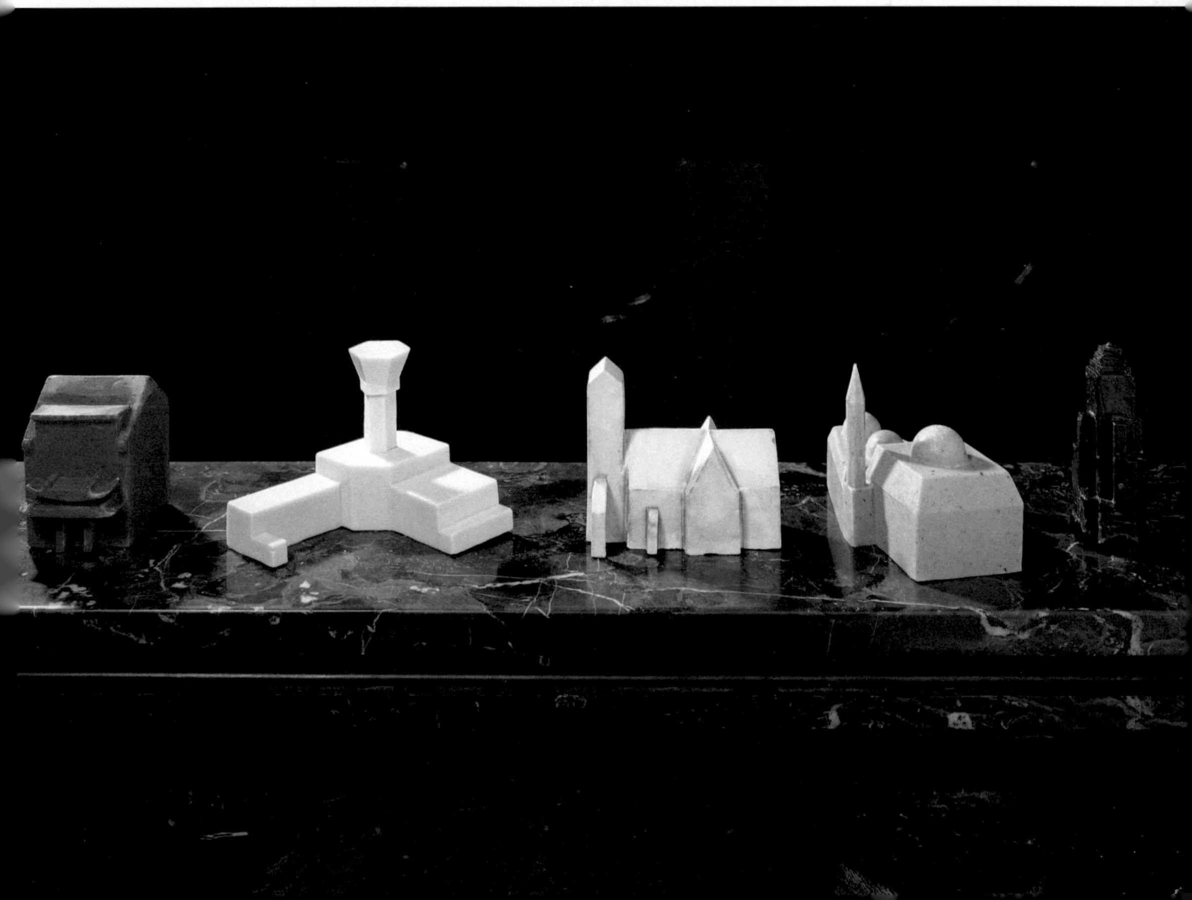

Simon Heijdens
Man and Communication [2002]

Opposite top and top left: Moving wallpaper, 2002. Materials: paper, thermochrome ink, silver.

Opposite bottom: Clean carpets, 2004. With a high-pressure sprayer and a template, grime is removed from the pavement in the shape of a carpet.

Top right: Reed, 2006

Right: Tree, Milan, 2004

Going Dutch: The Eindhoven Connection

Gert Staal

In 1941 the then German minister of propaganda paid a visit to the Venice Film Biennial. He watched the festival's opening film, 'La Corona di Ferro' (The Iron Crown) by the Italian director Alessandro Blasetti, which that year was to win the Golden Lion. It was no masterpiece. Herr Goebbels noted in his diary how appalled he had been. He was sure that no such monstrosity would ever have been produced in Germany, and concluded 'Italians are completely unsuited to making feature films'.

Once again it appears that one needs to be careful about attributing or denying artistic qualities to a particular nation or population group. It took more than 20 years for Italy to set up its own world-class film industry, as in the same period it succeeded in developing into a design country par excellence. Italian design has been considered a world leader since the 1960s. In their search for an explanation for this development, writers have been happy to refer to the country's highly developed cultural tradition. There was of course the aesthetic foundation of many centuries of civilisation and moreover the Italian predilection for outward show. This combination of factors must have been the source of the typically Italian approach to design.

PHYSICAL RESERVE

As far as that goes, the Dutch genetic passport is rather less obviously tailored to the design profession. The country is almost totally lacking in manufacturing industry of any significance. Since the days of Rembrandt and Vermeer the country has had little to bring to the European cultural stage except the early modernists in architecture and painting. And the Dutch have seldom had any feel for ostentatious display of fashionable clothing or exclusive everyday objects.

The British historian Simon Schama even recognised in this physical reserve the central feature of what made the wealth of the Dutch 17th century so exceptional. In his study, which appeared under the title 'The Embarrassment of Riches', he in fact characterised a culture that would in any event remain in existence until well into the 20th century. A culture of moderation, of marriages of convenience and of an overpowering understanding that ingenious solutions would be required if such a large number of people was to survive on such a small piece of marshy ground. This context enabled the creation of something like 'Dutch design'. In the last ten years countless attempts have been made to explain this concept. And the reactions to arguments for the absurdity of such attempts have been almost as numerous. Dutch design is at one and the same time an inescapable reality and a stubborn fiction.

When recently Forbo Flooring, producer of the internationally marketed Marmoleum floor covering, came on the market with the Marmoleum Dutch Design collection, the two perspectives converged in a bizarre way. In its own promotional material the manufacturer documented the unique character of its collection which, it said, was intended to thoroughly reflect the spirit of Dutch design. But in the same medium the designers involved in the project emphasised that they had mainly done whatever they wanted. In many voices, but with a reasonable degree of unanimity, the designers concluded that the nationalistic flag hung on the project by the manufacturer bore little relation to reality. Richard Hutten, often named as a typical representative of contemporary Dutch design, unhesitatingly described the concept as an imaginary quantity. According to him, Dutch design was 'an invention of the press'.

Aaron Betsky however, until recently director of the Netherlands Architecture Institute, thought he recognised what is really a typically Dutch position: 'In a world in which design these days means packaging, propaganda or advertising, Dutch design makes you think. It proposes objects and images that maybe don't always work more efficiently or smoothly than what those big in-house design studios can produce, and it lacks the zip and the pow those slick Brit star designers can come up with, but it does make you wonder.

The best Dutch design makes you aware that we live in an artificial environment we have made together and continue to remake. With irony, wit, and earnest criticism, it dissects the objects, images and spaces of everyday use right in front of you, and then refuses to put them back together again. Figure it out, Dutch designers say, that is what our culture is all about'.[1]

Thus anyone holding forth about Dutch design finds himself talking about a concept which is, to say the least, debatable. Going on to connect such a term with the products that have emerged from a single design course in the Netherlands, would seem to be a prescription for disaster.

Yet it is sensible to repeat here the attempt to see what people in recent years have thought they understood by Dutch design. And also to take yet one more serious look at the fictional character of design as a national phenomenon, and to determine its possible value. And then to apply the findings on both subjects to the development of what has by now become one of the world's most publicised educational establishments in the field of design, Design Academy Eindhoven. Praised by the New York Times and the Secretary of State for Foreign Trade in The Hague, recognised by the discriminating public at Milan's Salone del Mobile and described by Icon, the British architecture and design magazine, as 'the most influential organisation at the heart of the world's most influential national design culture'. [2]

In other words, is the concept of Dutch design really something invented by the press? Has it turned out to be a useful peg on which to hang ideas about the structure of design in the Netherlands, or is it primarily a marketing tool and should its value be determined chiefly by reference to its effect on exports? Is it perhaps a purely Dutch preoccupation to lay claim to a discipline in this way? Or were we talked into it by others? And finally, is it wise, in the first decade of the 21st century, to be so explicit about linking such a concept to a particular course?

DESIGN RENAISSANCE

However far-fetched the connection between a national design identity and a school may appear to be, it is one that in recent years

Improvvisare, Chelsea Hotel, New York, 2004. Design Academy Eindhoven graduates improvised with found materials and objects (Mark van der Gronden, Cynthia Hathaway, Joris Laarman, Christien Meindertsma, Reineke Otten, Marc van de Sande and Neeltje ten Westenend).

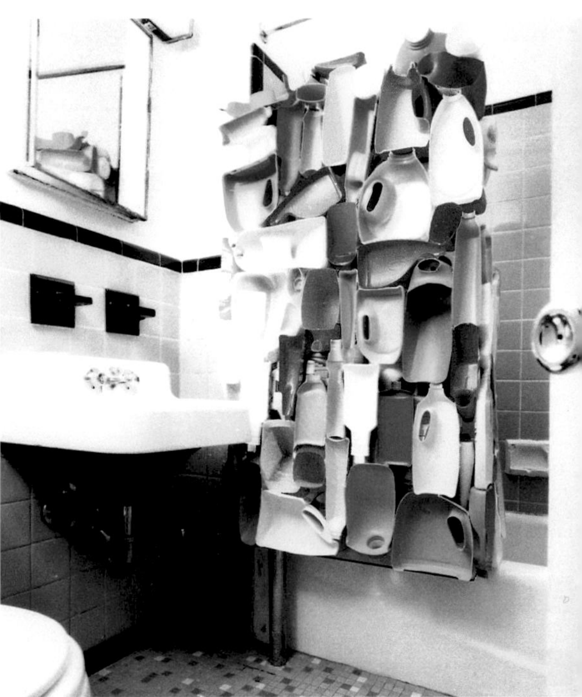

has been made with great regularity. When Icon magazine included Design Academy Eindhoven in the top five of the most influential players on the contemporary design stage, it referred explicitly to the role that the Netherlands is beginning to play. 'After a few years in the doldrums, the Dutch design scene is back as a major force', was the magazine's judgement in 2005. And instead of including an individual designer in the hit list – people have mentioned Maarten Baas, Bertjan Pot and Joris Laarman as possible candidates – the editors chose the training provided at Eindhoven as the exponent (or motor) for the renaissance in Dutch design.

Anyway, the connection is even made within the academy itself. For example, consideration was recently given to a proposal to concentrate the programme for the international master's degree course IM on training in the conceptual quality of Dutch design. However, the people who cause all the to-do about the 'Dutchness' of Dutch design are usually outsiders. Magazine editors, members of design competition juries, curators, gallery owners and export promoters are only too happy to talk about the specific nature of Dutch design, making repeated use of terms like conceptuality, austerity and humour – qualities which many see as most strongly personified in the work of Eindhoven students.

This year ArtEZ, the Institute for the Arts in Arnhem, another Dutch training centre for product designers, published the book 'Product Design Diversity'[3] which reviewed of the merits of its own educational programme by reference to the successes of former students. The authors took full advantage of the opportunity to place them in the context of the image that Dutch design has by now achieved. According to the compilers, modernistic Dutch architecture and graphic design has long known itself to be assured of international recognition. But that is not all. 'Since the 1990s Dutch Design has been enriched by high-profile product design, especially by the designers of Droog Design, who have attracted worldwide attention', wrote Jeroen van den Eijnde in the chapter 'Infiltranten van de industrie' [Infiltrators into industry].[4] Many of these designers, he found, 'have benefited from training ... at Design Academy Eindhoven or some other design course. Despite the obvious media success in past years, he does however recognise that the development of product design in the Netherlands has its drawbacks: 'Most Dutch designers do not easily get to understand complex production and market requirements'.

Put more briefly, Dutch design does well in the press, but not in the factory and not in the shop. Thus 'Product Design Diversity' puts into words what is probably the most common reaction to the design renaissance in the Netherlands, at least among designers and observers of the profession. Whereas outside the country Dutch design is perceived as a mark of quality, at home it generates either boastful euphoria of the kind on which the Economic Information Department appears to have the patent, or gloomy reflections on the part of people more directly involved in the profession.

This makes it all the more remarkable that both sides seldom raise any question about the reality content of the concept. How legitimate is it, in an open culture like that of the Netherlands, to insist so stubbornly on 'individuality' and 'otherness' by comparison with what are broadly speaking Anglo-Saxon, Latin and Central European cultures (or design cultures)? Can a country with such a mixed population and a political attitude that is ever more strongly oriented towards Europe really go on hammering away at its unique national position?

Yes, it can. And it does. As in France, a referendum amongst the Dutch population rejected the European constitution. It is true that that aroused dissatisfaction at government level, but government in turn went on to show its nationalistic pride. In recent years the universities have made serious efforts to draw up a canon of Dutch history. For educational purposes a list of national historic events and personalities has been identified which, if it was left to the Dutch government, every young resident of this country should know about, regardless of the fact that the young resident in question may only have lived here a few years, may perhaps have come from Kenya, or as a former resident of the Antilles or Surinam may have his own ideas about the illustrious past of Dutch seafarers, fort builders, traders and missionaries. Just wait: in a few years schoolchildren in an ethnic minority area in Rotterdam South will be rattling off the newest entries in the national canon: 'Viktor & Rolf, Hella Jongerius, Marcel Wanders, Rem Koolhaas, Jurgen Bey, Li Edelkoort...'

MANAGEMENT MODEL

Dutch history, and particularly that part associated with Calvinism and a more highly developed business sense, did in the first instance play a definite role in the formulation of whatever is specific to Dutch design. Like the landscape, naturally – or in this case would it be better to say the landscape unnaturally? For real nature has never stood much of a chance in the Netherlands, and some people believe that to be the main reason for the fact that every Dutchman is really a designer.

The country from the delta to the North Sea – the part of the country that the Dutch call the Randstad – is presented as the essential foundation for the nation's design mentality. Aaron Betsky for example referred to this in his book False Flat.[5] His attempted characterisation relies on the man-made landscape that the Dutch inhabit, and the management model they need to preserve and exploit that land.

The polders not only provide the Netherlands with living space and protection from the water. They are also responsible for the so-called 'polder model', the consultative structure which since time immemorial has ensured that everyone concerned has a voice in decision-making processes relating to spatial planning, security, industrial relations and even the preservation of a nature which is not really natural but designed.

This democratic principle has come to determine the way in which design is done in the Netherlands, whether in connection with architecture and urban design or products and communication. Consequently Dutch design has always had a very wide field of activity.

FOREIGN TOUR

Undoubtedly there were precedents, in the shape of occasional presentations or viewings during the 1960s and 1970s. But the origin of the idea that there might be such a thing as Dutch design probably lay in the early 1980s. Before this time individuals with a reputation, inside and outside the Netherlands, as significant designers, such as Mart Stam and Gerrit Rietveld for their furniture, a handful of classic typographers, Kho Liang Ie for his interior architecture and a firm like Total Design for its systematised designs, were well able to stand up to international comparison.

The mid-1970s saw the arrival of a generation of product designers which had established its reputation, even in the Netherlands, only in dribs and drabs. In 1980 an exhibition was sent travelling outside the country as a way of increasing public awareness. Gijs Bakker, previously known mainly as a jewellery designer, brought together a colourful group, much as he did almost 15 years later when, with Renny Ramakers, he provided the initial impetus for Droog Design. In line with foreign art policy, Bakker's exhibition 'Design from the Netherlands/Design aus den Niederlanden' was sent (with government subsidy) to various countries as a sign of a new self-awareness in the design world. At the end of the tour the exhibition was also put on in the Netherlands. This undertaking failed to bring about an international breakthrough by Dutch design, but the travelling exhibition was an important landmark for the professional group involved, and more especially for the designers. For the time being mainly for domestic consumption.

Around 1980 the design profession, and certainly the profession of product design, was still too young to be associated with generally valid pronouncements, let alone national characteristics. At that time people were mainly trying to argue the importance of design itself to a public that had still not really been won over to the idea. At such a moment international exposure was a more powerful argument in the Netherlands than the specifically Dutch character of the products.

These were mainly years of emancipation. The world of culture, as represented by museums and galleries, became noticeably more interested in design. And almost as a matter of course the part of the design world that was associated with the visual arts received by far the most attention. Not the anonymous engineers, but the designers who had trained at an art school. Furniture, lighting and jewellery, intellectually parented by a known name, largely determined the Dutch output at the time. Author's design gained a firm foothold, and the lack of any real industry in those years meant that all kinds of designers developed their own production lines to allow them to put even small editions on the market. Museums became their showrooms.

NATIONAL CHARACTERISTICS IN DESIGN

For the time being the rest of the world took little notice. Products only occasionally left the country, and then only for the purpose of exhibitions. For practically all designers international sales were a

Dutch Village, during ICFF 2005, at Weiss Studio, New York, 2005. Innovative traditions in design from the Netherlands (49 Design Academy Eindhoven graduates including the products of Jurgen Bey, Hella Jongerius and Job Smeets for Royal Tichelaar Makkum)

pipe-dream. Dutch design played little more than a walk-on part at major international design events like the Milan Triennial or the megalomaniac but highly influential exhibition and research project 'Design is Unsichtbar', held in Linz, Austria, in 1981. When in 1985 the forerunner of the London Design Museum – The Boilerhouse Project at the Victoria & Albert Museum – devoted an exhibition to 'National Characteristics in Design', many countries were represented, but not the Netherlands. The compilers collected icons of industrial production from Japan, the US, France, Germany, Russia, Great Britain, Sweden and of course Italy. These products were used to make spatial picture postcards, as it were, characterising the countries as childishly charming (Japan), coarse and amusing (Russia), obsessed with industrial anonymity (Germany) or simply with the better rural handicrafts (France) etc.

Often they were caricatures, subsequently provided in classic British style with comments putting them into context. So for example while the Germans might brim with what the exhibition called 'Teutonic efficiency', according to the museum anyone who looked more closely would also see in their products 'a load of fattening sugary sentimentality'.

At the time I tried to describe the missing Dutch entry to the exhibition for a Dutch paper by way of a review. Each country present was introduced by a so-called 'Premise'; I therefore had a go at composing a Dutch profile. 'The English compiler will complain about the suggestion of order and neatness in Dutch design, which stands in shrill contrast to what he encounters on site. The designs are dominated by the economical use of means and ideas, so that simplicity sometimes gives rise to products that not only seem, but actually are, unresponsive. The high population density compels such solutions, and a few centuries of Calvinism and five years of war have done little to encourage the designers to add excessive frills. Geometry is the key, even to the extent of determining the design layout of dreary and overcrowded little gardens. Nonetheless – as the piece would conclude – for the sake of the international market individual identity is anxiously suppressed in production. The trader must be able to handle foreign languages, but so must the designer'.[6]

PRAGMATISM AND LOVE OF EXPERIMENT

In the same year, 1985, the editors of Abitare, the Italian architecture and design magazine, produced a special issue on the Netherlands. Only four pages of editorial material were devoted to the design industry, the remainder being used for photo reports on flat polder country, a few high points from early 20th-century building production and a procession of advertisements intended finally to ensure international recognition for manufacturers of Dutch design. Despite all these advertisements, Dutch design was at the time by no means a significant factor. Abitare, it seemed, could hardly contain its laughter.

When the editors came back for a new special edition in 2002, the situation was completely changed. The government money that the Netherlands was prepared to put up for productions of this kind was still the same, but otherwise everything was different. Recently completed architectural projects turned up all over the special edition, and about a quarter of the magazine was occupied by designs illustrating the breadth of current Dutch design. And in fact the size – almost 300 pages – seemed inadequate to do full justice to the situation.

In its introduction Abitare drew attention to how remarkably different things were from how they had been in1985. Although the text referred exclusively to the architectural climate in 2002, the description also served as an effective characterisation of the environment within which the selected designers did their work: 'The Netherlands of today is more difficult to describe because there are no formulas and no acknowledged architectural figureheads to generalise from. Ever more vital and pluralistic, Dutch architecture impresses foreign observers with its pragmatism and love of experiment that make the country seem a paradise for architects, its social radicalism and utopianism, but also its open-minded rediscovery of anarchism, hedonism and consumerism'.[7]

This is a description which the management of Design Academy Eindhoven would gladly apply to its own courses. The signature of the school has increasingly become a mixture of pragmatic and activist design. The conceptual basis has by no means been abandoned, but at the same time the courses seem to have taken on board the need to avoid excessive autonomy in the work done by students. Designers should not only relate to a cultural or industrial reality, but should also take account of the desires, dreams and needs of the individual and the impact of their work on ever more complex societies.

SYMBIOTIC RELATIONSHIP

In a pursuit of this sort most foreign authors recognise the special appeal of Dutch design. Remarkably enough they usually project their characterisations on to a different subject, one that seems to all intents and purposes to coincide with Dutch design, namely Droog Design. The alpha and omega of Dutch product design. The vade mecum, conscience and laboratory for anyone who wants to think about the renewal of the profession. In recent years the perception has grown that the real design avant-garde is directed from its headquarters in Amsterdam's Staalstraat. This perception might well be at least as carefully designed as the products in the Droog collection.

Since 1993 its originators have exercised an unusually strict control over the image secured by their activities and ideas. Right up to the present day Droog Design has itself been the most important source of publications on Droog Design. It regularly supplies the market with new books, describing new projects or recapitulating its own history. It has talked the outside world into using a language and a frame of reference which not surprisingly has been adopted by many newspaper and magazine articles dealing with the Dutch design climate. As a result Droog is to some extent able to control the debate. It is my personal conviction that it is precisely this aspect – more even than its collections or the subjects it deals with – that makes Droog Design truly Dutch design. The product, the context and the perception are defined as an integrated design task.

Thus it might be that Dutch and Droog have become synonymous. That a direct relationship is often assumed with the Eindhoven training which is at the very least Dutch and possibly even Droog. The fact is that by far the greatest part of the collection was designed by students or ex-students of the academy. And that the lectureship of Gijs Bakker in particular has played an important role. He does not simply pass on his vision of design to new generations of Eindhoven students, but also offers them the prospect of a role in the professional design world after (and for some even during) their studies. A role which not surprisingly needs to conform to the vision which Droog Design uses to position itself culturally.

So far both the academy and the designer label have profited from their symbiotic relationship. It has helped the training to enlarge its international reputation and guaranteed the interest of a large group of potential students. But then again the education means that Renny Ramakers and Gijs Bakker find themselves close to the source of whatever talent and areas of interest turn up amongst the youngest groups of students. They get the pick of the crop and can make a significant contribution to shaping the specific type of designer that represents Droog Design.

How great the influence of Droog Design has been on the present image of Dutch design becomes all the clearer if we look back ten years or so. It is true that at that time Eindhoven Academy of Industrial Design cherished great ambitions, but in practice everything had to wait until Jan Lucassen, as chairman of the board, announced major changes in the 1996 exam catalogue. He spoke of 'the dynamic process of educational reform' in which the academy found itself. 'In the coming year this process of change will become apparent in a number of ways and will be made obvious by name changes, rehousing, the renewal of the educational process and the digitisation of the design process in the education itself'.[8]

This was a typically Dutch way of announcing something new. We're going to relocate, give the thing a different name, arrange things differently and adjust a few priorities, and we have bought in new technology. None of this sounds terribly impressive. And yet in fact it laid the basis for substantial innovation. That it still took a few years before there was any real change in the nature of design in Eindhoven, was all part of the pattern. Analysis, reconfiguration, investment and clever renewal are the tools used to organise Dutch design processes. This applies to Droog Design, and so must also be applicable to the renewal of an educational establishment.

INTERDISCIPLINARY FIELD OF ACTIVITY

What does all this mean for the concept of Dutch design? For example, is conceptualism an invention or the exclusive privilege of a group of designers who were born in or work in the North Sea delta?

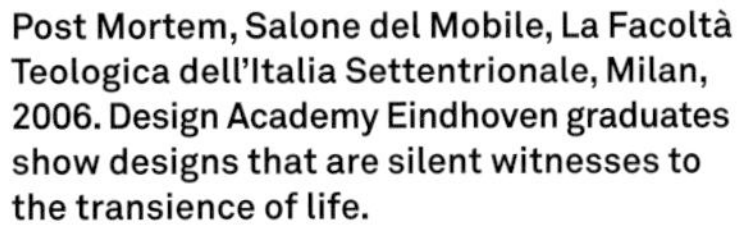

Post Mortem, Salone del Mobile, La Facoltà Teologica dell'Italia Settentrionale, Milan, 2006. Design Academy Eindhoven graduates show designs that are silent witnesses to the transience of life.

That seems debatable. Is it possible that the sum of qualities such as the economical use of resources, clarity and functionality is sufficiently characteristic to distinguish Dutch design from the product of its neighbours? When in 1994 the Museum für Angewandte Kunst in Cologne organised the exhibition 'Made in Holland. Design aus den Niederlanden', these were important keywords indicating the traditional status quo of the Dutch product.

But Gabriele Lueg, the curator, also discovered a more contemporary way of looking at things. Much more clearly than their colleagues in Germany, young Dutch designers had been struck by the necessity to 'stretch' the concept of design 'into an interdisciplinary field of activity'. Lueg did however think that they retained their individual identity, 'an identity which thanks to its unbroken tradition and very specific historico-cultural background still stands alone but nevertheless has achieved an international standard'.[9] According to Lueg, Dutch design was characterised by sincerity, common sense and modernity.

'Made in Holland' came at a crucial point, shortly after the first presentation by Droog Design which was dismissed with a shake of the head by the Italian designer Andrea Branzi as an expression of 'protestantism'. Others however saw in Droog Design the announcement of a new spirit in the world of design. The unexpected association with humour, irony, curiosity and sensuality so shocked the Italian designer and theoretician Mario Trimarchi, that he wondered 'might Dutch design perhaps be different from what Dutch design would wish to be?'[10]

Nevertheless the die was cast. A new design culture began to take shape, even if some people thought that it took until the fatal impact of two aircrafts on the World Trade Centre before the search for an alternative approach to design, production and consumption, of the kind that had taken shape in the Netherlands in the meantime, really got its way. Only when the smell of excess and sumptuous boredom spread through the western world did the Dutch approach achieve its true significance. Dutch design demands less in the way of usefulness than of obvious necessity. It is not by definition functional but more contextual and investigative.

Ron Arad, associated as lecturer with the Royal College of Art, recognises this quality in the Eindhoven graduates who turn up in London for a continuation course. 'For some reason, they are more informed and grazing in the right places for ideas – they're inquisitive. Though the Dutch style is often emergent in their work – we have a little giggle about that'.[11]

In other words there must be a reason, however personal it sometimes might be, for making a change in a product. Mere design generally goes down badly with the residents of the North Sea delta. They have no grounds for pride about their style.

PUBLIC-PRIVATE INTEREST

But is that sufficient basis for claiming validity for a concept like Dutch design, or is the result no more than the sum of a number of accidental variables? However strong the arguments might be for suspecting a compelling common foundation supporting Dutch design, I still tend to see it mainly as a useful mental exercise. Thinking about the greatest common factor helps one to think about the smallest common multiple. How does one use history to assess current developments? What steps turn out to be necessary to move from a period of stagnation to one of acceleration? Dutch design exists because it is non-existent. It was invented to make discussion possible, to allow a story to be told.

The story might concern the content of the design or the marketing of products, increasingly often the latter. After years of a sincere lack of interest, the Dutch government's economic sector has discovered design and has embraced Dutch design as a factor in the worldwide competitive struggle.

Forbo, the producer of Marmoleum Dutch Design, was not the first manufacturer to appropriate the Dutch design brand. Many others came before them, and undoubtedly countless more will follow. The question is whether recognition by the ministry of Economic Affairs and exploitation by producers will make any substantial contribution to the development of design in the Netherlands. Undoubtedly courses such as those offered by Design Academy Eindhoven will come to occupy a much more important position. Hopefully they will be supported by a growing public-private interest, but ultimately they will have to rely on their own inventiveness, on their power to reconfigure what already exists and so to give things a fresh meaning. It would be better to abandon any kind of nationalistic thinking. Forget Dutch design, and realise that by now the demand for necessity comes from the whole world.

[1] Alex Wiltshire, 3 Days in the Netherlands, Icon, no. 012, May 2004
[2] Icon 021, March 2005
[3] Jan Brand et al.: *Product Design Diversity*, ArtEZ Press, Arnhem 2007
[4] ibid., p.105
[5] Aaron Betsky & Adam Eeuwens: *False Flat: Why Dutch design is so Good*, Phaidon Press, London 2004
[6] Gert Staal: 'Een leegte in de negende straat', NRC Handelsblad, 14 June 1985
[7] Abitare no. 417, Speciale Olanda, May 2002
[8] *Graduation 96*, Eindhoven Academy of Industrial Design, 1996
[9] *Made in Holland. Design aus den Niederlanden*, Ernst Wasmuth Verlag, Tübbingen/Berlin 1994, p.10
[10] Ibid., p.33, quoted from Renny Ramakers' article 'Neue Tendenzen'
[11] Alex Wiltshire, 'Design Academy Eindhoven', Icon, no. 31, January 2006

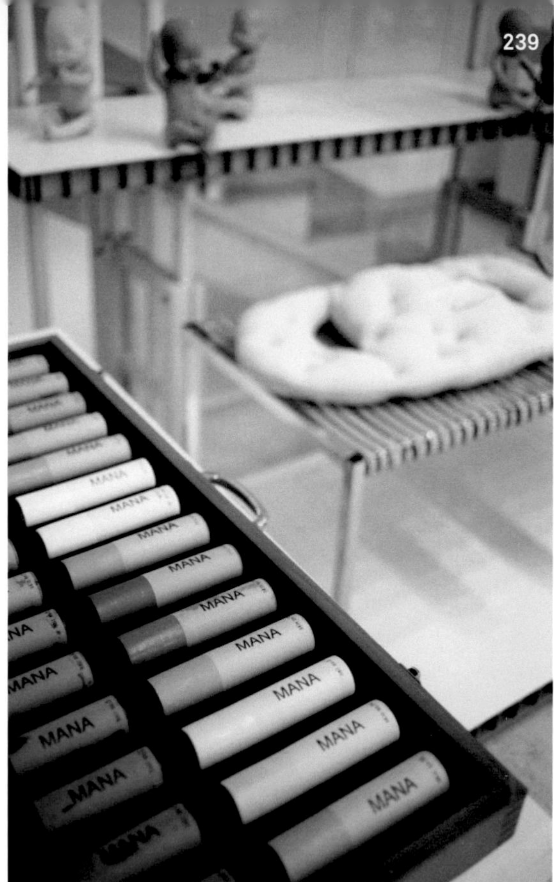

The Family of Form, Salone del Mobile, Museo Luciano Minguzzi, Milan, 2007
Three generations of Design Academy Eindhoven graduates show their views on the identity of design.

Marijn van der Poll

Man and Living [2002]

—

Modular Car, 2002. The user can saw, cut and sand his own car.

Do hit (Droog Design), 2000

Chairman (Lensvelt/Gispen), 2005

Neeltje ten Westenend

Man and Public Space [2003]

—

À votre service, 2003.
A new concept for the combination of traditional and functional clothing for the inhabitants Yport, an old French village.

Iris Toonen
Man and Identity [2003]
—
Spoons with Character, 2003

Basten Leijh

Man and Mobility [2003]

—

City bike concept, 2003

Raphael Navot

Man and Activity [2003]

—

Virtual vase, 2003

Christien Meindertsma
Atelier [2003]

—

Echt schaap.
The wool of a single sheep turned into a sweater, a scarf and socks.

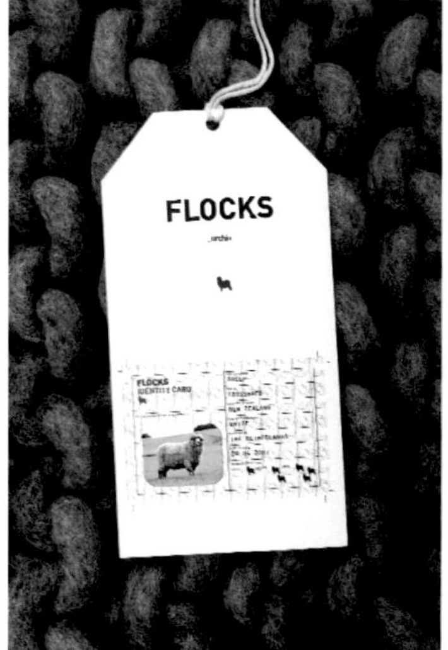

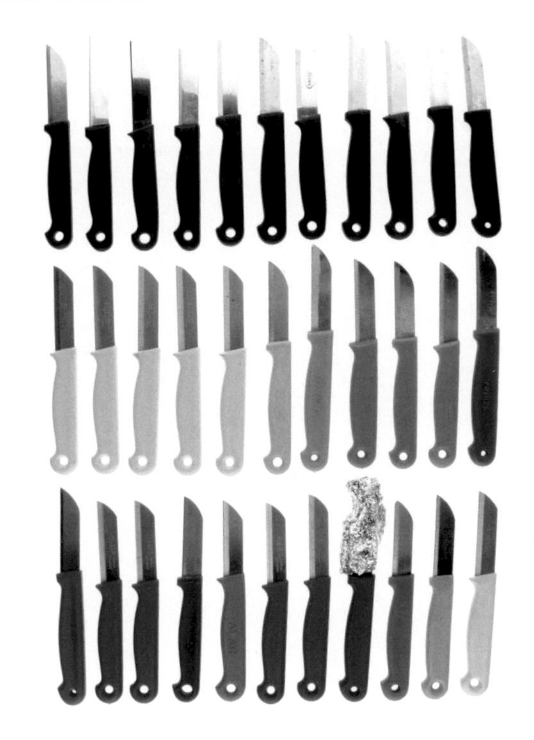

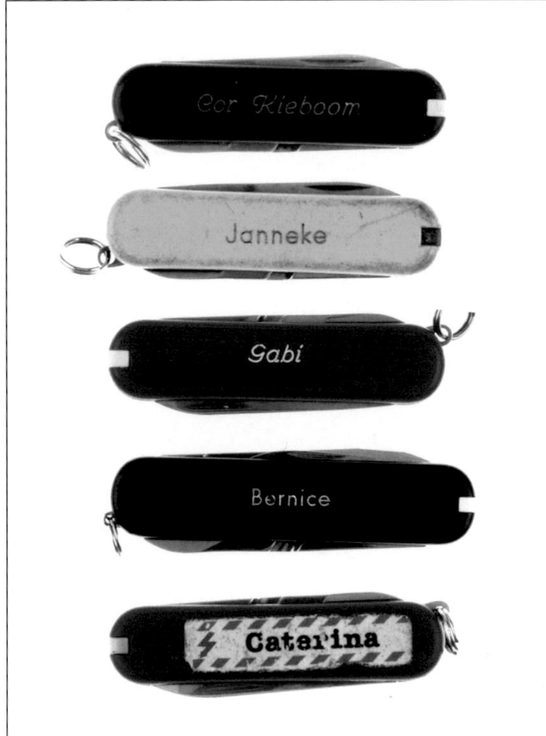

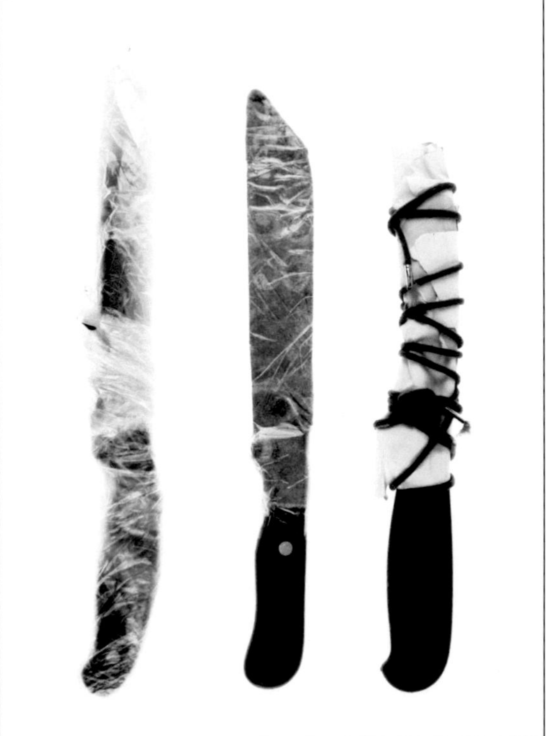

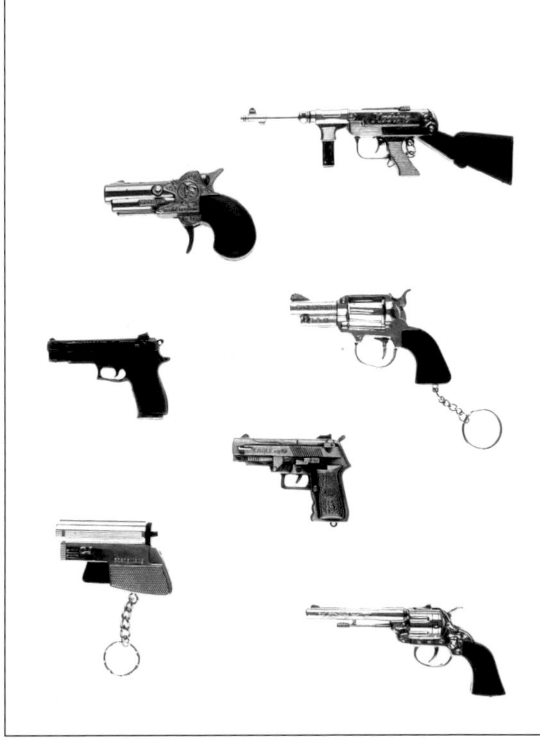

Checked baggage, 2003.
Inventory of all items confiscated
in one week at Schiphol Airport

Claire Warnier

Man and Identity [2003]

—

Personal jewellery made using a 3D model of a scan of the human body.

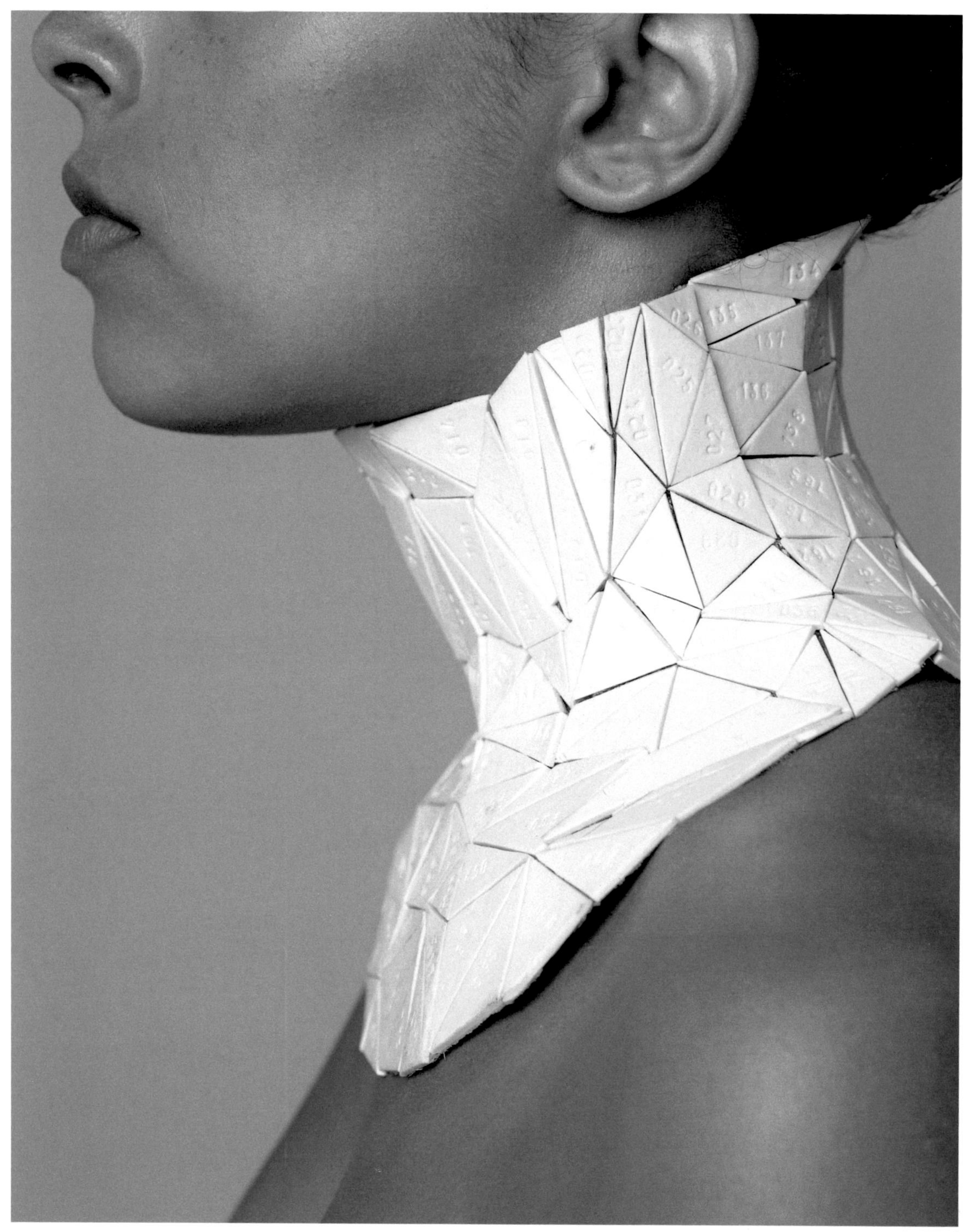

Sampling the past, 2004

Susan Verheijen

Man and Identity [2004]

—

Form-matic, 2004

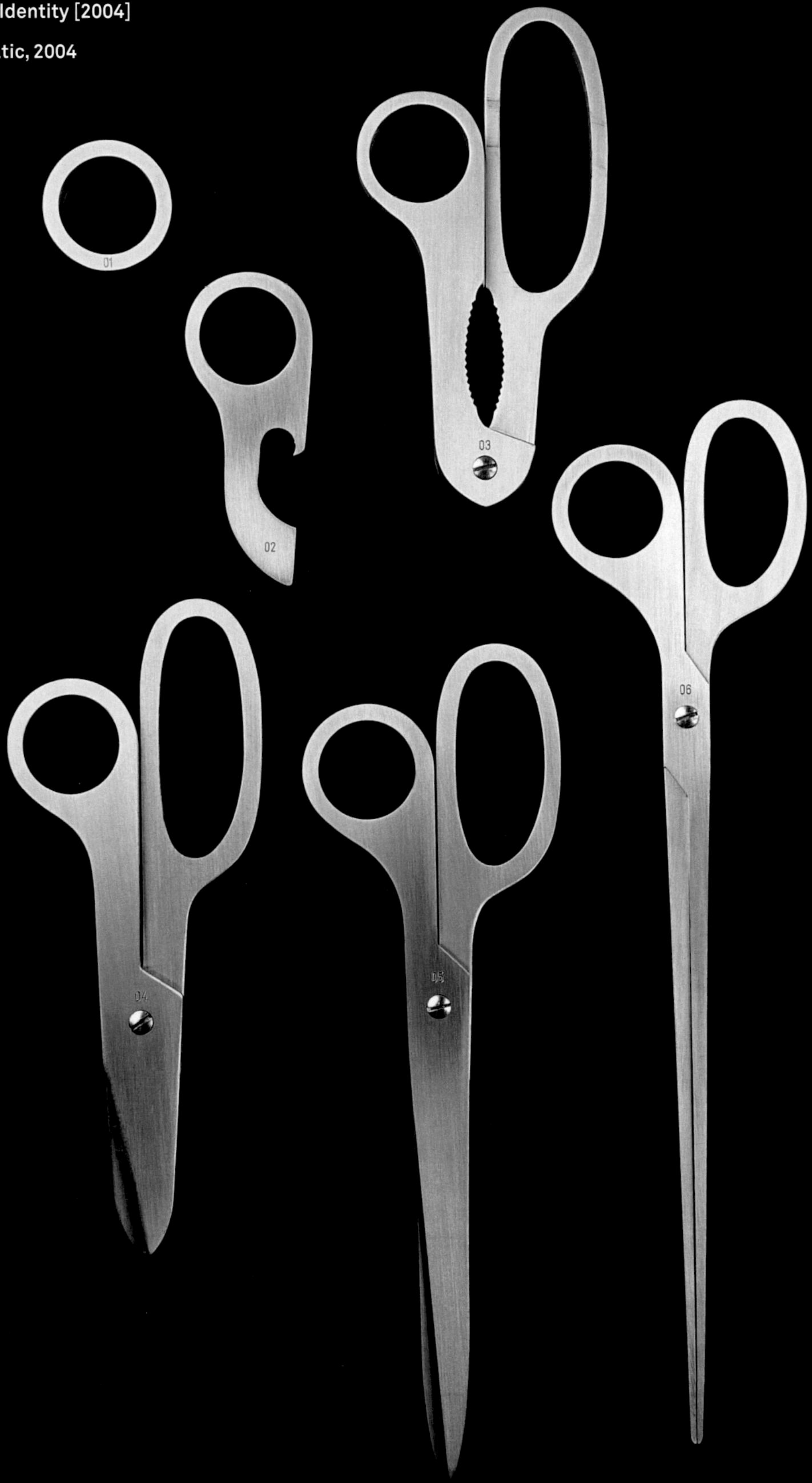

Ying Shen

Masters Funlab [2004]

—

Marry me. A declaration of self love, Shen married herself. The veil contained personal treasures.

Tristan Frencken
Man and Mobility [2003]
—
Stand up, 2003

Eric Klarenbeek
Man and Identity [2004]
—
Floating light, 2004

Above: Madame Rubens, 2003

Right: Tape-it, 2004
Stacked iron elements kept together by tape

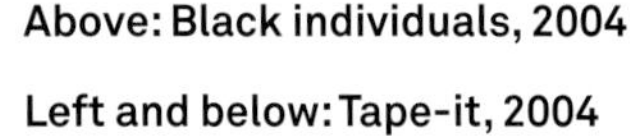

Above: Black individuals, 2004

Left and below: Tape-it, 2004

Joris Laarman (1979): 'In retrospect, I see that the academy offered me a platform. Beyond that, I didn't learn all that much of a practical nature.'

Joris Laarman wanted to be an inventor, or an architect. Or to enter some other profession that would afford him the freedom to create what he liked. He chose the art academy in Arnhem, but after six months the 19-year-old Laarman had had enough of 'chatting and drinking coffee'. A visit to deWitteDame in Eindhoven, home of Design Academy Eindhoven, felt like a homecoming. 'That gorgeous building was instantly compelling, and I immediately found the perfect combination of doing something serious in a professional way and being able to realize my dreams. And you also had the prospect of being able to earn a living at it later. That was so far removed from the subsidy culture that reigned in Arnhem at the time.' Isn't this remark somewhat strange coming from someone who has received a starter's subsidy from the Dutch state's BKVB Fund not once, but twice? 'That's true,' he laughs. 'Let's just say the atmosphere was rather musty.'

By his own reckoning, the now 28-year-old designer has little to complain about when it comes to budget and the freedom to do exactly what he wants. The amount of money now circulating in the field, which affords his enterprise the opportunity to experiment, cheers him to no end. 'So much money has become available to do things in the last several years – that really makes me very happy.'

Yet the ploughing still comes before the harvest. What were those first few years like in Eindhoven? 'The first year was really brilliant, perhaps the most enjoyable year of the whole programme,' he says. 'It was all about theory, which gave depth to a field I had always thought of as just the design of traffic signs or postage stamps – I hadn't realized the importance of it yet. Amazingly cool classes taught by instructors with unique characteristics. The mutual atmosphere was good, too; there was an unspoken competition that motivated all of us to get the best out of ourselves. Certain teachers accurately sensed what was going on, for that matter. One of them was Mathieu Meijers, who taught Colour 1 and 2. At one point he said, "There are people here who could well get top marks for this assignment." So everyone pulled an all-nighter in order to produce their best work. No one got "top marks", but we'd all improved anyway.'

Laarman considered himself an average student. Into the third year of the programme he was still struggling with the choices he'd made and the paths he'd chosen. 'The cliché of an art-academy student,' says Laarman. The turnabout came in the third year. 'I had switched specializations and selected Man and Living, a department with a close-knit team of teachers with whom I could talk about the object instead of about the space containing the object. I was still searching, but ultimately instructor Bart Guldemond gave me the right push. The guidance provided by the whole team was better than in previous years, but Bart was the only one who believed I would turn out all right.'

'In retrospect, I see that the academy offered me a platform. I was given the freedom to come up with something that made me happy. Beyond that, I didn't learn all that much of a practical nature. These days, 75 per cent of the time I'm involved in my business: earning money, making sure everyone has work, making sure the staff gets paid. Those are things you don't learn at the academy. Nor should you have to. That programme should be a sanctuary, and running a business is something you learn as you go along.'

His last year at school saw the emergence of Heatwave, the graduation project that would propel him like a comet into the design firmament. From one day to the next, Joris Laarman became a hot designer. 'A month after I graduated I had 16 potential clients. It was bizarre. I had no money, so I was working for a KPN telecommunications call centre. I'd have Japanese media visiting me in the morning, and in the afternoon I'd be on the phone selling internet subscriptions.' Laarman does not seem to have an explanation for the success of the radiator, but reflects: 'It was 2003, ten years after the founding of Droog Design, which after years of praise was suddenly attracting criticism. People were saying that the collective was doing nothing but producing museum pieces and that its designers were a bunch of poor working stiffs. That couldn't go on, obviously. Something had to turn the tide. And suddenly my radiator was in the Droog Design collection, which is remarkable in itself, because I actually *reject* the typical Droog style, content-wise. The radiator, with its decorative formal idiom, didn't seem to fit into the collection at all.'

The exclusively positive publicity the radiator generated does surprise Laarman. 'Not one negative thing has ever been written about Heatwave, something I find strange in retrospect. I mean, it's weird that my field doesn't have something like critiques or reviews. Everything seems to be written up without any criticism. It must have something to do with advertising revenue. It's a shame, because I am sincerely trying to produce something good, and doing so costs a lot of time and energy. After all that effort, it would be nice if the result were looked at critically. Criticism is also a form of recognition.'

Like every young designer whose graduation work immediately comes to the attention of the international media, Laarman had to prove that Heatwave, which was conceived within an academic context (and thus under the guidance of teachers), would not be his only hit. The proof is in Laarman's second successful design. His most recent product, Bone Chair, can compete with the radiator in every respect. The brand-new chair was discussed enthusiastically in virtually all international media, and Laarman is talking with the Museum of Modern Art in New York City about a possible acquisition. Vitra has also shown interest, as has the Centraal Museum in Utrecht.

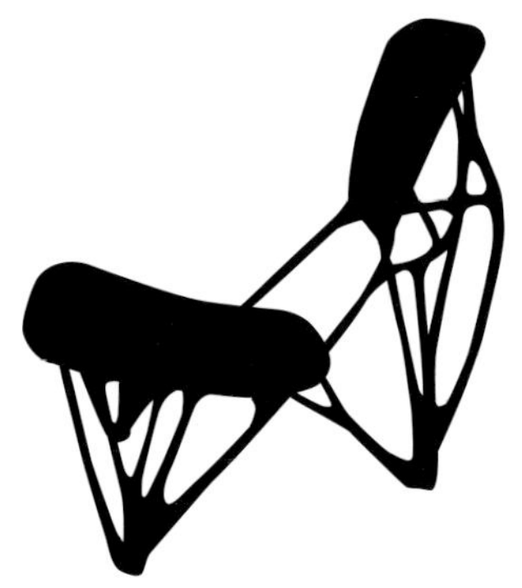

'My chair is riding the wave of the limited-editions hype; every single one has been sold. It couldn't get any better.' What does he think of the current 'design art' trend? 'Very interesting – it's what I like to do best, because you can experiment with new technologies and materials, as well as contribute to a discussion. But 80 per cent of the designers are making limited editions because they make money. Everyone is falling for it, without a shred of critique. People are paying hundreds of thousands for things that are sometimes completely pointless and might just as well be manufactured in China for a few pennies. It's too bad no one is pointing this out.'

Laarman's own criticism is sometimes outspoken but usually carefully packaged in diplomatic language. Wanders? 'I have a lot of respect for how he runs his firm, and I would have loved to have made that Knotted Chair myself; I think it's really brilliant. I admire his business instincts; his latest designs are okay.' Morrison? 'It's not my taste, but I still think what he does is good. Just like Grcic, who, for example, works with businesses that haven't reached the status of Vitra yet – I really appreciate what he's doing in that respect. He doesn't let things get to him. It's a good thing that Newson's chair sells for a million, but it's also good that IKEA has chairs made for a few cents. It all contributes to diversity. Imagine if everyone made decorative radiators – what would be the point?'

He finds it difficult to identify with colleagues, but he beliefs that he belongs to a generation of young designers who work without conventions and are able to make 'weird stuff'. His firm is located in an old building in a remote corner of Rotterdam's harbour area. He shares the space with Christien Meindertsma and Demakersvan (famous for the Cinderella table and Lace Fence). It is not a studio, but a laboratory. 'Yes, I call it that because I like having room to experiment,' he says. 'We've set up a company in collaboration with Demakersvan, and that allows us to do only the work we like. On a separate basis, I work for manufacturers like Cappellini and Flos, and I design for Princess, which represents an entirely different field: industrial design. Water kettles and toasters. The inside of a toaster, for instance, is standard. The technology in a toaster is always the same; as a designer, it's not something you have to consider. I'm involved only in the design of the container. But because even the exterior is boring, I'm always pushing the envelope. I really want to bring back the beauty displayed by such products, say, 60 years ago. I think,' he concludes, musingly, 'that a limited-edition toaster would be *so* cool to make.'

Martijn Goedegebuure

Joris Laarman

Man and Living [2003]

—

Ivy, 2003.
Decoration that works as a free-climbing wall.

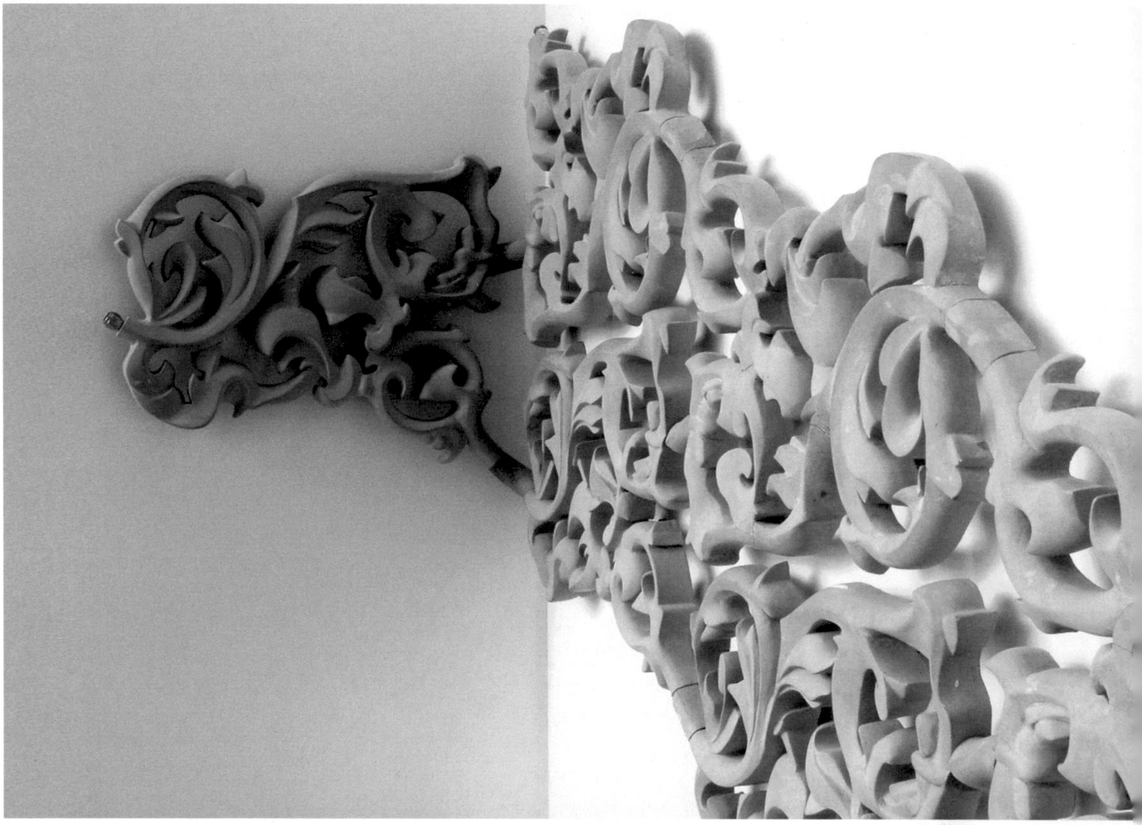

Opposite top: Heatwave, 2003
Reinventing functionality

Opposite bottom: Limited, 2003
Series of vases made by means of a production process that wears out quickly

Below: Bone Chair (Droog Design), 2007

Bas Warmoeskerken

Man and Living [2004]

—

Red revisited, 2004. Plastic products referring to old clay pottery

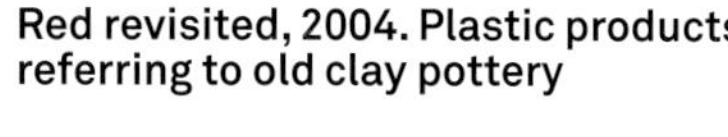

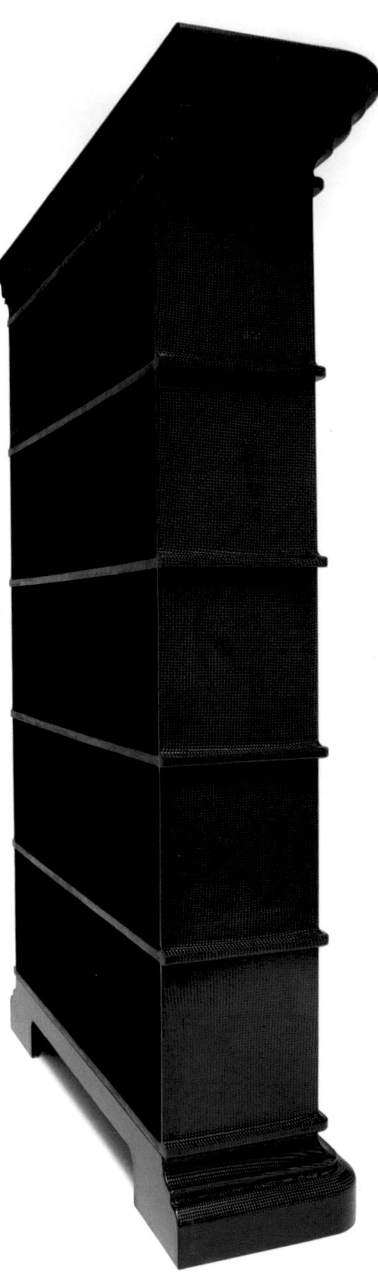

Heavy lightweight,
(Dry tech 3, Droog Design and
Technical University Delft), 2007

Franke Elshout

Man and Living [2005]

—

Showfood. A cookery book and kitchen apron enabling men to show off, 2005

Jan Dijkstra

Man and Living [2005]

—

Kitchenette, 2005

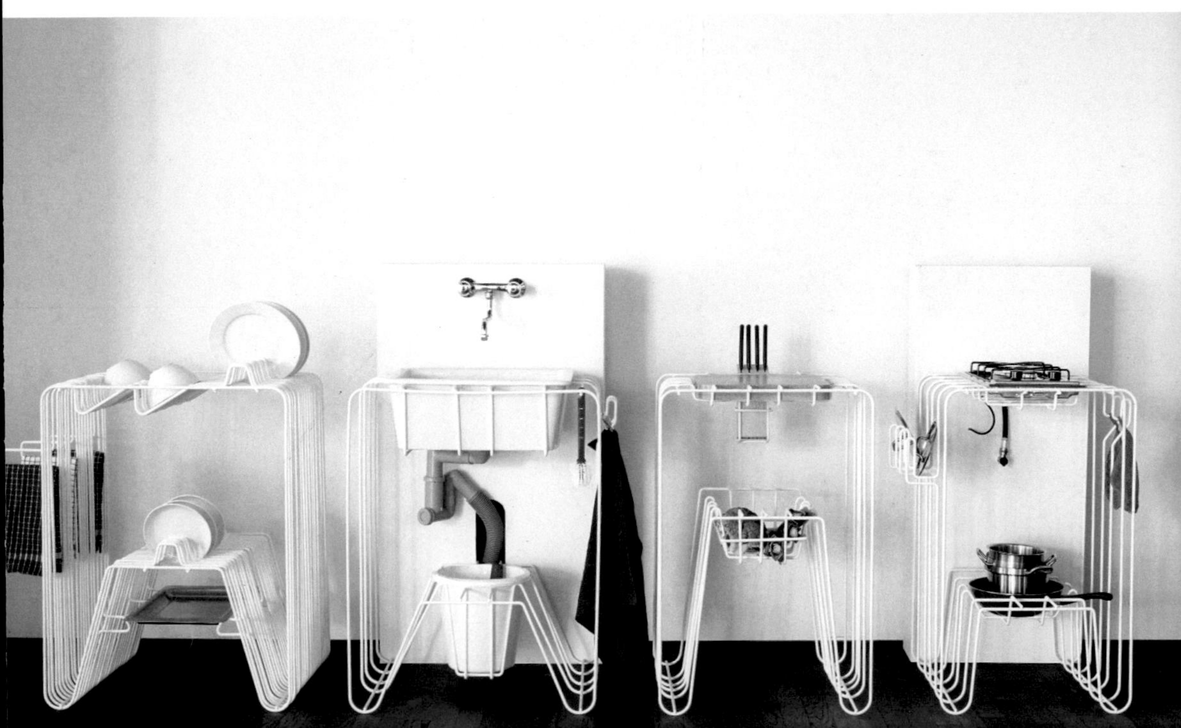

Susanne Philippson

Man and Living [2005]

—

Karakta, 2005

Sietze Kalkwijk

Man and Well-Being [2005]

—

Kydex Kitchen, 2005. MDF kitchen element coated with a high performance thermoplastic sheet called Kydex.

Mareike Gast

Man and Living [2005]

—

Refugee Radio, 2005. Radio waves in the air are used as an alternative power source for this radio.

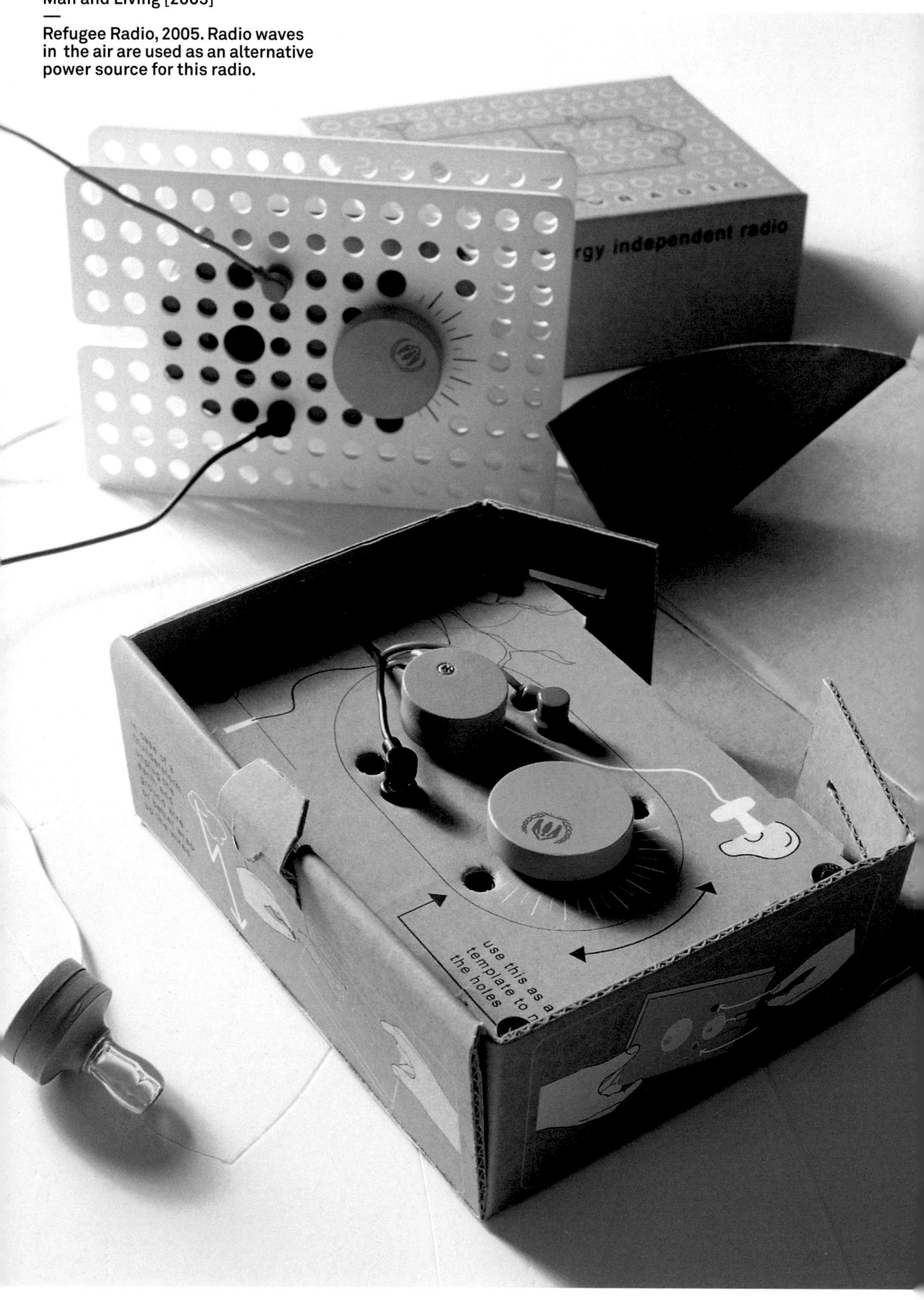

Mario Minale

Masters IM [2004]

—

106% red-blue rietveld chair

Sotiria Kornaropoulou

Masters IM [2005]

—

Cupboard House, 2005. A house in a house

Nami Mizuguchi
Man and Activity [2005]
—
Bookshelf = ladder, 2005

Rebecca Potger
Man and Activity [2005]

Daylight, 2005. A solar lamp. A stylized sun flower by day, stores up the energy it needs to function at night

Merel van Tellingen

Man and Well-Being [2005]

—

Ashes of the deceased turned into a functional memory, 2005.

Jelte van Abbema

Man and Communication [2006]

—

Virtureel, 2006. A word processor that explores the boundaries between man and machine.
A light touch is represented by a small font, etc.

Symbiosis,2006.
Printing with bacteria

Wouter Haarsma

Masters Man and Humanity [2006]

—

Crop coffee, 2006. A coffee system which connects the farmer directly to the consumer by an internet retail structure. Haarsma not only designed the retail system, but also the packaging of the green beans to be shipped, the devices one needs to roast, grind and brew the coffee at home, and accessories to serve the coffee.

Yvonne van Mol

Man and Identity [2005]

—

Mamamal, 2005. Various ceramic products from one mould.

Below: Multi Teacups

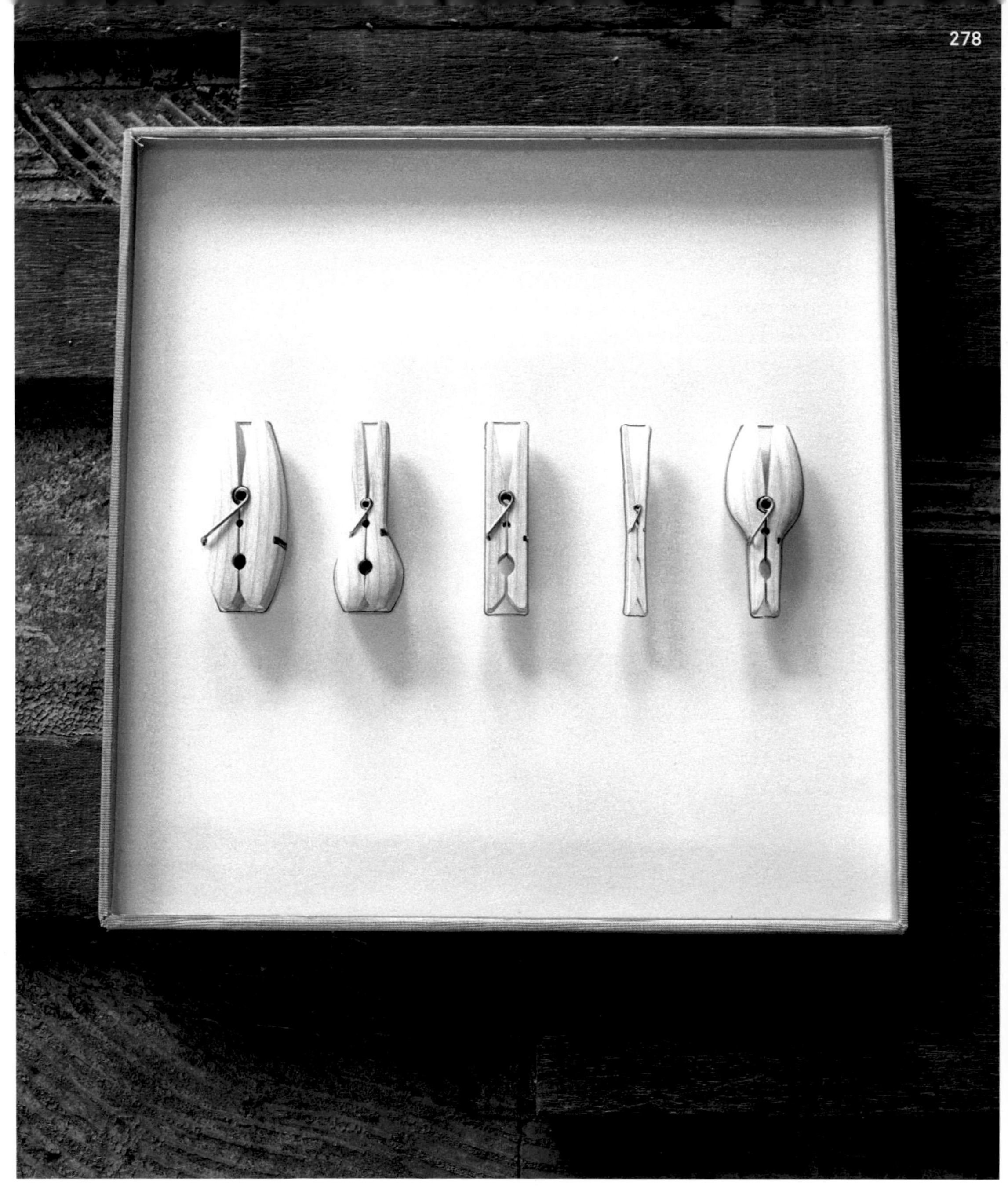

Leonie Martine Janssen

Man and Activity [2006]

—

I'mperfect? 2006. A representation of various body shapes in hundreds of pictograms as a basis for products.

Chung-Tang Ho

Masters IM [2006]

—

The volume of symbiosis, 2006.
A cupboard offering unexpected options for functionality.

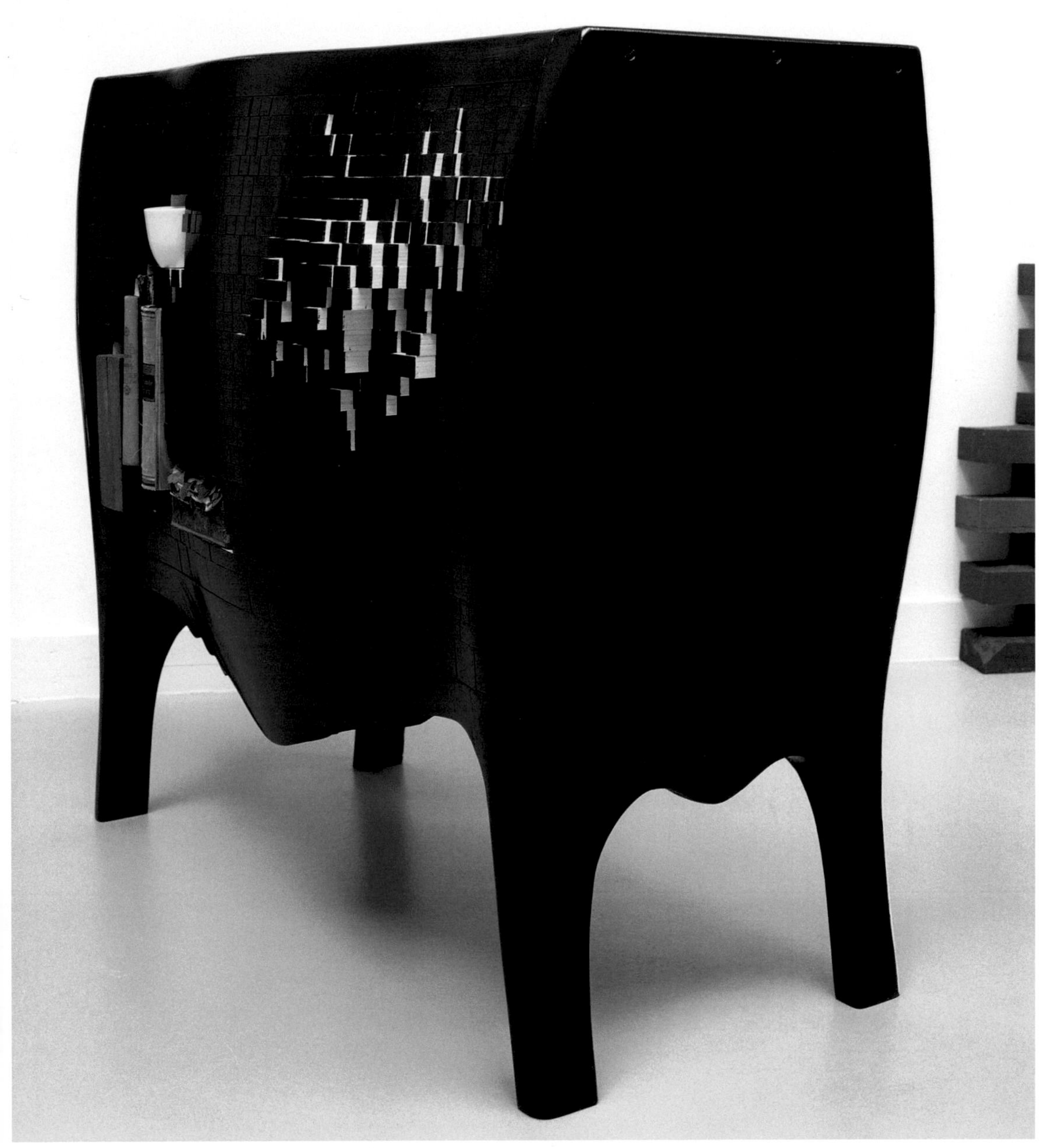

Sebastian Brajkovic

Man and Living [2006]

—

Lathe Chairs, 2006

Prothesis table, 2006

‘Lidewij Edelkoort gave an impressive speech. One could see three people nod in agreement while the rest of us didn’t understand one bit of it’, remember Judith de Graauw (1976), Joep and Jeroen Verhoeven (1976).

‘Those who had nodded in agreement left within a year. The rest of us understood already in the beginning that we were not supposed to understand what the hell she was talking about at that moment in time. And we survived’, muses Jeroen Verhoeven while remembering his first day in the academy. ‘I learned nothing that one might also learn in the books. That’s what’s so good about the academy. They teach you how to think in a dream world and one could never stuff books with that. The academy is like love, either it grasps you or it suffocates you’. Almost ten years later Verhoeven knows for sure he made the right decision to start his design career in Eindhoven. After all, when a major Dutch newspaper calls your graduation project ‘the most published design object of 2005’ (*de Volkskrant*, 3 May 2007), when that object is scooped up by prestigious museums like the MoMA in New York City and the Victoria & Albert in London, and when something you made as a student leads to countless major commissions almost before you’ve had time to frame your diploma, it’s safe to say your career is off to a flying start. The object in question is the Cinderella table, an intriguing combination of digital technology and traditional craftsmanship.

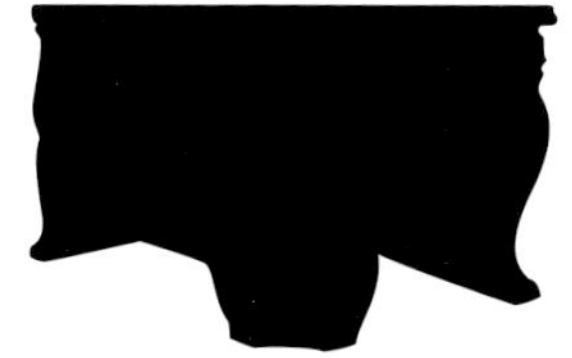

Jeroen Verhoeven graduated in 2004 with a degree from the academy's Atelier department, originally headed by Hella Jongerius and later by Dick van Hoff. (The department was discontinued when its speciality, a strong focus on handcrafted objects, became a division of the Compass Department.) Shortly after his exams in 2004, Jeroen Verhoeven entered into a collaborative enterprise with Judith de Graauw and his twin brother, Joep Verhoeven, who earned their degrees from the Atelier department and the Man and Living department, respectively. Jeroen's partners were off to a flying start as well. Judith de Graauw's Waiting Chairs and Lost & Found Stool soon found their way into various international magazines, and the latter is currently in production at Montis Furniture. For his graduation project, Joep Verhoeven came up with Lace Fence, his interpretation of an industrial-strength Heras fence. The orderly network of crisscrossed lines is interrupted here and there by an interwoven, lacelike decoration. Also discovered by the international press, Lace Fence has been exhibited at numerous shows, including the furniture fair in Cologne; was purchased by the likes of MVRDV Architects; and is now being manufactured by the metre by ID Productions in Bangalore, India, an enterprise set up by Demakersvan themselves.

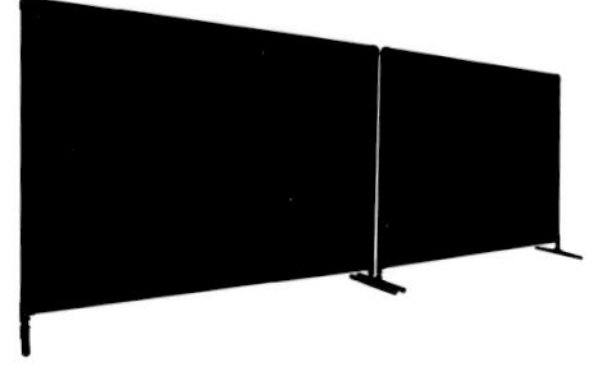

Overwhelming interest from the international press for Demakersvan has led to exhibitions at the Victoria & Albert Museum in London, the Boijmans Van Beuningen Museum in Rotterdam, the Kreo Gallery in Paris, the Cologne Furniture Fair a.k.a. IMM (at the stand displaying Joris Laarman's Ideal House) and the MoMA in New York City. Then, too, the young trio already has a long list of impressive industrial clients. In 2004 they showed great promise, and a mere three years later they seem to be making good on that promise. With boundless energy and enthusiasm they throw themselves into each commission that comes along, spend time developing independent projects and collaborate with other designers on a regular basis. De Graauw and the Verhoeven brothers call themselves dreamers. They want to push the boundaries that apply to their individual talents, to broaden their horizons, and to turn design inside out in pursuit of every possibility the profession has to offer. In practice, this means they work unremittingly day and night whenever a commission or a bright idea demands their full attention. They discuss 'good' and 'bad' design, 'good' and 'bad' designers, for hours on end; refer with unconcealed admiration to the designers they find 'brilliant'; and – without reservation or a trace of envy – take pleasure in the success of their peers: designers who are part of their generation. One of them is Joris Laarman, with whom they share a large studio in Rotterdam. Talking to the members of Demakersvan, you nearly come to the conclusion that Holland's youngest generation of designers is not burdened by a 'me first' mentality. Wherever possible, they involve others in their personal success.

Collaborations involving designers are not unique, nor is it unique that many of these partnerships begin while the participants are still at school. Like any number of other young design agencies, Demakersvan has its roots in work that de Graauw and the Verhoeven brothers produced while still at the Design Academy Eindhoven. In the meantime, the outfit has achieved a high level of professionalism. As a result, every project they work on nowadays involves vital decisions – who will shoulder the final responsibility, make the appropriate appointments, keep everything moving according to schedule – while in terms of creative content, even today no precise division of roles exists within the company. Collectively, they brainstorm. Collectively, they row. Collectively, they determine the how and why of each project. 'Quite often it begins with a misunderstanding. Having run into a brick wall of mutual incomprehension, for example, we sit around searching for words and some sort of common ground, and the very misunderstanding that started it all turns out to be a source of inspiration,' says de Graauw. 'Up to now, our ability to complement one another has been fantastic. As a matter of fact, we've always approached our work with the same attitude, as well as with a similar sense of irony and humour. That's the reason we decided to work together. It's not only more effective but also lots of fun.' While the twin brothers pepper the conversation with a steady barrage of one-liners, it's mainly de Graauw who manages to inject a note of logic and simplicity into the narrative. They are in complete agreement when it comes to their partners' 'specialities'. Jeroen comes up with the wildest ideas; Joep is exceptionally good at negotiating and making fast decisions; and de Graauw, the most rational of the three, has a knack for propelling all input in the right direction. Jeroen: 'More than anything else, we want to surprise ourselves. We question everything. Why like this and not like that?' de Graauw: 'The work is often based on a deficiency – on the lack of something – and you're looking for a counter reaction to what already exists. We start a lot of projects by asking ourselves how this particular problem was solved in the past. It can be very enlightening, for instance, to check out how people used the toilet round about 1800.' To date, their joint efforts have led to unexpected collaborative products and large projects. For instance the one that Demakersvan is working on with Joris Laarman and Tord Boontje. For a 20-villa resort in Shanghai, the five have designed an oxygen bar and 20 villas. Scheduled for completion in 2008, the complex will feature products designed by the team and produced by Artechnica. It's Demakersvan's first architectural project and their first large international commission.

How do the three young designers look back at the academy where they spent a longer period than the intended 4 year program (surprisingly almost all of the successful designers took their time in studying). Jeroen: 'What I liked about the academy is the struggle it caused. So many times I thought 'what the hell am I doing here, what do they teach me, why did I choose this kind of weird environment, it drives me crazy. Why is that couch not a house, why is the rain in the shower never real'. Once you enter your third year in the academy you start to accept it's a way of thinking which balances on the thin line between frustration, daydreaming, anger and euphoria. The academy let's you experience reality in a new way. The normal will never be the same again.'

Louise Schouwenberg

Demakersvan

Judith de Graauw
Atelier [2005]

Jeroen Verhoeven
Atelier [2005]

—

Below: Cinderella, 2004

Joep Verhoeven
Man and Living [2005]

—

Top: Lace fence, 2004

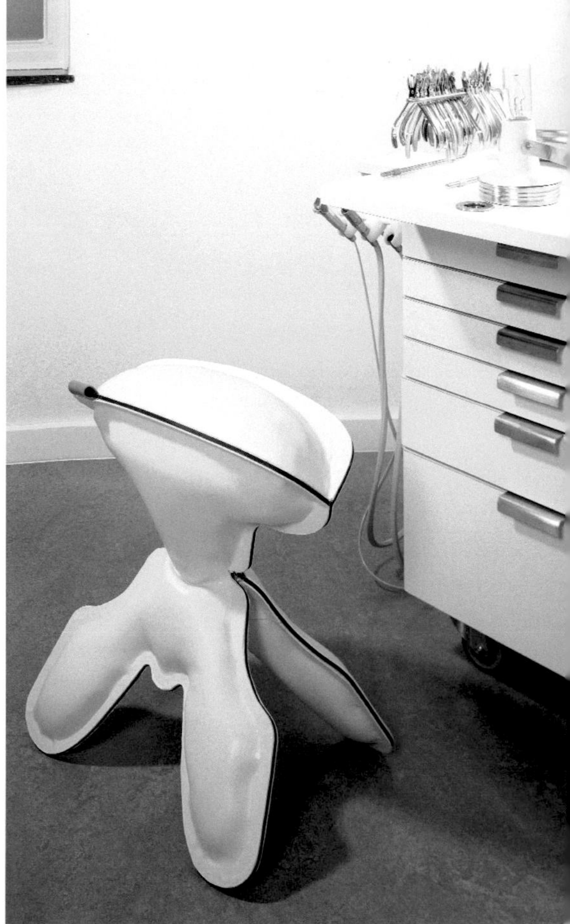

Judith de Graauw
Lost & found, 2004. A series of products lending new value to old emotions in our day and age

Top: Light Wind, 2006

Below: Light Fuse, 2006

Catharina ten Haaf
Man and Well-Being [2006]
—
Techne: the secret life of circuits, 2006.

Nadine Sterk

Atelier [2006]

—

Sleeping Beauty, 2006.
A lamp that develops like a living organism. Switch it on and it slowly starts growing by knitting its own lampshade.

Lotty Lindeman
Man and Living [2006]
—
Space/door, 2006

Sprouting, 2006. A chair that unfolds in the seating.

Ernst Ruijgrok

Man and Communication [2006]

—

New images for the Netherlands

Below: Smaak (taste), 2006

Lonny van Rijswijck

Atelier [2006]

—

Drawn From Clay, 2006.
Tableware made from clay that has been dug up in various parts of the Netherlands

Tatsuya Maemura
Man and Well-Being [2006]
—
Connectivity, 2006

Norihiko Terayama

Man and Living [2006]

—

Door in felt, 2006

Francisco Rojas
Masters IM [2006]
—
Brick experiments, 2006

—

Message in a box, 2006

Thomas Eurlings

Man and Identity [2006]

—

Total Access Jewelry, 2006

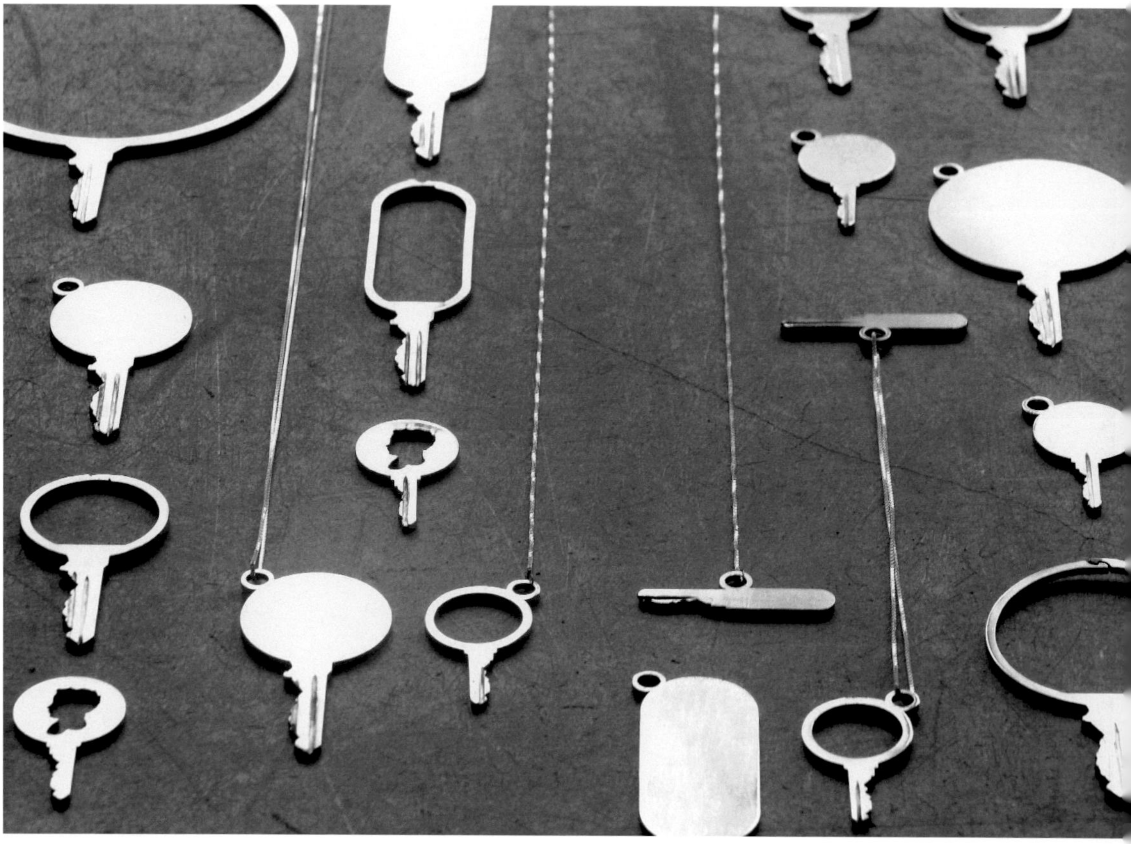

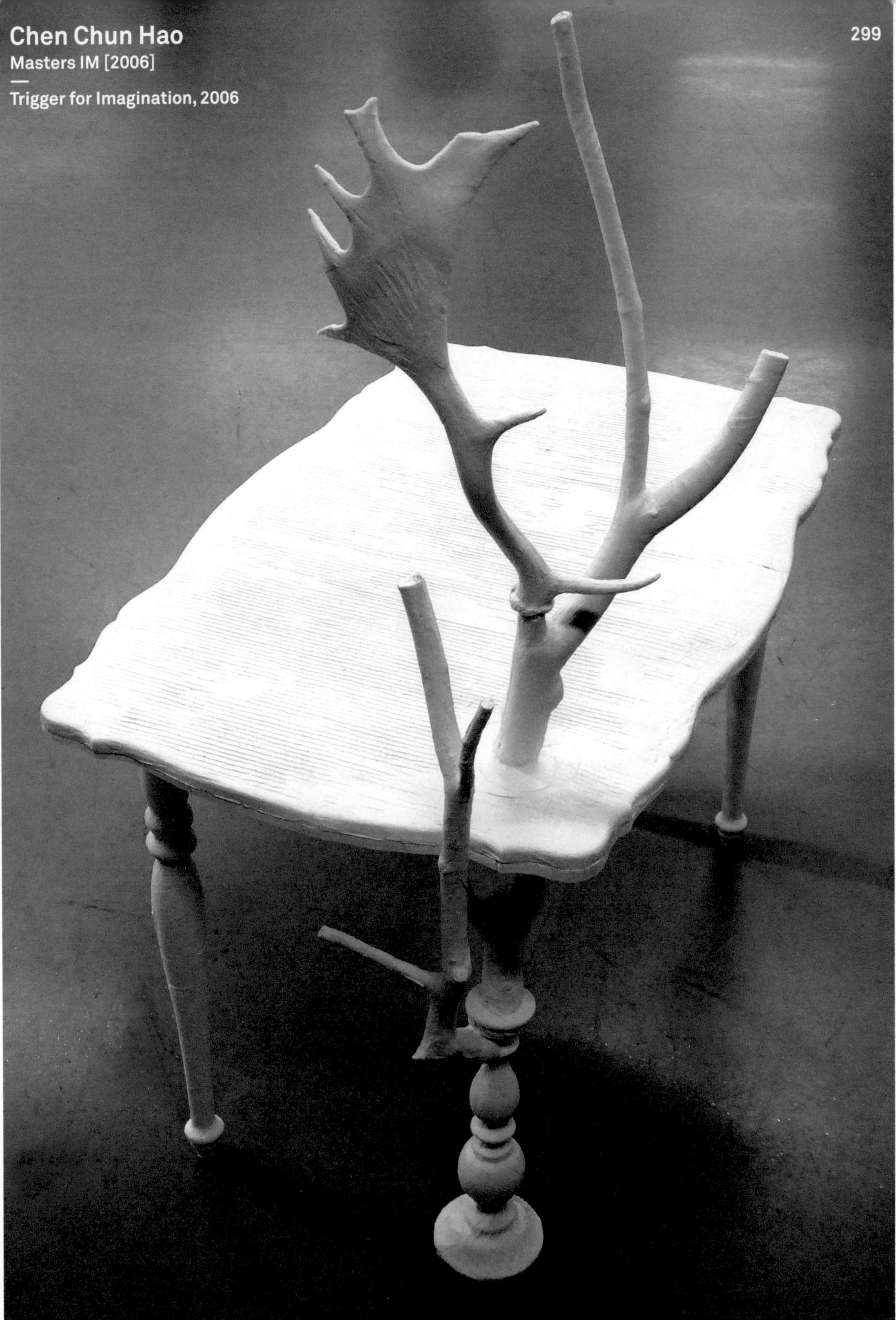

Chen Chun Hao
Masters IM [2006]

Trigger for Imagination, 2006

Tomáš Gabzdil Líbertiny

Masters IM [2006]

—

The Honeycomb Vase 'Made by Bees', 2006

Below: The Beeswax Amphora, 2006

Sylvia Siu Fung Lai

Man and Activity [2006]

—

'O'bject, 2006

Jeroen Wesselink

Man and Activity [2006]

—

Flocomachine, 2006. Stools made from discarded expansion vessels

Maarten Kolk

Man and Leisure [2006]

—

Doorgeschoten (Bolted) 2006
A book showing pictures from seedlings to withered stalks.

Agata Jaworska

Masters IM [2007]

—

Made in Transit: a supply chain concept for on the way growth, 2007

What is the meaning of a master thesis project in the context of Design Academy Eindhoven, renowned for it's conceptual approach to design? Right from the beginning I wanted to ask a contemporary question; How to apply this learned conceptual rigor to a pragmatic end, even (or especially) if it fell within a problem area typically not addressed by conceptual author-designers. I was convinced that the value of conceptual design is in how it applies its process of analysis to actual problems.

re-conceptualizing transport

I set out to find a unique angle on an ubiquitous reality – the globalized context of our production-consumption chains – wondering how the inevitable long-distance journey could be considered in the design of a product. Typically, design for transport means design for lightness or for compactness, driving innovations in lightweight materials and in new ways of stacking, folding, deflating, flat-packing, etc. I wondered if transportation could be given a new meaning, for no matter how efficiently the goods are packed, inventory in transit is trapped in a state of hibernation – it's essentially dead matter awaiting the factory or the consumer.

I hypothesized that if we could merge production with distribution, then we can redefine the role of transport from the mere *relocation* of goods to their simultaneous *transformation*, and translate that wasted time and space into valuable production time. Could this become a viable mode of production, one which replaces land-based factories, shortens the chain, saves labour, or produces custom products, and possibly only on demand? What sorts of products could most benefit from 'on the way' production?

from 'best before' to 'ready by'

Perhaps the industry that is fighting hardest against the detrimental effects of transport is the fresh food industry. From the moment of harvest, the living organism is removed from its source of life and begins a natural process of decay and so-called 'post-harvest technologies' are essentially a form of damage control that slow deterioration down. Modified atmosphere packaging and shipping containers, refrigerated vehicles and warehouses, gases that manipulate the ripening process, or expedited trips with air transport are measures that only slow the inevitable decay. The operational paradigm of the industry is preservation, and the winner of the race is the one who can stretch shelf life the furthest. *Made in Transit* reverses the paradigm from preserving freshness to enabling growth, for food grown along the way is automatically fresh upon arrival, and ready for harvest by the consumer.

mobile mushroom cultivation

Unless we're prepared to have trees grow on trucks, the *Made in Transit* concept doesn't apply equally to all commodities. Mushrooms seem promising since they need relatively simple conditions for growth and a relatively short growing period, and form bodies that are entirely edible yet highly perishable once picked. The application gains particular salience in a high labour-cost country like the Netherlands, where the mushroom industry is threatened by lower-wage countries like Poland and China, since it would entirely eliminate the cost of harvest labour. Growing on the way could also mean that even the most perishable varieties – too perishable to be traded in fresh form and therefore available only in canned form – could theoretically be available anywhere in fresh form.

Though growing mushrooms in their package on the way to the supermarket was intended to be realistic, scientifically it remains futuristic, and realization rests on further research and development, which at time of print is being initiated at the Netherlands' life science university, Wageningen University. In the end I didn't design a 'new' product that takes transport into account, but rather redesigned the way in which something very ordinary is produced in response to the global context, spurring the need for further research and development, if indeed the benefits of on the way production outweigh those of traditional farming.

Ming-lun Wu
Masters IM [2007]

—

The world as Identity, 2007

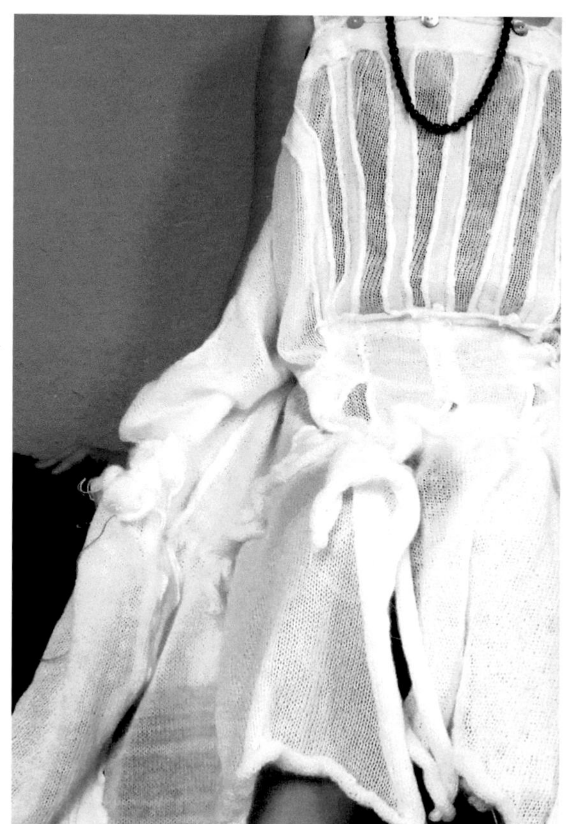

Julien Carretero

Masters IM [2007]

—

Theme & Variations, 2007

Ivana Borovnjak

Masters IM [2007]

—

Logic of Language vs. World of Objects, 2007

1. cup, *2. cup of structuralism,*
3. cup of coffee

1. cup, *2. white cup with golden edge,*
3. cosmogony origin

1. cup, *2. cup of structuralism,*
3. cup of coffee with milk

1. cup, *2. cup of structuralism,*
3. cup of sugar

1. cup, *2. cup of structuralism,*
3. cup of tea

1. cup, *2. cup of structuralim,*
3. cup of milk

1. cup, *2. cup of structuralism,*
3. cup of tea with milk

1. cup, *2. cup of structuralism,*
3. cup of milk with sugar

1. cup, *2. cup of structuralism,*
3. cup of a cup

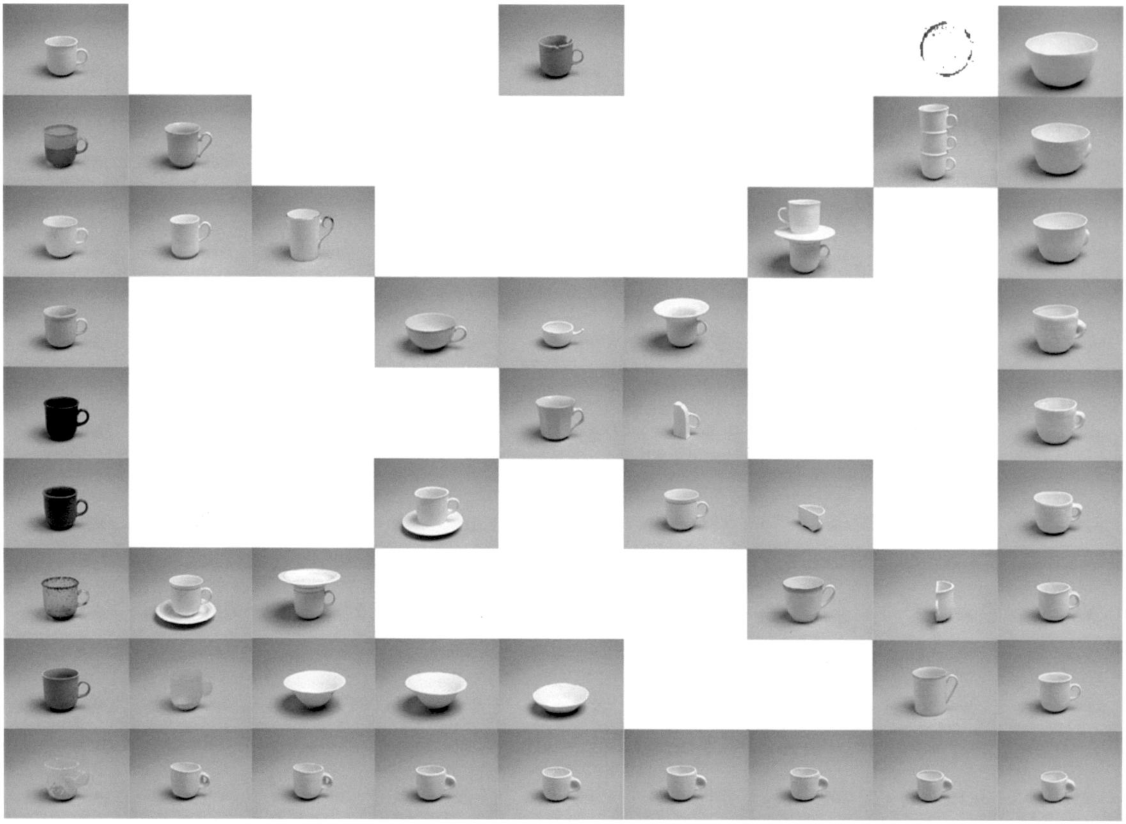

Hans Tan

Masters IM [2007]

—

The Imaginary Mass of Things, 2007. Tan investigated the many ways of lifting the weight of physical things.

Jonathan Ben-Tovim

Masters IM [2007]

—

Dangerously Safe, 2007

—
A Second Nature, 2007

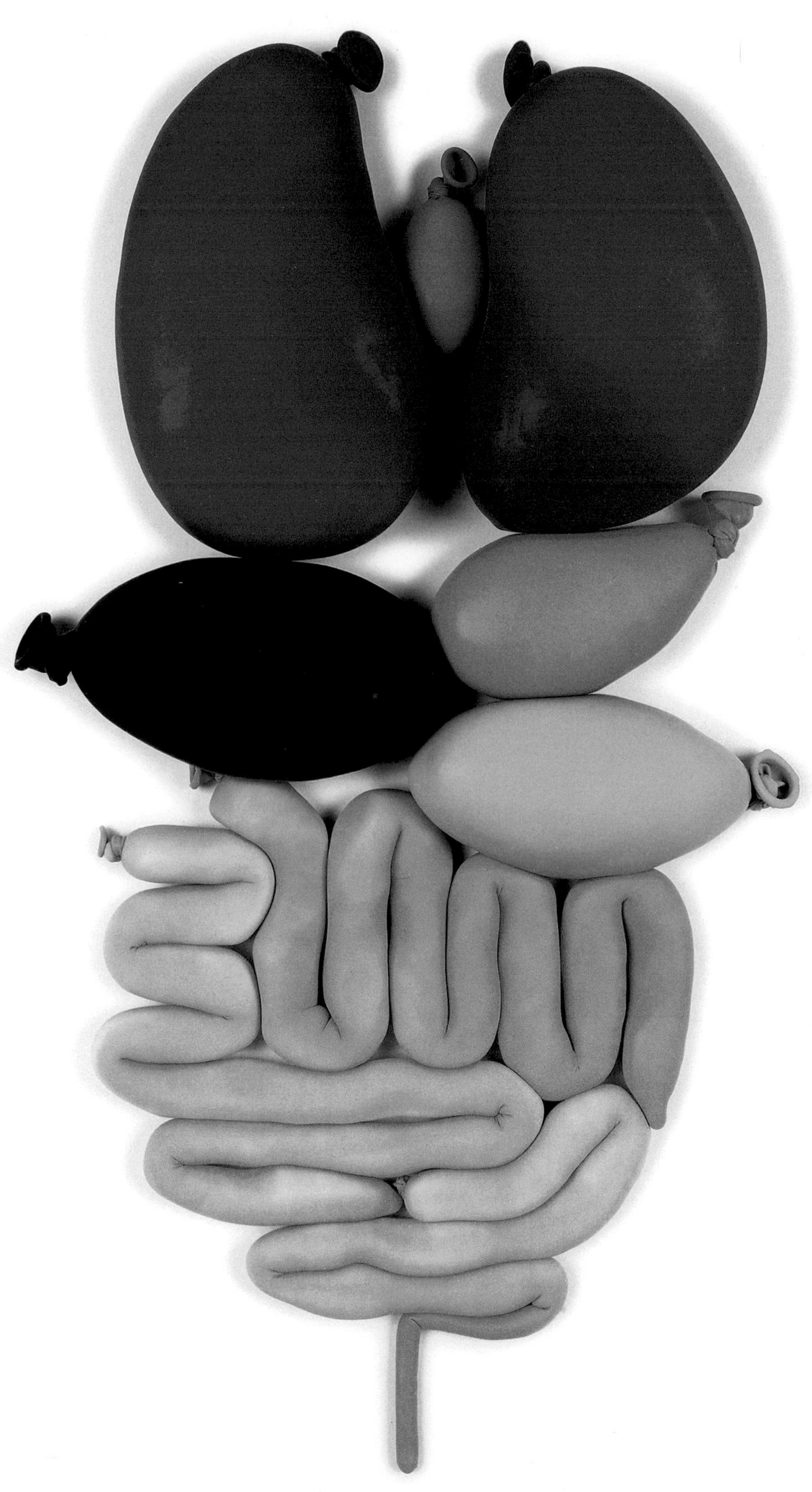

Design Academy Eindhoven

10,000 m²
6 floors
700 students
1,600 graduates (alumni)
110 lecturers
17 instructors
32 (other) staff members
Bachelor's programme:
  Design: 8 departments
  Compass: 4 departments
Master's programme:
  Design: 2 departments
  Source
7 workshops
1 design restaurant (deWitteTafel)
1 café for students and teaching staff (zBar)
28 nationalities
1 library

DESIGN ACADEMY EINDHOVEN CURRICULUM

Louise Schouwenberg

INTRODUCTION

Design Academy Eindhoven has a full-time bachelor's programme and a full-time master's programme that lead to Bachelor of Design (BDes) and Master of Design (MDes) degrees, respectively. The four-year bachelor's programme offers students a choice of eight departments in which to specialize. The academy accepts students who have successfully completed secondary school or intermediate vocational training (equivalent to Dutch HAVO, VWO or MBO-4) or who have earned comparable international diplomas at this level. The two-year master's programme currently consists of two departments. The master's programme accepts people who have earned degrees at the bachelor's level or who have equivalent work experience in the field of design.

In addition to the necessary diplomas and/or work experience, students applying for either programme are selected on the basis of artistic talent, as illustrated in their portfolios, *and* on motivation.

Approximately 85 per cent of those in the bachelor's programme are Dutch (100 per cent in 1957, 90 per cent in 1997); the percentage of Dutch students in the master's programme is about 5 percent. The foreign students come from Belgium, Germany, Japan, France, England, South Korea, Norway, Canada, Iceland, Israel, Taiwan, Iran, Austria, Denmark, USA, Brazil, Chile, China, Mexico, Turkey, Sweden, Latvia and Luxembourg.

In theory, undergraduate courses (bachelor's programme) are conducted in Dutch and postgraduate courses (master's programme) in English. In the first year of the bachelor's programme, a foundation course in English is available to non-Dutch students. To continue studying at the Design Academy Eindhoven, students in the bachelor's programme are required to learn the Dutch language in classes provided for them. In practice and to an increasing degree, however, courses in the second through fourth years of the bachelor's programme are also conducted in English, owing to the growing group of non-Dutch students attending the academy.

THE DESIGN ACADEMY EINDHOVEN BACHELOR'S PROGRAMME

Courses offered by the bachelor's programme differ from one another, but all have the same basic structure. Students explore and learn the design process by completing specific assignments under the close supervision of their teachers. Although discussions usually take place in groups, their main objective is to help the individual student with his or her personal development. The programme can be completed in four years. Included in those four years are formal lectures (including those by visiting lecturers), seminars, workshops, business-related projects, excursions, congresses and symposiums. Educational units in the bachelor's programme include eight design departments (each with a specific focus: communication, leisure, well-being, living, identity, public space, activity and mobility) and four Compass departments (atelier, lab, forum, market), each of which refers to an area of specialization.

The bachelor's programme is set up as follows:

1st year – Foundation course: basic curriculum with classes in the four Compass departments and an introduction to the eight design departments. At the end of the year, the student selects one of the eight in which to continue his or her education.

2nd year – Students enter their chosen design departments. They also attend classes in all four Compass departments.

3rd year – Students continue attending classes within their chosen design departments (some will have changed their minds at the end of the second year and chosen different departments, which they now enter). In addition, each student attends classes in either one or two of the four Compass departments, thus further narrowing down his or her preferred specialization.

4th year – A student who has successfully completed all four design modules is ready for the final phase of the programme. The first half of the fourth year consists of a traineeship intended to help prepare the student for a career in design. The academy has a work-placement database of creditable companies that have served Design Academy Eindhoven students well in the past. Students can also investigate potential workplaces on their own initiative. The traineeship can be divided among more than one design agency and/ or firm in the Netherlands and abroad. The ultimate choice of a trainee post is a mutual decision made by student and teachers.

The second half of the fourth year consists of preparation for final exams. During this period, students usually work on two projects: one of their own choice and the other either an assignment given by their teachers or a collaborative project with an external client, perhaps from the business world. The projects themselves are evaluated by a committee consisting of the department head, the teaching staff, the directorate and an external expert in the field of design. This committee bases its assessment of the graduation projects on three criteria that play a part in the design process: analysis/ concept development, creativity, execution/presentation.

Because each student follows an individual path through his or her years at the academy, exams take place twice a year. The results of these exams are displayed at an annual autumn Graduation Show.

THE EIGHT DEPARTMENTS OF THE BACHELOR'S PROGRAMME

__**Man and Communication**: This department explores and emphasizes the importance of visual communication. Included, for instance, is the study of various media in the area of information services, as well as research into specific societal target groups. Students in this department go on to work as graphic designers, as art/design directors for multimedia projects and in similar professions.

__**Man and Leisure**: Students in this department have an interest in how people spend their free time. Classes are centred on developing creative solutions for a growing phenomenon in Western society: activities that fill the hours in which we are not at work or asleep. Such solutions can take the form of intrinsic interpretations of leisure as a theme, including products, services and facilities.

__Man and Well-Being: In this department, students concentrate mainly on developing 'lifestyle' products and services. They tackle the question of how to translate ideas on the quality of life within areas of interest such as food, housing, body culture, cosmetics and care.

__Man and Living: Everything having to do with life in a domestic environment passes in review in this department, from the creation of layouts and atmospheres, which touches on interior architecture, to the design of chairs, tables, fabrics, dinner services and other home accessories. Attention is paid to various views on residential life, as well as on production methods and skills involved in traditional craftsmanship.

__Man and Identity: This department helps students analyse and understand the emotional value and sense of identity inherent in all types of products – for the home, the workplace, the body (clothing) and public space. Taking centre stage are textiles, experimentation with materials and techniques, future trends, semi-manufactured products, accessories and magazines.

__Man and Public Space: Public space is a complex terrain that demands intelligent analyses and cooperation between designers and external parties (both experts on and users of public space). Theory and analysis are vital resources in this department, where students learn to develop concepts, programmes, products and services geared to improving public space.

__Man and Activity: Here the crucial concern is the relationship between people and their workplaces. Current demands – relating to human interaction, interaction between people and products, flexibility, the incorporation of advanced technology and so forth – play important roles in the products and services that students develop in this department.

__Man and Mobility: A strong focus on design as it relates to physical movement is essential to the work done in this department. Students are confronted with key terms like efficiency, innovation, comfort and beauty and asked to consider the ethical, social and environmental issues associated with mobility.

THE FOUR COMPASS DEPARTMENTS OF THE BACHELOR'S PROGRAMME

In addition to courses within the eight design departments, throughout their years at Design Academy Eindhoven students follow a general programme created to furnish them with a foundation for future careers in design. The word 'compass' conveys this idea, and the Compass departments have been set up to guide students in making various choices, such as which design department to select at the end of year one. Compass courses vary from the more academic subjects (psychology, philosophy, economics, art history, design history and the like) to those centred on creative skills (introductory design, drawing and sketching, two- and three-dimensional forms, CAD technology, musical communication, ceramics, woodwork, textiles and so forth). Various subjects are taught within more than one Compass department, each time viewed in a different context.

Prior to 2005, general subjects now covered in the Compass departments were provided in addition to courses within the design departments, partly as courses belonging to a student's required programme of study and partly as elective courses. Since 2005, subjects have been grouped within the four Compass departments and have thus grown in importance within the overall programme without invalidating the underlying thought that they support, broaden and direct the work done in and by the design departments. At present, students can earn a degree only within one of the design departments. In the future, it may be possible to earn a degree within one of the Compass departments.

__Atelier: This Compass department concentrates mainly on traditional aspects of design. Courses include those on the theory of traditional techniques, the acquisition of artisanal and technical skills, and the in-depth analysis of design processes.

__Lab: Here students learn to incorporate technology into the design process. A strong focus is placed on technological innovation, skills, and the development of ideas on the use of technology within cultural and social contexts.

__Forum: Courses in this department include the history of art and design, as well as a theoretical study of the discipline as seen from a cultural perspective. Among other things, students learn to recognize the cultural and philosophical roots of the 'designed environment' and to understand how the media operate.

__Market: It's here that students investigate the economic and market-oriented side of the design profession, which includes dealing with supply and demand, understanding production and marketing options, and discerning economic patterns.

THE MASTER'S PROGRAMME

In addition to an emphasis on the development of personal viewpoints and distinctive signatures, which dominates the bachelor's programme, the master's programme stresses the areas of research and analysis. Postgraduate assignments have a higher level of complexity. Shaping so-called author designers (with personal viewpoints and distinctive signatures) is now paired with illuminating the context in which design and designers are taught to play their roles.

The English-language master's programme differs from course to course, as does the bachelor's programme, but each course has the same basic structure. Under the close supervision of their teachers, students examine the design process through themes and specific projects assigned by the teachers, as well as through self-assigned projects. Although discussions usually take place in groups, their main objective is to help the individual student with his or her personal development.

The programme can be completed in two years, during which time students participate in formal lectures (including those by visiting lecturers), seminars, workshops, business-related projects, excursions, congresses and symposiums.

New students can select one of two departments: Man and Humanity or IM: Conceptual Design in Context. At the same time, they follow a general lecture and workshop programme known as Source. Like the Compass courses that accompany the bachelor's programme, Source provides a comprehensive foundation for courses within the design departments. Because most of the students are from countries other than the Netherlands, Source gives special attention to the history and significance of Dutch design.

The master's programme is set up as follows:

1st year – The first year is divided into three trimesters, each lasting three months. Students work on specific thematic assignments. At least one trimester is spent on a collaborative project with an external partner.

2nd year – During the second year, each student comes up with a personal thematic project and, after a period of intensive study and research, develops related concepts and design proposals. To earn a master's degree, each student completes a thesis (elaborating on the chosen theme both theoretically and visually) and presents design proposals.

THE DEPARTMENTS OF THE MASTER'S PROGRAMME

IM: Conceptual Design in Context

IM is aimed at a conceptual and contextual approach to design. Using socially relevant themes as a basis for each unit of study, students explore and analyse a number of complex issues. Each thematic unit ends with students' design proposals. The department is headed by Droog Design (Gijs Bakker and Renny Ramakers), a Dutch platform for contemporary design. A team of research mentors and alternating visiting mentors supervises students during the research and design phases.

FunLab (currently part of the IM Department)
FunLab, with its focus on 'experience design', was devoted to all sorts of leisure activities. Heading the department were a number of alternating curators, among whom Ed Annink, Guus Beumer and Cynthia Hathaway.

Man and Humanity

Man and Humanity is aimed at humanitarian design and sustainable living. The department gives students a foundation in socially correct design, with an accent on matters such as sustainable design and social issues in disadvantaged areas, including the Third World. Heading the department is Indian designer Satyendra Pakhalé; students are supervised by a team of mentors and visiting mentors.

GENERAL INFORMATION

EXCHANGE PROGRAMMES

Students wishing to broaden their horizons can also participate in exchange programmes with a number of European design institutes. The period involved is normally one semester. Participating schools are the Royal College of Art, London; University of Art and Design, Helsinki; ECAL, Lausanne; Ravensbourne College of Design, London; Kingston University, London; Free University of Bolzano/Faculty Art and Design, Bolzano, Italy; ENSCI 'Les Ateliers', Paris; Elisava, Barcelona; Hochschule für Gestaltung Offenbach, Frankfurt; Istituto Europeo di Design, Milan; Rhode Island School of Design, Providence. In addition to participating in exchange programmes involving schools outside the Netherlands, students occasionally work together with their counterparts at the Industrial Design Department of the University of Technology Eindhoven.

LECTORATE

From September 2002 to September 2006, the Design Academy Eindhoven had a Sustainable Design lectorate, headed by Ursula Tischner, MA, a specialist in environmental and sustainable design. Tomorrow Matters, a new lectorate introduced in September 2006, explores the role of materials in innovative product design.

COLLABORATION WITH BUSINESS PARTNERS

Friends of the Academy, an organization that supports the Design Academy Eindhoven, consists of a group of businesses that act as school sponsors. Joint projects emerging from their sponsorship involve businesses and students in both the bachelor's and master's programmes.

GRADUATION SHOW

Work by the academy's most recent graduates takes centre stage at the annual Graduation Show. From 1991 to 2001, this exhibition took place in the Beurs van Berlage in Amsterdam. It is currently held at deWitteDame, the monumental building that also accommodates the Design Academy Eindhoven. The Graduation Show is the main event of Dutch Design Week, during which the city of Eindhoven hosts a variety of design-related activities and exhibitions. The Graduation Show is open to the public, as well as to representatives from the business world and the media.

AWARDS

At the Graduation Show, a small internal jury awards the René Smeets Prize to the *most innovative* design of the year. The winner receives 2,000 and a street sign bearing his or her name, which remains at the entrance to the academy.

Another award presented during the Graduation Show is the Melkweg Prize, which goes to the person judged by the jury to be the *most natural and original* talent of the year. This student also receives 2000, as well as active supervision by people and organizations able to contribute to a successful start to his or her career.

The *most technically inventive* graduates receive the Willie Wortel Prize: a bunch of carrots.

DIRECTORATE, DEPARTMENT HEADS, LECTURERS

DIRECTORATE

Lidewij Edelkoort, Director and Chairwoman of Design Academy Eindhoven's Board of Governors
Anne Mieke Eggenkamp, Director of Education and member of Design Academy Eindhoven's Board of Governors
Annette Noks, Head of Human Resources and Organization
Edwin Pelser, Head of Communication and External Affairs
Nol Manders, Head of Finances and Administration

BACHELOR'S PROGRAMME: DEPARTMENT HEADS AND LECTURERS SINCE 2002

Man and Communication – Head: Annelys de Vet (who recently replaced Anthon Beeke); lecturers and former lecturers: Vincent van Baar, Petra Janssen, Lode Coen, Boudewijn van Noppen, Steve Pille, Ewoud Traast, Edwin Vollenbergh, Max Kisman, Chris Vermaas, Aaf van Essen, Rene Knip

Man and Activity – Head: Oscar Peña; lecturers and former lecturers: Wytse Rodenburg, Jane Worthington, Damian O'Sullivan, Satyendra Pakhale, Andrew Hartman, Natassia Jacobs, Chris Koens, Marko Macura, Joanne Mycroft

Man and Mobility – Head: Axel Enthoven; lecturers and former lecturers: Karina van Eeten, Dick van Hoff, Rik de Reuver, Huib Seegers, Dorian van der Brempt, Frans Hegge, Bas Sturm, Farida O'Seery, Jelle Zijlstra, Bart Carpentier, Peter Ketel, Siep Wijsenbeek, Oscar Zaalberg

Man and Identity – Head: Marty Lamers (who recently replaced Ulf Moritz); lecturers and former lecturers: Annet Haak, Gerhard Belgraver, Saskia van Gelder, Mariëtte Zinsmeister, Helen de Leur, Arie Vervelde, Josephine Colsen, Niels Klavers, Shirley Muijrers, Paul Linse

Man and Leisure – Head: Irene Droogleever Fortuyn (who replaced Lidewij Edelkoort in 1992); lecturers and former lecturers: Wineke van Muiswinkel, Marc van den Bossche, Matthijs van Cruijsen, Kim van Leuken, Jan Melis, Eibert Draisma, Ina Meijer, Niels van Eijk, Elly Uijttenbroek, Anne Mieke Eggenkamp, Henk Ovink, Saskia van Stein, Emmanuel Babled

Man and Public Space – Head: Liesbeth van der Pol (who recently replaced Marijke van der Wijst); lecturers and former lecturers: Hans van der Markt, Ester van de Wiel, Wim de Vos, Eva Pfannes, Herman Kerkdijk, Natassia Jacobs, Matthijs van Cruijsen, Arie van Rangelrooy, Caspar Slijpen

Man and Living – Head: Bas van Tol (who recently replaced Gijs Bakker; Hella Jongerius and the duo Louise Schouwenberg/Jurgen Bey filled this post in the interval); lecturers and former lecturers: Vincent de Rijk, Peer de Bruijn, Miriam van der Lubbe, Chantal van Heeswijk, Bart Guldemond, Wieki Somers, Gerard van den Berg, Tom Couvee, Piet Hein Eek, Dinie Besems, Ineke Hans, Menno Stoffelsen, Ellie Uyttenbroek, Joost Grootens, Ulrike Möntmann, Jan Hoekstra, Anja Koops

Man and Well-Being – Head: Ilse Crawford; lecturers and former lecturers: Lisa Smith, Jan Boelen, Aldo Bakker, Stef Bakker, Tessa Blokland, Kathy Stertzig, Stijn Roodnat, Arnout Visser, Annemartine van Kesteren, Bettina Neuhaus, Irene van Peer, Dinie Besems, Jeroen Bodewits, Luk van der Hallen, Peter de Cupere, Linde Hermans

Atelier – Atelier was discontinued when its speciality, a strong focus on handcrafted objects, became part of the Compass departments. Previous department heads were Hella Jongerius and Dick van Hoff. Lecturers included Miriam van der Lubbe, Jurgen Bey, Louise Schouwenberg, Chantal van Heeswijk, Peter Hopman and Timo de Rijk.

COMPASS DEPARTMENTS

Forum – Head: Michiel Schwarz; lecturers and former lecturers: Gerhard Belgraver, Jacqueline Cové, Jos Delbroek, Michael Gibbs, Wim Janssen, Theo Poel, Christian van der Heijden, Johannes Steeghs, Wilma Sütö, Nadia Palliser, Mariska van den Berg

Atelier – Head: Bernardine Walrecht; lecturers and former lecturers: Rien Derks, Wendy Doodson, Pieter van Evert, David Geraerts, Teun Hocks, Mathieu Meyers, Fred Nagengast, Liesbeth Fit, Miriam van der Lubbe, Debra Solomon

Lab – Head: Jurriënne Ossewold; lecturers and former lecturers: Gerard Blaauw, Arnoud Breedveld, Horst Rickels, Werner Schippers, Frank Scholten, Xavier de Clippeleir, Adrian Silvestri, Yoka Stada, Marieke Sonneveld, Olaf Stevens, Toni Mazel

Market – Head: Walter Maria; lecturers and former lecturers: Ton de Gouw, Luk van der Hallen, Nannet van der Kleijn, Sandra Oom, Peter Thijs, Rony Platenkamp, Willem van Weelden, Godert van Hardenbroek

MASTER'S PROGRAMME: DEPARTMENT HEADS AND LECTURERS SINCE 2002

IM: Conceptual Design in Context – Head: Gijs Bakker and Renny Ramakers (Droog Design); coordinator: Wendel ten Arve; (visiting) lecturers: Jurgen Bey, Joost Grootens, Louise Schouwenberg, Ronald Rietveld, Madje Vollaers, Ted Noten, Chris Kabel, Barbara Visser, Allan Wexler, Edouard Francois, Matali Crasset, Ton Matton, Jago van Bergen, Wieki Somers, Joris Laarman, Tyler Whisnand, Pieter van Os

FunLab (now part of the IM Department) – Curators and (visiting) lecturers: Guus Beumer, Cynthia Hathaway, Ed Annink, Herman Verkerk, Kessels Kramer, Joost Swarte, George Brugman, Alan Murray

Man and Humanity – Head: Satyendra Pakhalé (who replaced Lucy Orta); coordinator: Aimilia Mouzaki; (visiting) lecturers: Toni Mazel, Erna Beumers,

Dick van Hoff, Frank Buschmann, Herman Kuijer, Graham Hollick, Jota Castro, Birgitta de Vos, Ursula Tischner, Marina Martinez Garcia, Aldo Bakker, Bas Raijmakers

Source – Head: Frans Parthesius; lecturers and workshop instructors include Martí Guixé, Ton Matton, Thimo te Duits, James Auger, Alan Murray, Tyler Whisnand, Antonia Mazel, Jurriënne Ossewold, Ursula Tischner, Ted Noten, Tobie Kerridge, Dominic Robson, Irma Boom, Anne Marie Commandeur, Kees Dorst, Gert Staal, Susanne Mosmans, Timo de Rijk and Susanne Piët.

DESIGNERS INDEX

PHOTOGRAPHY CREDITS

Arcfoto *88*
Abry, Stephan *265–267, 271*
Anthierens, Eric *280, 281*
Barenbrug, Max *119–121*
Bey, Jurgen *54–59*
Blersch, Josef *264*
Boontje, Tord *64–67*
Bruessing, Alec *220*
Cleijne, Edgar *158*
Cramers, Ingmar *287*
Eek, Piet Hein *72–77*
Gurp, Vincent van *254, 294, 295, 303*
Herfst, Walter *63*
Holmer, Marjan *253, 277, 288, 298*
Houten, Maarten van *208*
Hulst, René van der *274, 289, 302, 311*
Hutten, Richard *83–87*
Johnson, Lane *231*
JongeriusLab *94–99*
Jukkema, Miep *297*
Kämena, Ralph *62, 63*
Koning, Fleur *194*
Kramer, Luuk *103*
Kramer, Raoul *285, 286*
Laarman, Joris *259–261*
Langenberg, Jules van den *254*
Leenders, Mariëlle *304*
Lehmann, Claus *235, 239*
Loermans, Marsel *58, 192*
Lucas, Sander *299*
Maat, Hermen *46*
Maharam NY *61*
Manduzio, Matteo *115*
Manson, Phil *157*
Mars, Hans van der *245*
Mesman, René *43*
Mol, Yvonne van *277*
Nicolas, Daniel *Cover, 1, 2, 8–17, 153, 222, 223*
Nieuwenhuis, Bart *44, 45*
Nymphenburg *61*
Omlo, Anouk *240*
Ooms, Gijs *264*
Peen, Melissa *292*
Peijnenburg, Ruud *103*
Pigalle, Sabine *243, 246, 248, 250, 262, 273*
Pilet, Bianca *152*
Pot, Bertjan *185–189*
Princen, Bas *101, 158, 159, 178, 179*
Riele, José van *193, 249, 268, 272, 275, 278, 293, 301*
Rueschendorf, Grischa *88, 89*
Ryall, Vaughan *154*
Schmalgemeijer, Marcel *108–111*
Schwartz, Johannes *221, 286*
Somers, Elian *196*
Stigter, Peter *177*
Studio Edelkoort *60*
Studio Job *165–171*
Studio's Müller en van Tol *42, 43*
Teixeira, Ruy *244, 252*
Visser, Bernard *28*
Vogelzang, Marije *216–219*
Witte, Jonas de *43, 45*
Won Suh, Myiung *307*
Zedelius, Vincent *131, 137, 141, 147*

Photos of the Graduation Projects from the period 1989–2007 have been collected from the archives of Design Academy Eindhoven. Unless otherwise stated the pictures are from Edward Aghina, Hans van der Mars, Henk Visser and Peter Walvius.
Photos on pages which are not listed above are the responsibility of the individual designers.

HOUSE OF CONCEPTS
DESIGN ACADEMY EINDHOVEN

Publisher
Frame Publishers
www.framemag.com

Compiled and edited by
Louise Schouwenberg, Gert Staal and Joost Grootens

Texts
Louise Schouwenberg, Gert Staal, Hedwig Saam, Martijn Goedegebuure, Ed van Hinte and Renson van Tilborg

Production
Marlous Willems

Graphic design
Joost Grootens
with Jonas Habermacher

Translation
InOtherWords (Donna de Vries-Hermansader) and Arthur Payman

Colour reproduction
NerocVGM

Printing
Livonia Print

ISBN 978-90-77174-17-3

Frame Publishers
Lijnbaansgracht 87
1015 GZ Amsterdam
Netherlands
www.framemag.com

Printed in Latvia
987654321

Acknowledgements
Many thanks to Bas Berck, who's idea to make a book on Design Academy Eindhoven popped up in the fall of 2006, one year before it actually appeared (Berck, a Design Academy Eindhoven student from 1986–1992, the former coordinator of the Design Academy Eindhoven's cultural and commercial affairs 2003–2005, has worked as project manager for Merkx+Girod architects since 2005).

Special thanks as well to all the people of Design Academy Eindhoven who have helped us to gather all the necessary information: Antoinette Klawer, Martina Thijssen, Yolande van Kessel, Arjo de Vries, Henri Beelen, Nol Manders, Annette Noks, Annet Daamen, Lia Sipkes, Edward Aghina, former and current heads, teachers and students we talked to.